ADULT CHILDREN
Being One, Having One & What Goes In-Between

WISING UP ANTHOLOGIES

ILLNESS & GRACE: TERROR & TRANSFORMATION

FAMILIES: *The Frontline of Pluralism*

LOVE AFTER 70

DOUBLE LIVES, REINVENTION & THOSE WE LEAVE BEHIND

VIEW FROM THE BED: VIEW FROM THE BEDSIDE

SHIFTING BALANCE SHEETS:
Women's Stories of Naturalized Citizenship & Cultural Attachment

COMPLEX ALLEGIANCES:
Constellations of Immigration, Citizenship, & Belonging

DARING TO REPAIR: *What Is It, Who Does It & Why?*

CONNECTED: *What Remains As We All Change*

CREATIVITY & CONSTRAINT

SIBLINGS: *Our First Macrocosm*

THE KINDNESS OF STRANGERS

SURPRISED BY JOY

CROSSING CLASS: *The Invisible Wall*

RE-CREATING OUR COMMON CHORD

GOODNESS

FLIP SIDES
Truth, Fair Play & Other Myths We Live By: Spot Cleaning Our Dirty Laundry

ADULT CHILDREN
Being One, Having One & What Goes In-Between

*Heather Tosteson, Charles D. Brockett,
Kerry Langan & Michele Markarian*
Editors

Wising Up Press

Wising Up Press
P.O. Box 2122
Decatur, GA 30031-2122
www.universaltable.org

Copyright © 2021 by Wising Up Press

All rights reserved. No part of this book may be used or reproduced in any manner whatsoever without written permission, except in the case of brief quotations embodied in critical articles or reviews.

Catalogue-in-Publication data is on file with the Library of Congress.
LCCN: 2021949705

Wising Up ISBN: 978-1-7376940-0-7

To Those Who Raised Us—
And Those We Raised—
And All The Growth Involved
For All, For All . . .

CONTENTS

HEATHER TOSTESON
Adult Children — 1

I. ROLE REVERSAL

JUDITH SANDERS
Helping Mom Downsize — 12

CAROL BARRETT
Portrait — 15

PAMELA HARTMANN
Don't Remember This — 16

ALISA CHILDRESS
Pleading for Answers — 24

ALEXIS DAVID
Picking Up My Dad from the Hospital — 29
Mourning Doves — 30

JOAN DOBBIE
Conversation Before Sleep — 32

MICHELE MARKARIAN
My Mother's Mother — 35

JANET LUNDER HANAFIN
'Round the Bend — 37

SHARON LASK MUNSON
If by Chance There Is Memory in Your Slumber — 42
Oh, Mom — 44

LAURA GLAVES
In the Silence — 46

II. ASSUMING ADULTHOOD

CHRIS WOOD
Her First — 50

JOANELL SERRA
This Skin No One Can Claim — 51
Pandemic, Poolside — 53

STEPHANIE HART
Birthday Cake Dress — 56

SERA DAVID
> *Undercurrent* — 59

CATHERINE HAYES
> *A Fear of Motherhood* — 65

JENNIFER PALMER
> *Reflections* — 70

III. LETTING GO

MADLYNN HABER
> *One Perfect Moment* — 86

LISA MOLINA
> *When We Held Hands* — 88

JUDITH SANDERS
> *Bus Ride Through Rome* — 91
> *My Friends' Children* — 92

MK PUNKY
> *Precious Boy* — 94

CAROL BARRETT
> *Lobster Bisque* — 96

TERRI WATROUS BERRY
> *On Guard* — 98
> *Pure Condensed Owl Shit* — 100

MARK BLICKLEY
> *Han's Solo* — 102

DEBBIE PETERS
> *Delinquent Account* — 106

THEA HEARD
> *Transgressions* — 107

J. WEST
> *Interiors: Table, as Is with Blue Dog* — 115

JOAN GERSTEIN
> *Dead Weight* — 120
> *Some Days I Scarcely Think of You* — 121

HEATHER TOSTESON
> *Call Waiting* — 122

NANCY WICK
> *He Did It His Way* — 125

PAULA BROWN
Finding Dad *132*

PAUL SOHAR
My Crutch *136*
The Reaper *138*
The Candle *139*

IV. GENERATIONS

GAYLE BELL
Reflections *142*
Down Home Blues *143*
Homegoing *144*

MELANIE REITZEL
Back in the Day *146*

PATRICIA BARONE
The Fall of Our Adolescence *155*
Old Children *156*
Time's Arrow *158*

LORI CLOSTER
Surviving Family *159*

RICHARD LEIS
Pangaea Proxima *172*
Panthalassa *174*
Juniper Tree, Boy and Bird *175*

SHERRY SHAHAN
Little House in the Redwoods *178*

PAMELA BROTHERS DENYES
You May Not Know *184*

A.P. QUILT
Instructions on How to Survive *186*

KATE MEYER-CURREY
Mother's Day Card *188*

DEBORAH SCHMEDEMANN
Title Nine Daughter *192*

JOAN DOBBIE
My Mother Is Alive *197*

PENELOPE STARR
Tattoo *204*

V. REVISIONS

GARY YOUNG
"My Youngest Son Considers" — 214

BETH CHRISTENSEN
Insomnia — 215

MK PUNKY
Ego Death — 225
Pround Mama — 226

AROONEY
Elegy for Darleen — 227
My Father Turning — 230
Lament of a Lated Orphan — 232
On Seeing My Mother in the Frankfurt Airport — 234

JAN CALLNER
Okay, God — 237

LAURA GLAVES
The Price Was Too High — 247

MELVIN STERNE
The Rest of the Story — 252

LAURENCE SNYDAL
Daddy — 263
My Father's Mantel Clock — 264

MARK TARALLO
Four Fathers — 266

LOWELL JAEGER
We'd Planned — 279
Some Things Pass By and Never Come Back — 280
Who's That? — 281

MARY KAY RUMMEL
Son et Lumiére: Chartre — 282
Returning — 284

MELODIE CORRIGALL
Winter Birds — 286

ACKNOWLEDGMENTS — 291
CONTRIBUTORS — 294
EDITORS — 302

HEATHER TOSTESON

ADULT CHILDREN:
Being One, Having One & What Goes In-Between

Where It All Began

Often the ideas for our anthologies take years to gestate, either because we're not ready to share them or others aren't as interested as we in exploring the topic. If I look through my files, I realize that this anthology has been turning around in my head—and life—for a very long time. In the fall of 2013 I wrote a possible anthology call that began: "Adult To Adult: *Is it possible with those we raised or those who raised us?* . . . When asked, most parents will say their most important task is nurturing their children to adulthood. But when both are adult, is the relationship between them ever adult to adult?"

I wrote that call at a point in my life when my son was going through a difficult separation from his wife. My husband and I were in Mexico at the time, busily editing the anthology *Connected: What Remains as We All Change*. My son was in New York and not answering calls. My anxiety was acute—and had no realistic place to go. What could I, at sixty-two, really do to ease the challenges he faced at forty? I was living again, however briefly, in Mexico, the country where my own choices had posed challenges for him, in his adolescence, that he had experienced as unbearable—creating a lasting rage at me which he also sometimes found unbearable. He told me this in his own early thirties as we sat in a delicatessen in Boston, gathering there for my father's 80th birthday. I took it both as a gesture of confidence—he was speaking his truth—and also a source of anguish, since we can't rewrite the past, only refuse to repeat it.

However, in Mexico, those many years later, at very different stages in both our lives, my son now several years older than I had been when I brought him there, I was assailed with memories of his early childhood, of the fierce protectiveness I felt for him as a young single mother—and with something more solid than guilt for the formidable challenges he had faced in his early teens when I uprooted both of us for "pinche, putamadre love" as I wrote in a poem. I could, at last, bear to *feel* what that experience might have been like for him. But it had taken me a good eight years and a return to those locations, although in very different—and better—circumstances, to be able to bear that knowledge and that guilt.

I also understood that my current angst was stripping my son of all the years of his own intentional maturation, all the many many adult choices he had made that had nothing to do with me or those choices I made in his adolescence. I titled that series of poems, "Letters to my Son, Twenty Years a Man." I've never shared them with him, nor do I think he would have any interest in reading them. He has his story and I have mine. I'm sure you would hear powerful, abiding affection in each of our stories, but the stories don't neatly mesh. Nor should they.

He made this clear to me by his resolute silence when, recently, in celebration of his forty-ninth birthday we were walking a South Carolina beach and I was sharing with him some of the stories included in this anthology—and the questions and insights that were arising from reading them. *Whatever.* He turned the conversation to issues of his own concern: challenges and intrigues at his workplace, savings accounts, housing markets.

I gazed out at the ocean, a little miffed. Couldn't he see he might be one of the underlying inspirations for the all this? ("Far too clearly," my husband would say later with a hearty laugh, "and he's wisely not taking the bait.") As we walked on, I saw a wonderful set of triplets, fair-haired boys of about four, gathering at the water's edge—their young parents and a little two-year-old sister gamely tagging behind. I imagined what those boys would remember of their childhood, what kind of mind meld they might develop as an identical trio. How their little sister would position herself over the years.

Over the next two days, we would pass that young family several times as we rode our bicycles along the sand. Each time the boys spoke to my imagination—as did their father, gently cajoling and firmly corralling them. Finally, just before we left, impulsively I stopped and asked if I could take a photo of them. I probably was thinking of just photographing the triplets, but the parents understood it as a group portrait and eagerly agreed. The mother, a beautiful, sylph-thin redhead in a bikini, joined us, pulling in the most recalcitrant of the boys. I told the parents how impressed I was each time I passed at what a wonderful job they were doing at what could only be a challenging task. Both parents beamed. "Thank you so much. We know it will get easier in the future," the mother said, reaching out to catch her daughter's hand as the father hurried off toward the water in pursuit of the boys.

I looked at her beautiful smile and her flat, tanned belly and I wondered, as I'm sure she often did, *How did all this amazing life come out of one small being?*

Revisiting this topic of adult children in our current anthology call, my questions are obviously much what they were before. *Can* we ever be in a fully adult relationship with those who raised us, or they with us? What does that adult-adult relationship look like? These questions are especially salient now that our life spans are increasing and we spend decades longer together as adults. Many of the markers of adulthood—child-bearing age and economic self-sufficiency are also being extended, so the natural equalizers and transitions between generations are not coming into play as early or as clearly. We also often live at a distance from our families of origin, so our interactions are fewer and more symbolically charged.

All adults are, by definition, adult children. But adult child is a squinting construction, the emphasis often shifting in ways that reflect the tension in the condition, an ambiguity reflected in some of the dominant stories we tell about familial relations. On that same beach trip, I observed to my son that he, as have all our children, had lived a number of years longer as an independent adult than he had lived with me. He in turn observed with a smile that I had now lived with my husband longer than I had with him. Unspoken was the question of whether this reality had made it into our inner narrative—or shared—narratives.

Grievance Stories

Several narratives are dominant if you scan the books that come up under the search term "adult children". The first is "adult children of—" stories, which focus on parental inadequacies and our vulnerability to them. We all have them of course, but this type of story/grouping holds out a suggestion that we all have a "right" to an untroubled childhood with adequate parents. Another theme is estrangement—parents who feel rejected by their adult children. A third is the sandwiched adult—usually female—responsible for caring for both aging parents and children who are "emerging adults." What struck me is that these are at some level all grievance stories, but without any clearly defined, realistic standard to orient or mitigate the sense of injustice and loss because they all also involve ambiguous and often competing definitions of adulthood.

As I read through several of these books, I found myself going back to Erik Erikson's life stages in search of a workable definition of adulthood, especially the emphasis on the virtues we need to develop to have a rich adulthood: love, care, wisdom. These are all active, performative states. They are more about giving than receiving, more about generous relation than simple self-sufficiency. They are about proportion, context, change.

The tension between our needs for care and autonomy shift constantly. The difference between the adult state and the child's is that as adults we consciously choose, we see ourselves, we evaluate ourselves, by an assumption of agency. An assumption that is not always true, certainly never unqualifiedly so. We choose to have children, but we do not choose the children we have anymore than children choose their parents. In our stories of our childhood, we often strip out that sense of ourselves as agents, forces to reckoned with. The triplets on the beach, in their stories of their childhood, probably will not have any sense of the formidable dedication and hope, the sheer energy that went into shepherding them to adulthood—at least until they have children of their own. They will probably always remember where their beguiling young parents fell short. They may never be open to hearing the alternative story—because it so tries the child in any of us to be asked to understand the intensity of the demands (as well as the delights) our very being placed on our parents.

Bearing the Gaze

The psychologist Jerome Bruner in his discussions of the role of narrative describes it as one of our most effective ways of creating a sense of shared reality. Family stories, the ones shared at the dinner table, are of this nature. Our own private takes are constantly being qualified, elaborated, challenged until we have a story we can share with strangers. The ones we write from, not so often. We often write to get our own story straight, to find our unique solid ground, or own blend of chance and intention, responsibility and vulnerability. We usually don't write these for our families but for the world at large. At some level, we know our stories are contestable, but we'd like, just for a moment, for them to seem oracular. (This may explain why we had more writers than ever before choose to publish under pseudonyms for this anthology.)

Do we want to know how our parents *really* see us? I asked my husband. Or how our children *really* see us? Absolutely not, he said immediately. I agree, but I've begun to wonder why that is—what would have to shift to make us all able to bear the gaze—to really see ourselves as others see us. This reluctance to bear the gaze has a lot to do with agency and internal accountability. Parents choose to have their children, that is at the heart of the relationship. They continue, even when their children are adults, to need that relationship more than their children do. Which makes sense, of course. They *chose* it. It says something about their identity, their adulthood. What they don't want to hear, of course, are the limits of that choice—the ways they may have failed to be the person they wanted to be—or the one their children wanted them to be. Life, raw life, is rarely an extenuating circumstance from a child's perspective, neither is human fallibility. But the adult child's grievance story leaves out an essential truth: *without you, I would not be.*

Most of the books on adult-adult estrangement between parents and adult children emphasize the importance of staying out of our adult children's choices about how to live their own lives. On the other hand, part of raising a child to adulthood is to hold out a future, or futures, *for* them—to believe in those possibilities as real and realizable so they can too. But these possibilities can restrict as well as motivate. It is often harder than we imagined to say, "It isn't important what we think about your life choices. It *is* important that we respect your right—and responsibility—to make them." No adult child particularly wants to hear how they have disappointed their parents by exercising their own judgment. The estranged parent grievance story leaves out that to be a parent is to raise an *adult*, someone who can choose independently and differently, someone who is *free* to leave us and follow their own dreams, ones that may bear no relation at all to those we had for them.

But what happens when the balances between autonomy and care shift again as parents age? What has to shift in the adult child's understanding of their own story to be able to make this transition from autonomy from their parents to care for them? Where do they now need to step in rather step back? What *do* we owe those who gave us life? Who cared for us when we were not yet capable of caring for ourselves? I actually find my step-daughter most alive to these questions, not only because of her experience as a social worker working for years with seniors and with hospice, seeing first hand how differently families respond to these challenges, but also because she experienced an unusual, tragic number of deaths—grandparents, uncle and mother—as a late teen. She assumes, most generously, that she will have a substantial role to play as we age, indeed has been casing out homes for us for the last twenty years. We, still in denial, quickly turn the conversations to the more immediate needs of her children.

But in the last few months, this question of aging and adult children has been particularly live to me as I have been an unwilling observer of the painful family dynamics of a close friend and her husband in their eighties and nineties. She has serious dementia; he is increasingly infirm but determined that they stay together in their home, which they can't keep clean and which is physically unsafe for them. They expect their two adult children, both childless themselves, to physically care for them as their situations worsen, which is not possible. It is not even clear where these expectations came from since neither of them did this for their own parents. Their two adult children, concerned about their parents but at vehement odds about how to respond, spend their time fighting with each other, afraid to directly provoke their father's wrath or jeopardize their inheritance. It is as if they are expecting, in their fifties, adult *children*, that someone will come in and arbitrate. There are so many opportunities both for agency and care that are lost here, I stay up listing them as a way of reminding myself that they exist.

Reading the selections for this anthology has been both solace and affirmation. For we meet here people exploring in careful, caring ways so many dimensions of this fascinating question: how can we, *adult* children, meet each other faithfully at so many of life's stages.

*

We begin, with *Role Reversal*, at the end of life, with adult children assuming care of their parents, whose health and memory are failing. Family stories are beginning to dissolve or be turned upside down, old grievances have little purchase when there is no one to hold responsible anymore. It is both a time of loss and new interpretations—and often high humor.

In the second section, *Assuming Adulthood*, we have an interesting set of stories, primarily by younger writers, that explore what it means to claim your own adulthood, to actively choose the standards you will live by. Will you choose to have children if you have been asked to assume adult responsibility for a younger sibling? What does it mean to go to college at the same time your mother does? What allows you to choose the partner who matches your own goals for your future, not your parents?

The third section, *Letting Go*, explores the expectations we need to release, at many different points in relationships, in order to create an adult to adult relationship that honors the agency of both parties. As they travel, a mother consciously stops narrating the experience for her adolescent son, making space for his own observations; a father gently punctures his son's assumptions about his own life choices; mothers release expectations—and hopes—that distort their adult children's temperaments and actual life choices; and, poignantly, a father mourns the death of his adult daughter whom he expected to outlive him.

In *Generations*, we see how stories repeat, and change, over generations, as do definitions of adulthood. There is a keen appreciation in these poems and stories of strengths and demonstrations of care passed down, absorbed. A daughter sees in her high-living but emotionally mature parents a model for a sophisticated and constructive adulthood for herself; large families of siblings accept their shared positioning; a mother accepts that she has inherited from her family, dominated by an autocratic grandmother, as large an inheritance of love as of grievance. In a grandmother's stability, a young girl finds some level of support and protection from her father's alcoholism. Mothers find strength in their adult daughters, adult daughters in their mothers. A woman discovers surprising affinities with a daughter she gave up for adoption forty years earlier.

In the last section, *Revisions*, adult children discover unexpected dimensions of their own lives or those of their parents, especially the lives of their fathers, discoveries that open possibilities for new stories and richer understandings. A woman finds the source of her chronic insomnia in early loss; a peripatetic man with equally nomadic family members glimpses them in a variety of countries and conditions; a daughter whose father has dementia discovers mementos that tell a story he was never able to share; a man discovers that his father was not the man he understood him to be—rather both more and less; a son begins to see his father, when hospitalized, in a very different light; a farmer's widow quietly sets out to live the life she wants, not the one her children expect of her.

We hope you find in these poems and short stories and memoirs echoes of your own experiences—and also invitations to new responses and possibilities. We did.

Bibliography

Beck, Julie. "When Are You Really an Adult?" *The Atlantic*. January 5, 2016.

Bouvard, Marguerite Guzmán. *Mothers of Adult Children*. New York: Lexington Books, 2013.

Bruner, Jerome. "The Narrative Construction of 'Reality'." *Psychoanalysis and Development: Representations and Narratives*. Eds. Massimo Ammaniti and Daniel N. Stern. New York: New York University Press, 1994. 15-35.

Coleman, Joshua. *Rules of Estrangement: Why Adult Children Cut Ties and How to Heal the Conflict*. New York: Harmony Books, 2020.

Erikson, Erik. "Human Strength and the Cycle of Generations." *The Erik Erikson Reader*. Ed. Robert Coles. New York: W.W. Norton, 2000. 188-225.

Isay, Jane. *Walking on Eggshells: Navigating the Delicate Relationship Between Adult Children and Parents*. New York: Doubleday, 2007.

Pew Research Center. "Majority of Americans Say Parents Are Doing Too Much for Their Young Adult Children." October 23, 2019.

Psychological and Counseling Services, University of New Hampshire. "Emerging Adulthood." Handout based on Arnett, J.J. *Emerging Adulthood: The Winding Road from Late Teens Through the Twenties*. Oxford University Press, 2014.

I
ROLE REVERSAL

JUDITH SANDERS

HELPING MOM DOWNSIZE

We've switched places:
She's in the passenger seat,
too old to drive.

From the trunk the DPW guy
unloads bundles of wire hangers
that held her designer outfits.

Bargains nabbed
with Bernese and Leila
and Milly and Flo.

Her eyes, rimmed with mascara,
now pocked with floaters,
can no longer detect the stains.

Back, we bag towels for the Vets.
The silver earrings Dad bought her
were stolen at the estate sale.

Frida gave her that ashtray.
This pitcher's all that's left
of the wedding china.

The turkey roasting pan
sold for a song
from a free classified.

Please take the spring-form pan,
perfect
for Chocolate Mousse Cake.

Out with fifth-grade compositions,
Grandma's citizenship homework,
Dad's Army discharge card.

No one will want this desk lamp
though it gives such good light.
The college textbook has mold.

•

I haul trash and stack boxes,
flaunting gorilla strength.
Soon, home to my warm husband,

to closets stuffed with sheets and pots
that might be useful someday,
to photos I don't yet have to throw away.

Here, I yank out picture hooks
from blanks framed with dust,
ghosts of paintings sold.

I dump the spices,
coil extension cords,
unplug the phone.

•

Out the door for the last time.
Key in the mailbox
for the young couple moving in.

Pluck a last chrysanthemum.
She wobbles, leaning on her cane.
Each dip could gape into a grave.

Such a good mop, she'd cried
when the DPW guy tossed it
into the dumpster.

She who took a bus to Mexico.
She who sped down icy mountains
on her Flexible Flyer.

CAROL BARRETT

PORTRAIT

My mother admitted to missing her full-length mirror, years since we moved them, my father now gone ahead to check out the scenery, Mother leaning more and more on her "pushcart" walker. I mount the new mirror by her closet, trim teal border to greet each new morning, near a button to press by 10 a.m. to say you are alright. I rub oil of olive on the gummy spot left by the sticker. Some things can be fixed. A sister tells me the mirror is too high. Mom is shrinking, and lower is better. Lower it goes.

Eons ago, I invited a friend to help go through my closet, weed out what didn't work, coach me on wardrobe fidelity. Her presence yielded a parade of hats and scarves, removal of boxy denim dresses. She intoned on flow and jewel tones, insisted I needed a full-length mirror. How could I know what I looked like, otherwise? My farm roots resisted, but she prevailed. This is not a world of sheep and chickens.

Now, almost 5 p.m. My mother says *time to go to dinner, you need to brush your hair,* increasing ardor the second and third refrains. I remind myself at least the salad bar will be good, retreat to her new mirror, take in the aging portrait, slim barrettes to hold bangs I am growing out, the rest looking just as I left it that morning, falling casually to my shoulders, hunched now to echo her height.

I tell her my hair is fine, check her oxygen tank, her keys. Annoyed, she gives up on my appearance, its temporary fix. I lean on the rail in the elevator, hold the door for her. The next day she will haul out her scrapbooks, show me the picture after my daughter was born, curls of a frizzy perm blooming. *Your hair looked so nice then* she will tell me. There is not much time left for corrections.

PAMELA HARTMANN

DON'T REMEMBER THIS

Caroline flung herself into active waiting mode. After twenty-five years of writing textbooks in English as a Foreign Language, she had received notice that the only publishing house for which she had ever worked was closing its EFL Department and expanding STEM. She didn't know anything about STEM. Stunned, she did nothing for days before summoning the energy to send out updated resumes.

Six months later, still jobless, her daily routine had morphed into ritual. She got up at 7:00 and assembled breakfast: coffee and two eggs, boiled, not fried, and a bowl of blueberries—for memory, they said. It was imperative not to check texts or email until 9:00, not to check the mailbox until 1:00. When the phone rang, she had to let it ring three times for fear of appearing too eager.

She had spent these months cleaning out closets, washing windows, catching up on email, working in the garden, going to the gym, taking classes. And she waited, uneasy with her suspicion that ritual was the refuge of the desperate.

Afternoon. Late summer. As she did every day, she called her mother.
"How are you, Mom?"
"Same old, same old."
"Are they treating you well? You're feeling okay?"
"Oh, ready to run a race."
"Yeah. I know."
"So are you enjoying your vacation?" her mother asked every afternoon.
"It's not a vacation."
"I know that. So what are you doing these days?"
"Well, I had my Modern Greek class last night, you know."
"You did? You didn't tell me about that. Why are you doing that?"
Caroline sighed. "I lived there one year, remember? In Greece?"

"You did?"

It was a long time ago—almost thirty years now. Her father had grumbled about how impractical it was, to be majoring in Classics.

"Oh? But why do you want to learn—what's that language again?" her mother said.

"Greek." Caroline thought a moment. The truth behind her impulse to sign up for the class was hard to articulate. She settled for a lesser truth. "I guess because it feels like progress to be learning something."

"Are you happy?" her mother asked, as she did each day.

"I'm fine."

"But are you happy?"

"I can't say *happy*. That's putting it too strongly, but I'm doing fine. I'm trying to take advantage of this time."

"Wouldn't you be happier if you were busy?"

"I'm keeping busy."

"Oh, Honey, I'm so sorry you're not happy."

"I'm doing okay. Are *you* okay?"

"Ready to run a race."

For a short time during Caroline's childhood, her parents were swept up in the wave of enthusiasm for *The Power of Positive Thinking*. A collection of self-affirming slogans was taped to the refrigerator, each copied in her mother's meticulous hand. Now, decades later, one of these slogans would invade her thoughts at odd moments—a chirpy, unwelcome mantra. *Every day in every way I am getting better and better!* It stuck in her mind like a burr.

In the morning, Caroline turned her attention to the garden, as she did every morning. Her plan six months earlier, in spring, had been to plant a Mediterranean herb garden, terraced on the hillside. She thought of it as a Greco-Roman hanging garden of Babylon. But first she had to prepare the space. The yard was huge, an overgrown tangle neglected in recent years when work had consumed her time. Now she had nothing but time. She pruned Coastal Oak and Monterey Pine, thinned California Lilac, tore out coyote bush, and endlessly weeded. In spring, the ground had been soft from the winter rains, the weeds easy to pull. The repetition of motions was restful, almost addictive. There was satisfaction in feeling the roots give way, over and over—*thwick, thwick, thwick*—in adding one more weed to the pile, in standing up to survey her achievement. *Every day in every way* . . . But now, in summer, the ground was hard, the heat oppressive. It drove her indoors. She called her mother.

"How are you doing?"

"Same old, same old. Ready to run a race. Are you working?"

"I'm working in the garden."

"You know what I mean. Do you have money?" her mother asked.

"I'm okay for now. I have some savings."

"But you like to be busy. Haven't you heard from that man yet?"

"What man?"

"The one who was coming back from New York."

"Do you mean the editor?"

"Yes. When is he coming back from New York?"

"He's not coming back from New York. He *lives* in New York. There's no *back*."

"Oh? I thought he was coming back."

"No, Mom. That was last year. He came out here for meetings."

"Oh. Well. Wasn't he going to give you some work?"

"He gave me a lot of work, but that was last year. He took early retirement."

"Really? You didn't tell me that. So you're not working?"

"Not that kind of work."

"But don't you want to be working?"

"I'm doing fine. I'm getting a lot done."

"But wouldn't you be happier if you were working?"

"Of course. But there's nothing I can do about that right now."

"But you want to be working."

"Yes."

"Because it must be expensive to keep me in this place. I don't want to be a burden."

"You're not a burden, Mom. You're paying for yourself. I just write the checks."

"But I don't have that kind of money."

"You have enough. You sold your house at a good time." Caroline's throat tightened around the lie.

"I did? Oh, I'm so relieved. I've been worried about that."

In the late afternoon, Caroline pulled on exercise gear and tucked her Greek vocabulary cards into her gym bag.

Almost thirty years before, she had returned from a dazzling year in Greece to find her life suddenly diminished. She couldn't bring herself to contact the friends she had made there, didn't respond to their letters or calls. She was ashamed at how her life had stalled while theirs, surely, had not. She imagined Jonathan trekking from Ephesus to Cappadocia, picking up Turkish along the way, to add to his arsenal of languages; Alex, with boundless energy, guiding visiting scholars by Jeep around lesser-known sites on Rhodes; Sarah and James excavating southern Mexico and perfecting their Nahuatl.

Her father had been right. Classics was a poor choice of major. Caroline slogged through her senior year and then two years of graduate school, where possibilities narrowed since she couldn't afford the trajectory to a PhD. The deeper she got into the coursework, the more weary of it she grew, her Master's thesis—"The Hephaisteion: From Temple to Church to Foreigners' Graveyard"—a terrible luxury for someone who needed to begin supporting herself. It was too late to start over in a different major, even if she could think of what that might be. Mired in student loans, she searched for work in a job market limited for a person with an MA in Classics.

She picked up small jobs writing supplemental textbook materials, surprised to find she liked the work. The jobs multiplied. In time, she worked her way up to creating her own series of books. It challenged her, made her feel taut, focused. She had found her calling without seeking it out. In between projects, the publisher sent her on speaking tours to colleges in Latin America and Asia. "Can't you send me to Greece next time?" she would ask. "Ha ha," the marketing people said, as if this were a joke. "No need for textbooks there. Everyone in Greece already speaks English."

At the gym, Caroline set the treadmill on an incline and propped her flashcards on the tray, to practice the language for which there was no need but which she was studying, anyway, in a free class at St. Sophia's Orthodox Church. The only non-Greek-American in the group, she made up for her disadvantage by applying an arsenal of study techniques she had used in her EFL books, culled from linguistics research. *The brain retains chunks better than bits,* researchers said, so on one side of each card she had written ten

Greek words, each one a "bit," nestled into the phrase in which she had found it, its "chunk." On the other side were the English translations. For an hour, she walked uphill and memorized vocabulary.

It was pointless, she knew—this compulsion to recapture a language she had left behind nearly a lifetime ago. But Greece had shaped her, and that year, she had been happy. All these years later, she would open a jar of oregano or bury her face in a cluster of fresh basil and—in an exquisite flash of pleasure and pain—inhale her first night in Athens, at an outdoor taverna on the slope of Mt. Lycavettos, with a garland of lights strung overhead and the Acropolis floodlit in the distance. It was her first experience in a foreign country, and she felt heady with the sensory assault: the blend of aromas floating from the kitchen, the burn of *retsina* on her throat, the soft notes of a bouzouki. Intoxicated with wine and anticipation for the year ahead, she and a clutch of other students—strangers until that night—shared roast chicken oozing with lemon and garlic, dipped crusty bread into the olive oil of a communal village salad, and fell into the immediate kinship of people unmoored from familiar, sheltered harbors.

Marble monuments and turquoise sea provided the background in the movie of her life that year, which crystallized into a series of scenes recalled and recounted so many times that she wondered where the truth lay—each scene frozen in time like an old snapshot from the family album, the original occasion now just a memory of a memory in an endless hall of imperfect mirrors.

Still, today, the sound of waves curling onto a pebbled shore transported her to a languid afternoon swim on Crete with her boyfriend of a short time that first semester. Her body held the physical memory of emerging from the Aegean—feet crunching through coarse sand, skin tingling with salt and sun. They sprawled side by side on the hot beach, face down, chins propped on fists. "Look," he said in Greek. "Do you see the sand?" She thought she had misunderstood. It was a peculiar question. But then she did look more closely. The sand was not sand—but billions of unimaginably tiny seashells. How could she not have noticed this before? She scooped up a warm handful and let it run through her fingers: multitudes of miniature corkscrews, snails, clams. Then she stretched arms and legs to the four directions, a universe of primordial creatures beneath her body. For one moment of pure, distilled joy, she felt the roundness of the Earth.

Ah! she thought. *Now it begins! This is what my life will be like!*

But it was a false start.

※

Now, so many years later, Caroline found pleasure in the familiar feel of Greek on her tongue and in the challenge of reaching out for new words, folding them into her memory. One word, though, clung in her mind without effort. She didn't need to transfer it from her notes to a flashcard, didn't even need to cocoon it in a phrase for context.

"Don't try to remember this," the instructor had said. "It's not a real word, so you'll never need it, of course."

The students scribbled furiously, anyway: *pothoglistres*. Nikos Kazantzakis had invented the word to describe Helen of Troy. She had "passion-gliding-down-her-shoulders" beauty. The class was charmed.

Caroline found herself forming the word on her lips, whispering it as she climbed the treadmill. *Pothoglistres*. She considered the use to which she might put this technique: *Don't remember the declension of neuter nouns. Absolutely do not remember the conjugation of passive voice verbs.*

※

The next day, she took stock. The closets were cleaned out, the ground was too hard for planting, and the Greek class would soon be over. Caroline's savings were almost depleted. Some nights she slept ten hours. Some she didn't sleep at all.

"Are you doing okay?" she asked her mother.

"Ready to run a race. Are you happy?"

"I'm okay."

"But I want you to be *happy*."

"All right. I'm happy."

"You don't sound happy."

Caroline sighed. "I'm happy, all right? Happy, happy, happy." She heard how pathetic she sounded.

"Really? Has that man come back from New York?"

Caroline felt strangled. "No. He hasn't. He won't. Ever. What do you want me to say? What do you want to hear? You keep asking the same question over and over and over, so the only thing I can figure is that you don't like my answer. Do you want to hear that I'm miserable, that I'm curled up in a ball? *What do you want from me*? No, he hasn't come back from New York. He *lives* in New York, and now he's not working, either. There's *no work*, so *please* don't ask again because I can't bear to hear it, and my answer will always be the same."

Her mother abruptly hung up. A knot formed in the pit of Caroline's stomach. She knew she had put a hex on everything.

※

In the garage, she found a fearsome three-pronged tool that she dragged into the garden. She gripped the waist-high handle and used all of her strength to thrust the prongs into the soil, to twist, to loosen the weeds. Over and over and over. The ground was like concrete, and she didn't have the right center of gravity. The roots did not give way with a satisfying *thwick*. But she kept stabbing into the dead ground and replaying the conversation with her mother. Over and over and over. Then she gave up and went into the house.

"How are you doing, Mom?"
"Same old, same old."
"I'm sorry I was rude."
"Were you rude?"
"I shouldn't have said those things."
"I don't remember what you said."
"I guess that's good."
"Are you working?"
Caroline paused. "Yes. I have a big project."
"So that man came back from New York?"
"Yes. He came back. He gave me a lot of work."
"Oh, Honey," her mother said. "I'm so sorry you have to work so hard. When can you take a vacation?"
Caroline took a deep breath. "It's okay, Mom. I'm happy."
Do not remember this, she thought. *Absolutely do not remember this.*

ALISA CHILDRESS

PLEADING FOR ANSWERS

The room had unbelievably shiny floors. Almost reflective. My mom sat next to me. This woman, who was once taxed with raising me, with my health and safety. She took me to doctor appointments, to the dentist, to church. She looked after my physical and spiritual well-being. Today, we were sitting together in this room, waiting for a doctor. She was waiting for her doctor, Dr. A.

Despite driving for thirty minutes and getting on multiple expressways, she had not realized that we were not at her doctor's office, which is only blocks from her home. And in a much different and much older building, one without the impossibly shiny floors. We were in the cancer unit, which on Thursdays is on loan to the memory care team. As I sat, I wondered if I was sitting in the same room my dad was in when he first received his terminal diagnosis.

While she was waiting for her primary care doctor, I was waiting for a neuropsychologist. For someone who could give me answers as to why my mother did not seem to realize why she was not in her usual doctor's office. Why she did not know who I was at times, or her husband, or her best friend of over fifty years. Or her grandchildren, including my mostly grown son.

Now, I am tasked with taking her to the doctor and seeing to her mental and physical well-being. We waited for several minutes until a lovely, young nurse entered. During this short wait, my mother commented on the floors dozens of times. She told me several times that she liked them. Each time it was as though it was her first time seeing them, and she had not commented on them less than a minute before.

"Look at these floors."

"Yeah. The floors are super shiny. Think someone waxed them last night?"

"Why are we here. Are you sick?"

"No. You are at the doctor's."

"Oh. Where is Dr. A? Why is it taking so long? Should we leave? Did you see these floors?!"

"I know. They are shiny. Would you like a magazine?" I pull out the *Better Homes and Gardens* from the basket by my chair. She has always liked the pictures. She was always interested in home decorating and kept a beautiful house. At least, in the before times.

"No. Thanks. Why are we here? Are you sick?"

"No. We are at your doctor."

"I feel fine. Wow. Look at these floors."

She is beyond the point of being able to tell me what she likes about these floors. Whether it is the brown color, the fake streak of marble, or the shininess that makes it difficult to notice the color or see the fake marble streak. I assume that it is the shininess and say that I imagine that someone just recently polished them. I mention the doors, which are primarily tempered glass set into a distressed wooden frame. I like the doors. I hope this will take the conversation away from the floor as I do not think I can bear to hear about them again.

I take out my phone and show her pictures of the family. "Who is that?" I am showing her my son's senior picture.

"That is Josh."

"I don't think I know him."

"He is your grandson. My baby."

"Oh. I don't know anything about that. Just look at those floors."

The sweet, young, blond nurse comes into the room, introducing herself as April. I pull my mother's Covid-required mask back up over her nose. April is pleasant and smiles through her mask as she talks. She asks my mother her name.

"Beverly."

My mom stares blankly when Nurse April asks for her last name. We waited a few moments. I was confident that she was going to say "Netherton." She identifies with this name now. It was her maiden name, two marriages ago.

The first marriage, to my father, lasted seven years. Then there was a long period of being single, in which she seriously contemplated becoming a nun. She then met and dated my step-father for many years. They have been married for twenty-six years and counting. She has not been a Netherton since she first married at twenty years old, over fifty years ago.

I wait for her to respond, but she says nothing, so I tell the nurse that her last name is Ralston. The nurse confirms this on her computer and asks her who I am. Again, we wait to see how Mom will respond. She tells her that I am her daughter. April asks for my name, and Mom replies, "Alisa," again with no last name. My mother has become adept at responding with the information she still has access to without letting others see the increasing gaps in her memory.

Months ago, I asked Mom if she worries about her memory, and she does not seem to be aware that she is any different than she was before. She does not realize that she can no longer drive or write a check, sort her medications, or fix a meal. This last one is a massive loss as she was an excellent cook.

Mom does not seem to realize that she has forgotten things and people. She seems to be happy. She never seemed truly happy before. I never remember her when she was not depressed, anxious, and worried. It is as though she has forgotten to worry. She has forgotten those things that she always worried about, car wrecks and cancer and the fear that her loved ones (mostly me) would go to hell.

We talk to the nurse. My mother tells April that she is there for a check-up with Dr. A and asks if he is in today. We simultaneously respond "no," which makes me feel better. If a dementia professional responds to her the same way I do, I must be doing the right thing. As though there is a right thing.

When she was in charge of me, I always assumed there was a right and wrong way to do things. When I was small, I thought that, since she was the adult, my adult, the one in charge of my care, that, of course, she knew the right way.

When I was a teenager, I had that same assuredness of right and wrong ways to do things. I had that sense of justice and certainty that can only exist in adolescence. And I was equally sure that she was doing everything the wrong way. I wonder if my son thinks the same of me. If so, he does not let on. He is much more polite and kind than I was at his age.

As an adult, I see that there is no absolute right and wrong way to do anything. My son is on the precipice of adulthood, and I am even more uncertain about parenting than when he was an infant. When I am in charge of my mother, I wish very much that there is a right way. A shining light. A beacon that would come down and tell me what to do. Now that I am the adult in charge, I desperately wish I was not.

April asks, "Why are you here? What do you want to know?"

"My step-father and I have very different ideas of what is necessary for Mom's care and well-being. I want to know what exactly we need to do to keep her safe."

"Ok. I want to make sure that we address all your concerns in our report. That you get the answers you are looking for."

I feel a little hope that I will learn the right way. I allow myself to believe that these professionals are the adults in the room. They will give me a paper to take home that will serve as the adult in the room. It will tell me how to care for my mom, who is quickly becoming less and less recognizable. It feels very surreal, co-parenting my mother. Especially with a man I did not meet until I was in high school and who has very different ideas than me

"I want a diagnosis and a prognosis. Dr. A diagnosed her with early-onset Alzheimer's, and I'm sure he's right. There have been so many issues for several years. But then he pulled the diagnosis out of thin air. There were no tests. He did not recommend an evaluation. Maybe something else is in play. Something that could be treated."

She is taking notes on her computer.

"Mostly, I want recommendations on how to best take care of her. To keep her safe. My stepdad took away her keys a few months ago."

"Finally," I think to myself. I do not say that he did this long after I thought he should. Long after other friends and family thought it was safe. After mystery dings started appearing that she could not explain or remember. After she lost her car in a Walmart parking lot and had a stranger drive her home. After she got lost on the way home from a mall she had gone to thousands of times.

"He has unplugged the stove so that she cannot cook." Again, I leave out that he waited to do this until she left the water running in the sink for several hours, and it occurred to him that she could do this with the fire on the gas stove.

"But, he leaves her at home alone while he is at work. For eight to ten hours at a time. The rest of her family and friends feel like this is a bad decision." The thought of this gives me a pit in my stomach like we are inviting danger, and I feel like I might have more footing if a professional tells us this.

Her alone time has been a point of contention for many months now. She has locked herself out of the house and had to go to a neighbor's house.

She stayed with them until he was able to get there with the key. He let her in the house, ensured she was settled in and left to return to his job.

She calls people dozens of times each day. I once counted forty-seven calls in five hours. I answered eight times as I was working and could not answer every time, even though I had a twinge of guilt every single time I ignored her call. She would never have let my calls go unanswered. Each time she called, she did not remember speaking to me before, and it was not clear that she knew who I was.

My step-father, Mike, says he thinks that the day will come when she cannot be left alone, "but we are not there, yet." He used this phrase when he would not take away her keys, even when everyone else told him he needed to. He does not want to take away her autonomy and does not understand the gravity of the situation. He loves her and is in denial.

And, even though it is on the tip of my tongue, I am afraid to mention my worry that this will happen to me. This thing that is happening to Mom at such a young age.

She asked me when we started noticing things. I told her that I saw things years ago, small things in her early sixties. It became apparent when she was hospitalized for a blood clot around sixty-five years old and did not know where she was the entire time. She tried to leave, pulling out an IV, on her way to the door. She had just been given morphine and was asleep. I stepped out for a quick lunch and returned twenty minutes later to find a trail of blood on the floor. She was lying down as two frazzled nurses tried to put a new IV back in her arm.

I saw it happen to my grandmother when she was in her eighties. I saw it happen to two of my grandmother's aunts and heard tales of dementia in my grandmother's sister. I see it occur over and over and over to the women in my family, and I wonder when it will come for me. Occasionally, I forget a common word or the artist who performed a song that has been swimming in my head since 1983. I assure myself that this happens to everyone or that it is stress, but I worry. I worry that I am beginning to slip away and am just as unaware of it as my mother is.

ALEXIS DAVID

PICKING UP MY DAD FROM THE HOSPITAL

I want to cut the iris in the garden,
I want to pour rainwater over my feet.
The pansies sit like hopeful children,
waiting for their parents to come home.

You are like the apricots in *Le Puy-en-Velay,*
as kind as baseball leather.
My father, your beard
grown out into a white scruff—
something between sailor and forget.

You pull your legs out of the car.
You're wearing my blue wool socks.

We stand for a moment.
You don't want me to help.
You want to tell me about the hospital,
want to tell me about the cleaner.
He didn't want to be a cleaner in a hospital:
didn't go to high school,
wished he had.

He asked for your ginger ale.
You gave it to him
(of course you did).

MOURNING DOVES

My dad asks me to follow him to the backyard.
"I call her Mommy. Call her Mommy!"
"I'm not calling her mommy," I say.

Why does my dad think this bird is his mom?

The mourning dove is on the nest,
huddled and surrounded by pieces of wheat bread.
The bread is obviously from my dad,
"I just thought she might like that."

His own mother used to bring him candy bars.
She cleaned houses in the East Side of Buffalo,
let him come with her.
He got to watch TV in the empty houses of strangers.

Now, my dad cleans relentlessly:
licks his pointer finger,
gently places it on six fallen crumbs on the kitchen floor
throws them away,
and then wipes his hand on jeans that he bought twenty-six years ago.

The mourning dove's baby birds are under her,
like two strange critics.

He brings out three worms every day.
He looks up "Mourning Doves" on YouTube
and watches videos of the babies leaving the nest.

There are some beliefs that are part of my skin:
waste not want not
save your money
love your family more than anything else.

He comes to my house today,
drinks coffee,
tells me, his voice nearly shaking, "The babies just fall out of the nest and then
fly away from the mom. Gone. That's it."
His mother died from pneumonia the day after I was born.
I was always told not to live more than one day's drive away.

Now, he stands in my kitchen.
He asks me if he is keeping me from my work.
"No," I say.
"Want a cookie?" I ask.
Like I am packing his nest with bread.

All children are critics,
watching their parents watch them.

JOAN DOBBIE

CONVERSATION BEFORE SLEEP

For my Mom 1913-2002

She knew I'd be writing about it
after she died.

Are you taking notes?
(Her voice almost demanding.)

No, I said.
Did you take your evening pills?

No, she said. *Do I have to?*

Yes

*I think you should write a novel about my life.
I've had a very interesting life.*

I've already written about your life.
Besides, I'm a poet not a novelist.

*Novels sell better.
You need to write a novel.*

Alright. I'll think about it, okay?
You need to take your night pills.

Do I have to take the yuck medicine?

Yes

Alright, if you say so. But it makes me sick.

You'll be sicker if you don't take it.
Anyhow, Barb says you need to take it.

Alright, if Barb says so then I have to take it.
Are you sure I have to take it?

Yes. No.—Okay. I'll ask Barb tomorrow.
Maybe you can stop taking it.

Good. But do I still have to take it tonight?

Yes

Okay, if you say so. I do everything I'm told.
Will you get me a cigarette?

No. Yes. Okay, here.
But you have to sit up to smoke it.

You should start on that novel, you know, while
you still have me around to answer questions.

Maybe tomorrow. I have to
think about it, okay?

Okay, tomorrow. By the way,
are you taking notes?

MICHELE MARKARIAN

MY MOTHER'S MOTHER

"This is my sister," says my mother, beaming and patting my arm. "No. No—wait. This is my *mother*."

"I'm your daughter, Ma," I reply, somewhat testily. It is my mother's birthday, and I have bought enough of her favorite Chinese food to share with the table at her nursing home, which I do.

Arlene, a woman who is just a few years younger than my mother and whose own mother is 103, looks at me shrewdly. Arlene visits her mother almost every day, even though her mother can be sharp and dismissive. This Arlene chalks up to old age.

I would like to chalk my mother's behavior up to old age, but really, she is who she always was, only a little more concentrated.

"Stay with me tonight," my mother demands. "I can't be alone. My fiancé isn't speaking to me." This is new, my mother's boy-crazy side. Every week there's a new fiancé, with some kind of roadblock to marital happiness—another girlfriend, a possessive mother, a demanding job.

"I can't, Ma."

"Why not?" My mother's mouth sets itself in a hard line.

"I have tickets to the theater—"

"Always the theater with you!" Her eyes narrow to slits.

"More eggplant?" I hold out the dish to Arlene's mom, who ignores me.

"So selfish!" My mother is enraged, looking at me in the way she always did. It doesn't matter that I am the only one of her three children who is here to celebrate her birthday. I am also her health care proxy, power of attorney, executor. I handle her finances. Yet I am about to let her push my buttons, the ones that she has created.

"Besides, Ma, there's no bed for me here." This is undeniably true. Nursing homes do not allow sleepovers.

"Selfish, selfish, selfish. Always do whatever you want. Always have, always will. I'm disgusted. And sad." She pushes aside the present I bought.

"I'm not selfish, you're selfish," I spit out. "Who do you think takes care of you?" Across the table, Arlene gives me the fisheye.

"I'm sorry you're sad," Arlene says in a kind tone, cocking her head thoughtfully at my mother. I get it; Arlene thinks that this is a new dynamic, one involving a once-caring, loving mother and her selfish, willful daughter. Arlene doesn't understand that my mother has always been unhappy, has always been a black hole of need, one that no action or deed can ever fill. She's insatiable, my mother. No amount of growing up or therapy can stop me from wanting to put up a wall. At some point, the insults will worsen—"You have ice water running through your veins" was a favorite one throughout my teenage years—and I'll have to freeze, tune her out, keep her unhappiness at bay.

Today she's worn out. "Get a nurse to take me to my room," she murmurs. I bag up the Chinese food and write her name on the bag for her floor's refrigerator and tell the aids she wants to take a nap.

I follow them to her room. She is sitting in her wheelchair while they make up her bed and prepare to lift her onto it.

"I love you, but only sometimes," my mother calls over to me.

"I love you sometimes, too," I say. The nurses look uncomfortable. My mother starts to laugh, and so do I.

JANET LUNDER HANAFIN

'ROUND THE BEND

"Hello?"
"Hi, Mama, it's Evie."
"Who?"
"Evie, Mama, your—"
"Evie?"
"Yes, Mama. How are you? Is this a good time to talk?"
"I'm in jail!"
"Oh, Mama, you're not in jail."
"I am. I can't go anywhere. I can't go to bingo. I can't go to mahjong. I can't go to the mail room. I can't even go to church."
"Yesterday you said you went to church."
"I don't think I went to church yesterday. What day is this?"
"Monday."
"Well, I didn't go to church yesterday."
"That nice girl in the blue uniform came and took you to church yesterday, Mama. Don't you remember? You said three little girls came and sang before the sermon."
"Well, I don't remember. But you know, I can get out of here any time. I know the secret number. I just punch it in and I can get out whenever I want. It's on the wall by the red door."
"You don't want to do that, Mama. What if you can't get back in?"
"Why would I want to get back in?"
"Well, all your things are in your room, for one thing... Have you been playing any games, the dice game or Crazy 8s?"
"They steal you blind in here, you know."
"Is something missing?"
"My pink duster."
"Duster?"

"You know, that pink one with the black lace around the collar that I wear over my pajamas to watch TV on Saturday night."

"Oh, your old housecoat. You haven't had that in years."

"I did. I did! That's a terrible thing to say to me. I know that girl in the blue outfit stole it. She said pink was a good color on me, and I could just tell she'd walk off with it as soon as she got the chance."

"That housecoat wore out before I even left for college."

"Who is this?"

"Evie."

"Evelyn? You were named after my grandmother, you know. She was a very beautiful woman, but very crabby. After she got old nobody liked her. I don't know why I ever named you Evelyn."

"Have you been to lunch, Mama?"

"We don't have lunch here at noon. We have dinner, like on the farm."

"At noon?"

"Of course. When else would you have dinner?"

"What did you have for dinner then?"

"Oh, it was a lot of work! Swiss steak from when we butchered that cow. And mashed potatoes, and beans from the garden. I got Gloria to pick them. The beans are great this year. That yellow bowl was full. Evie won't go in the garden. She's afraid of the garden spiders. I baked those rolls your dad likes, and we had Jello. Bernice brought over plum pies for dessert. I'd never think of making plums into pie, but they were OK. It's too bad she doesn't know how to do a decent crust."

"Mama, I think you're remembering—"

"Of course I'm remembering. I'm not senile, you know. I don't have to make notes like that crazy old lady next door. She's really 'round the bend. Her whole table is covered with those sticky notes. What to tell her kids, what to tell the doctor, what TV channel—"

"I think you were remembering things you did a long time ago, when we were growing up. You don't have to cook for farm crews any more."

"They were baling the south forty. Only four of them, your dad and Bill, and those Peterson boys. John is big enough to drive the tractor with the flatbed now . . . They lock you in here, you know."

"I know, Mama. I know you aren't happy about that."

"And my green pen is gone. I can't find it anywhere. I'm sure it was stolen. They rob you blind here. I can't even write a grocery list without it."

"Did you look under the table?"

"I never thought of that. Just a minute . . . Well, aren't you smart? That's right where it was. You know, Christy and Brendan came by for dinner yesterday after church. Christy is expecting another baby. Did you know that?

"Yes. She called me a couple of weeks ago and told me, and said they'd plan to have lunch with you. Did you have a good visit?"

"Yes, we did. I don't know why she's telling everybody about the baby already. She isn't even showing yet. When I was young, you didn't go around telling everybody. They have a girl. Marissa, I think. Strange name. Very modern. Christy said they're having a boy. I don't know how she'd know that."

"A little boy will be nice, Mama. Did you have a good lunch, uh, dinner?"

"Very good. The meals here are always good. They do a very nice job with broccoli. We never had that when I was growing up. It's quite a new vegetable. Sometimes it's mushy. I think they steam it here, and it is always very pretty, bright green."

"Do you remember what else you had for lunch?

"Spam."

"Spam?"

"Yes. You know that pink meat. You get a key with it, but I can't remember what for."

"It was to open the can. Spam, Mama? Did they really give you Spam?"

"Maybe not. I think it was some kind of chicken with a mushroom sauce, and wild rice. I prefer white rice, but wild rice is kind of the in thing to serve now. Do you know how to make it?"

"Yes, but I don't do it too often."

"Well, what have you been doing since the last time you called?"

"Um . . . let's see. The choir is singing for a big church festival next week, so we had an extra rehearsal last Saturday."

"You sing in a choir?

"Ah, yes."

"A church choir?"

"Yes."

"Well. What church?

"Our church, Lakeside Lutheran."

"We don't have a choir here. People are too old to stand up. And they're way too old to stay in tune. That lady who used to play the piano died, and the one who directed the choir, back when we had a choir, got moved to memory care."

"And George and I went to the lake for a couple of days."

"Oh, the lake. I remember going there. Did you go out on the boat?"

"Not this time. It was pretty rainy."

"Well, I don't think you should go out in the boat. Boats are very dangerous. My uncle fell out of a canoe and drowned."

"Yes, I remember that."

"I don't know how you'd remember. You weren't even born yet."

"I remember you telling me about it."

"Telling you about what?"

"That Uncle Reynolds fell out of a canoe."

"I don't know why I'd tell you a horrible thing like that. He drowned, you know. I wouldn't tell a little child about that."

"And we went to see Gloria and Frank's new house."

"Who?"

"Gloria and Frank. My sister, your oldest daughter."

"Who is Frank?"

"Her husband. They bought a new house."

"A new house? Where?"

"It's about four miles from their old place. It's a townhouse, a little smaller than their other one."

"Oh, a house in town. They'll like that. Gloria never did like living so far out in the country. But what is Frank going to do in town?"

"They're both retired, Mama."

"Retired? Are they moving to Florida?

"No. Why would they do that?"

"Isn't that where everybody moves when they retire? Then, when they get really old, they move in with their children, if they're lucky and their children will have them."

"No, they didn't move to Florida, and they're not moving in with their children because they don't have any children."

"I wonder why not. Do you suppose something was wrong with Frank? I'm sure Gloria was perfectly all right. It must have been something wrong with Frank."

"They're going to remodel the kitchen, so they're busy picking out appliances."

"That's nice. I hope they get a dishwasher. I always wanted a dishwasher, but I guess you could say I had two of them. You girls were pretty good dishwashers."

"I'm glad you remember that, Mama."

"You were really good workers, on the farm, in the garden. Do you remember all those chickens you raised, and sold the eggs yourself?"

"How could I forget that?"

"And you even knew how to milk the cows. Not many of your friends can say that, I'll bet."

"And drive a tractor, Mama. We could all do that."

"John took my car away."

"That was a long time ago, and you said you were glad to get rid of it."

"They lock you in here, you know. I might as well be in jail."

"I'm sorry about that. Listen, Mama, I have to go, but I'll call you in a couple of days. I love you."

"But I can get out any time I want. You just punch in the secret number by the red door, and bingo! You're out. It's the same as our old phone number on the farm, 7-7-2-5-9 . . . Bye, Gloria. I love you, too."

SHARON LASK MUNSON

IF BY CHANCE THERE IS MEMORY IN YOUR SLUMBER

In sleep, do you slip-slide back
recall me, your middle daughter,
fine brown hair braided, ribboned?

While you nap
are you back in the red brick house
peeling parsnips, chopping onions

or are you a child yourself,
clutching your own mother's
firm warm hand?

I enter your narrow bedroom
glimpse the hills of your body
under the blue afghan,
your snow-white hair matted, tousled.

You stir, utter sounds I can't unravel.
It's been a year since we last spoke.

I settle myself on the padded rocker,
gaze out the window at the gray sky,
listen to thunderstorms pummel the roof,
throaty black crows in the yard, cawing.

Where do you go when your eyes close?
Is your mind an empty slate
that greets you upon wakening

or if by chance
there is memory in your slumber,
I wish you, my darling mother,
the sweetest of dreams.

OH, MOM

I clean out shelves in my linen closet
where I store bath towels, sheets

and the few things left that belonged to you.
I reach far into the back, behind clutter

and extract your beige leather shoes
the ones you wore toward the end

lace up oxfords, extra deep
with the scuff on the side where they rubbed.

It was the scuff that brought the tears,
that jaunty clip to your walk.

LAURA GLAVES

IN THE SILENCE

I slip inside Mom's room
early one evening
and find her awake in bed.

In the dim light,
I sit next to her,
just behind the bed rail.

Her brown eyes shine brightly.
She smiles that lopsided grin,
lifting the left corner of her lips.

I bend down and kiss her cheek.
She wrestles her left hand
from beneath the blankets.

Her fingertips trace my forehead,
then fall to my temple.

Tenderly, she strokes the contours
of my cheek. Never lifting her hand,
she caresses the curve of my chin.

Over and over again

Then she lifts her left hand
and strokes my silky hair
from the crown of my head
to the nape of my neck.

Over and over again

In the silence, her message is clear.

I love you,
I love you,
I love you.

Over and over again

II
ASSUMING ADULTHOOD

CHRIS WOOD

HER FIRST

I browse the card aisle,
read each Mother's Day card.
I cannot find the right sentiment,
the right theme to describe our relationship.

I blush remembering I was inside her once,
floating in amniotic fluid, connected by a cord.
That link, bond broken while she was in a state
of forced slumber. She didn't feel the split,
the cutting away.

She gave me life, yet I don't know her
or her me. Or do I? We are mirrors,
introverts, finding comfort in solace,
reflecting on our own thoughts,
neither expressing them very well.

My smile matches hers, yet
she seems lost, frozen in time, held back
or locked in a prison of her own making.

I face mine head on, walk through
the valley of my pain, my truth,
and like who I am.
                    Does she?

JOANELL SERRA

THIS SKIN NO ONE CAN CLAIM

You shake when the cops pull your car over, because Trayvon Martin. Because George Floyd. Because that Latin kid in Santa Rosa was 13 when he lifted his water gun, just playing. Look what happened to him. The heavy breather writes a fat ticket, making sure to dot the I's and cross the T's.

At work, your co worker takes your trembling body aside, "Let me tell you about being Black in this town." *I'm not Black*, you could say. But you feel her fear and determination. Not white either, according to the rules of colonization.

Your thoughts drift to the lake, the way the water breaks for the hull of the boat. To polished wood, and to pine trees and to deforestation. To agate blue water and fresh cut blood. Your mind lands on the topic of color.

I'm Brown. You're the shade of the Redwood tree sliced open, the circle near the outer edge of the trunk. Deep brown, solid brown, shining brown skin stretched over the hard muscles of a boy descended from Mayan athletes. Not a boy anymore, either. At the edge of grown, just polishing off this process of maturation. A man.

Yes a man, who runs like the wind, fuck the pain in your knees, spine, hips. Runs without stopping until you're free. Free of the schools designed by a prison architect. Free of the flashing lights thrown on for intimidation. Free of the lily-white suburbs that screen at the gate for pigmentation. Free of fear you'll be trapped in the churning stagnation of your peers. Free of the hope that a can of spray paint and a wall will bring real transformation. Free of resignation.

You're free to practice your own form of meditation, down on your knees, murmuring love songs to our dog. Planting spicy Thai peppers in my garden. Cooking wild caught salmon for the family, while discussing the intricacies of grape cultivation.

Free to squint at the sky and offer your own narration. Maybe the sun is sinking or maybe it's rising. Maybe you're offering a declaration to the future or a performing a thorough examination of your past.

But here's our joint revelation:

Either way the horizon is,
    at this moment,
        the most stunning shade of Brown.

PANDEMIC, POOLSIDE

the baby possum floats in the pool one morning
swollen with death
we gather that evening
as we do this summer
the scent of honeysuckle in the breeze

we sip, my sons and I
waiting until another appears
eyes closed
weaving like a drunken toddler
towards a death by drowning

we hustle to create obstacles
patio furniture, the cooler
bright flashlights
I search for a corkscrew
clearly, we need more wine

the youngest, almost twenty
grabs oven mitts
don't touch it
his brother warns
they all of have rabies, I think

Undaunted, Joe scoops up the cherub
they have a lot of babies
his brother continues
scrolling
because so many of them don't make it

we grow quiet, contemplating this
Joe places the baby back in the bushes,
near Mama possum
with a shallow water bowl
also, actually, most don't have rabies

maybe I made that up
we stay up late, vigilant
it's July 2020—
my sons and I, inebriated
desperate to save one life

STEPHANIE HART

BIRTHDAY CAKE DRESS

"Happy birthday, darling," my mother says, running a knuckle against my cheek. She heats an English muffin and lavishes it with jam and butter just for me. We sit opposite each other at our kitchen table in Brooklyn in morning light, sipping coffee and talking.

"You are so young and lovely," my mother says. "I remember when I was your age." The muscles in her face tighten; her green eyes narrow and I can tell she is seeing herself in another time and place. "My mother was already dead, so our house in Newark was dusty and quiet. My father was out with his new girl friend, Jenny; you know the one he married."

"Did you like her?"

My mother shakes her head. "She wasn't my mother. Do you know what I did on my eighteenth birthday?"

"Yes," I say.

My mother tells the story again. "I bought myself a present and wrapped it for myself. It was a long shimmering summer dress from Bamburgers department store in downtown Newark. I tried it on in front of a full-length mirror, thinking how lonely and beautiful I looked."

My mother takes my hand and presses it. We watch each other for what seems a long time.

She stands up and leads me into the foyer where a box wrapped in red and white paisley paper rests on a thin yellow table. "Open it darling. I can't wait for you to see what I got for you."

I pull off the ribbon, the paper, and the lid. A dress made of tiers of white cotton emerges.

"Isn't it lovely?" my mother says. The joy and need on her face makes me afraid. I can feel her thinking. "All my love is in this dress. You must treasure it."

That evening my mother, my stepfather, and my father, who I rarely see, along with his new wife, Annette and I go out for dinner. My friends, Kara and Brian, join us for desert. I am wearing the dress my mother gave me with a thin strand of pearls around my neck.

The chicken is tender, but my father is not. His face is etched in angry lines. "I've almost forgotten what you look like, Steph." Since my mother's remarriage and my decision to go to high school in Brooklyn, he has regarded me as a turncoat, and I avoid him whenever I can. He laughs with a little puff of air. "Too bad you didn't get into an ivy league college like your father, the Harvard man."

Annette and I are wary of each other. She smiles at me, showing horse-like teeth. She smacks her silverware against her plate, and wipes her mouth in an elaborate gesture.

My mother is wearing a white silk dress that clings to her. She tosses back her head; her smile is dazzling and my father's new wife seems to shrink from it. My stepfather, decked out in a lime green suit, is talking about a court case he won fifteen years ago. My mother thrusts her chin in his direction to show that she is listening.

The following summer my stepfather will die; my mother will take a lover. My father will develop a rare blood disease and recover completely. When I fail to give him the care and attention he demands, the chasm of resentment between us will deepen. Tonight when the cake and Kara and Brian arrive, we all regard each other with forced cheer.

"Blow out the candles," my mother says. "Go ahead, make a wish."

"You're getting up there," my father says. And my stepfather chuckles in agreement. "Happy Birthday," Annette says with a slight lisp. And Kara, Brian and I try not to giggle.

The cake is the color of my new dress and has the same lace-like pattern. There is one brilliant candle in the middle and several other smaller ones. I stand up and close my eyes and the room becomes dark. I feel the warmth of the candles against my cheeks. Suddenly I am flying above the table and out the window into the open sky like a figure in a Chagall painting. Kara and Brian join me, and we glide over the buildings, leaving the city and my family beneath us.

SERA DAVID

UNDERCURRENT

She better not wave. Just the thought of that possibility made my cheeks feel hot.

Walking into the cafeteria as a college freshman was hard enough—flashbacks of my high school lunchroom reminded me of the awkwardness of looking for someone to sit with—but when I saw her, I felt even more like an embarrassed kid. There, holding court in the cafeteria of the college that was supposed to represent my independence, my freedom, and my adulthood, was my mother.

Known as the Parents-On-Campus program, mothers and fathers of full-time undergraduate students were eligible to take regular undergraduate courses tuition-free on a space-available basis. Parents could audit courses or take them for credit; they could pursue an interest or seek a degree. A great benefit for my mom as she always wanted to go to college—that dream was put on hold when my siblings and I were born in quick succession.

Not so great a benefit for me, because really, who wants to go to college with her mom?

When we learned about the free courses for parents, my mom was ecstatic; I never saw her so excited before. About anything. It made my decision harder.

I was choosing between this college and a larger state university. Both were within driving distance from our house. I felt more at home on the smaller campus, but was reconsidering after envisioning my mom on the college grounds. But then the guilt hit. My parents were helping to pay tuition. And I could help my mom realize her dream. After all she did for me, this was something I could do for her. Her face beamed when I submitted my acceptance. It made me feel good. Until the first day of school approached.

We did lay some ground rules, like we wouldn't carpool and we wouldn't register to take the same class at the same time. Thankfully, we had different majors—I was in computer science and she was in journalism—but it was a liberal arts college, so there were classes that we were both required to take.

We hadn't discussed the cafeteria though. Now, she was chatting up a table of other older classmates (or professors?) while I was seemingly lost. I quickly looked down, not wanting to make eye contact. *She better not wave.*

I lived at home freshman year to save money. My parents' typical questions of "How was school today?" or "Tell me about your day" ended pretty quickly when I responded sarcastically, "Just an average day going to college with my mommy."

I spent that year avoiding my mom on campus. I sat at the opposite end of the cafeteria with my back turned to her table. If we passed each other in the hallways, I looked the other way, pretending to be in a hurry.

Sophomore year, I moved into a one-bedroom apartment not far from campus. I had worked for a small computer company ever since I got my driver's license when I turned sixteen. I felt pretty independent and grown up already, having a job in my field and paying my own rent. The company very generously paid tuition for any of my classes that were related to business or computer science. Since those classes made up the majority of my course load, it was a huge help financially. They didn't know that they were indirectly funding my mother's degree as well.

I was no longer dependent on my parents for housing or money. I was excited to be moving into my own place and it was fun to have my mom help decorate it. I liked spending time with her—away from college. As I grew older, she seemed like more of a friend than a mother.

But the grown-up me I was trying to be still felt like I regressed every time I saw my mom on campus, particularly in the cafeteria. I adjusted my schedule to the extent I could, but I still needed to eat before heading to work after classes. And more importantly, it was my chance to be with Mike. He was my first love—I didn't have a boyfriend in high school—and I wanted to spend every free minute with him. I hadn't introduced him to my mom yet. Part of me wanted to share my joy with her, but part of me was afraid it might change things. If Mike knew my mom was in the cafeteria, I thought it would be natural for him to be more guarded. I didn't want to lose his carefree displays of affection. But if I brought him home to meet my parents, would he recognize my mom? What if they had a class together? Was seeing her in the cafeteria holding *me* back? I thought for the millionth time, *college isn't supposed to be like this.*

Maybe she would notice that I was always sitting with the same guy. I sure noticed that *she* was always sitting with the same guy. Seemed to me they were getting too friendly. Something about the body language. Especially when they were sitting alone.

Being married to my dad couldn't be easy. After years of bearing the brunt of his alcoholism, she finally gave him an ultimatum: get treatment or get out. He went through rehab when I was in high school and, so far, remained sober. But now, she appeared to be the one looking for trouble. It occurred to me that I sounded like the parent. I did some checking and learned that the guy she was always sitting with was a journalism professor. He was married and had three kids. I felt betrayed and somehow also complicit.

Maybe part of growing up was realizing that parents had their own dreams, their own desires, their own lives beyond their roles as parents. But it seemed like every time I told myself to just live my own life and let my mom live hers, she would find a way to tangle them up. My mom joined the school paper as a staff writer. When she told me that she was writing an article about the Parents-On-Campus program, I was upset. It wasn't enough that we were living it, now she wanted to advertise it? I insisted that she leave me out and informed her that everything I ever said was off the record.

When the newspaper came out, her article was on the front page. Of course. But it didn't mention that she herself was in the program and had a daughter attending the college. Only a small percentage of parents took advantage of the program, but understandably, they seemed to gravitate towards each other, so she had plenty of material and quotes. She wrote about a student who was not thrilled when he learned his mother registered for one of his classes; his mom promised not to sit by him or talk to him. I could definitely relate to him, but another mother and son actually chose to take a class together. Maybe I was too self-conscious, or immature, but as much as I loved my mom, I didn't want college to be a mother-daughter activity.

My mom grinned when I congratulated her on her front-page article. When I finally told her that I had a serious boyfriend, her response was simply, "I know, I see you together all the time." I cringed; I didn't appreciate being watched, even though I had been watching her as well.

I tried to give her a knowing look as I said, "I see you too." When she didn't say anything, I pressed on. "You know he's married, right? He has three kids." I paused before I admitted, "I don't understand."

She said quietly, "You can't know other peoples' relationships."

I realized the truth in that. As a young child, growing up afraid of my father and his alcoholic rages, I wondered why my mom didn't (and I wished she would) divorce him. Now, my dad was sober, but complained about her taking classes. I thought it was because she became more focused on coursework than housework. He was used to a clean home, fresh laundry, dinner on the table, and her attention. But maybe he knew that going to college would open doors for her, change the dynamic, weaken his control.

I shook my head. "It's still wrong."

"I didn't ask for your approval."

I didn't know what else to say. The whole conversation was sideways and backwards.

As I walked away, she said, "I hoped you'd be happy that I'm happy."

Was it childish to want parents I could respect, whose behavior I wanted to emulate? I endured years with a drunk dad and now I had to witness my mother's flirtation? Was I being too immature? Too judgmental? Should I just be happy for her?

Junior year, my mother and I coexisted on campus. Outside of the cafeteria, we inhabited different buildings; she spent most of the time in the journalism center while I was usually in the computer lab or study rooms.

I disapproved of her relationship with the professor, but didn't talk about it. As a child of an alcoholic, I learned not to talk about hard truths. I compartmentalized. I tried to keep school, home, and work separated. Mike was the exception. I introduced him to my parents at our house. By then, I told him about my mom and reluctantly pointed out her presence in the cafeteria. He claimed it didn't bother him, but he was definitely more relaxed when she wasn't in the room. Fortunately, since Mike majored in business, he did not have any classes with her.

When the yearbooks came out, I did what I think most people do first—I looked for pictures of myself. Then I looked at photos of my boyfriend. Then I did what few people would do—I looked for pictures of my mother. I wondered if, someday, I would look back at this time and find humor in going to college with my mom, or wish that I handled it better. But I still didn't ask her to sign my yearbook.

I thought I would be the first person in my family to graduate from college. That was before my mom piggybacked on my life. Although it wasn't a competition, it felt like she beat me at everything. She graduated a year before me. At least I didn't have to worry about graduating together; alphabetically, she would have walked in front of me. In the end, she chose not to participate in the ceremony, but she graduated with highest honors—Summa Cum Laude. The cynical part of me wanted to complain that she got As by literally kissing up to the professor. But I knew that it couldn't have been easy for her to go to school with twenty-year olds. She really worked hard and deserved an education and the opportunity to follow her own dreams and not just support her kids' dreams.

I would graduate a year later—Magna Cum Laude. Second place. In photos taken after my graduation ceremony, the groupings and expressions reveal the awkwardness of that day. The pictures were taken by the journalism professor—he fancied himself a photographer. My father also attended my graduation, but stood slightly apart. My parents were separated by then.

Maybe my mother gained confidence while going to college, maybe she was waiting until she was in a position to provide for herself, or maybe she was waiting for the right person, but she finally filed for divorce. The professor filed for divorce too. His wife was blindsided. His kids were distraught. When their dad proposed to my mom, his kids vowed not to go to the wedding. So many lives impacted. I felt sorry for my (sober) dad, the professor's wife, my siblings, and soon-to-be step-siblings.

And for what? Was it really love? Or did she see him as the answer to some of her problems? To me, he appeared loud, impatient, short-tempered, sometimes obnoxious. He reminded me of my father when he was drinking. Why was she drawn to that type? Didn't she know that she deserved better?

Maybe she saw something in him that I didn't see. Maybe love does that.

Who was I to understand the forces of their love? My love for my boyfriend was a tsunami while my love for my mother was a constant battle of undercurrents. I pushed her away, and she still loved me. She disappointed me, and I still loved her.

We may not have waved in the college cafeteria, but we waved at graduation, and we waved at each other's weddings.

CATHERINE HAYES

A FEAR OF MOTHERHOOD

Are you pregnant or nursing?

I can always feel my heart rate go up whenever I hear someone ask me this question, not because it's true but because I'm scared of the fate that has already been assumed for me simply because I am a woman. It seems like this question always comes up at every single medical appointment I go to no matter what branch of medicine it is—primary care, therapy, even when I went to get a root canal I was asked this question. I always feel a sense of relief when I answer no and sometimes it's so palpable that I even make that exaggerated face that says "oh hell no"—the widened eyes, the head shake, and the enunciation of the negative word.

Ever since I was a little girl, my parents always told me that I have choices in life. They always told me to go on and have a career before settling down to have a family, that my life as a woman was not just defined by the idea of one day getting married and having children. Society says otherwise since I've been asked questions like this ever since I turned sixteen. At only twenty-one, I know that there is no pressure to become a mother and that I have the freedom to go have a career right now, but what about in the future? If I feel such relief at being able to say no, what will I feel like if I one day have to say yes?

The role of caregiver is not a foreign one, and in a way, I already am a mother. I have been for many years now and no matter how old I grow or how old any potential children I might one day have if I do change my mind will be, there will always be one person who is dependent on me for the rest of her life: my autistic sister Caroline.

She is low enough on the spectrum that she is unable to live alone and properly take care of herself. I have to help her with almost every aspect of her life; making sure she has proper dress for the different seasons, that she is in good health and hygiene, that she is living her best life with the vocational skills she has. She cries, she throws tantrums and needs support in all aspects of her life. She is like my child and she always will be. This role in a way was forced on me, but I never resented it and I'm only too happy to care for my little sister; she needs me and I am the only person she has apart from our parents.

When I was nineteen, the role of caregiver for my sister was made permanent when I became her legal guardian. Since then, I have taken a larger role in helping my parents to care for Caroline and manage her daily affairs; attending her Individualized Educational Program (IEP) meetings at school, making sure she attends her extracurriculars, and making sure that she receives the services she needs from the Department of Developmental Services.

My parents recognize the role I stepped into and the impact it will have on my future, and it was my father who voiced that recognition to me one day when we were standing in the middle of Target after Caroline got the dolls she wanted from the toy department.

Your mother and I chose to have kids, but it was something that was almost forced upon you. You didn't get to make that choice.

I have been a caregiver and a "mother" for so long, I'm afraid of going through it all over again. I don't know if I have the strength to raise a child or children and my sister. Even when my children are grown and gone, my sister will still need me by her side. What if I have a child with special needs myself? What would I do if I were to have more than one person dependent on me for the rest of their life? Who would take care of Caroline when I was gone if I didn't have children of my own?

I've always heard that one of the best benefits of having kids is that you'll have someone to take care of you when you're older. What about someone to take care of the younger autistic sister? My mother's side of the family is fractured beyond repair and no member of that side of our family cares about us. My father's side is the complete opposite and we all have such a close bond with one another, but the problem is they all live over in England and we live in America. While I receive the emotional support I need from them, I have no one besides my parents to help with physical support and one question that always plagues my mind is, what am I going to do when they're gone?

Having children shouldn't just be about getting free, future helpers though. I always find myself overcome with a sense of guilt when I think about potentially having kids and realizing that no matter how many times

I ponder the matter, I always find myself frightened at the prospect and my mind remains unchanged. This expectation of motherhood is becoming suffocating, and like a loyal pet seems to follow me wherever I go.

My mom is one of those women who was excellent at motherhood and growing up I had so many friends say to me that they wished my mom could adopt them or have my mom come and hang out with them for the day, just the two of them. When she first found out she was pregnant with me, my mom made a conscious decision that she was going to be different from her own mother, who failed in every area of parenting where my mother herself succeeded. My mom is such a loving and caring person and my father's mother once said to her soon after they had my sister and I that it would have been a crime if someone like my mom didn't have children.

She loved working as the school nurse when I was in elementary school, always gushing to me about the adorable kindergartners who would come in with a lost tooth and tell her about learning their ABC's. She'd always go on about how cute they were and I always loved hearing her stories. As a camp counselor, I worked with kids that age and I could see why she loved them; I even thought about being an elementary school teacher for a time myself because of working with those kids. However, every one of these conversations always ends with my Dad making a light-hearted joke about giving my mom grandkids.

You hear that? It's all up to you Katie.

I don't know what things will look like when you have a kid but . . .

You could have your old crib when you have a kid one day, but it's so old I don't know if it'll pass the safety guidelines of the future.

She's never said it outright, but I know my mom would be thrilled to be a grandmother one day and I believe she expects me to start a family with my husband one day. My younger sister has such severe autism she can never marry or have children, so any hope my mother has of having grandchildren rests with me. When I was younger I would laugh about it with them because the idea of having children was so far into the future at that point that the thought rarely crossed my mind except in those conversations. Now as I grow older, and the expectation of motherhood draws closer, I find myself becoming panicked that I will disappoint her and grapple with the idea that I might have to have a child, despite my fear, so as to not live with the guilt of taking something away from her. With this feeling of guilt comes so many questions as to how this will alter our close bond.

Would I break her heart by not having kids? What if I adopted? Will this somehow hurt our relationship? Despite all of this conflict within myself, I cannot escape the fear that grasps my heart every time I think about having to give birth and become a mother.

I might one day change my mind, were I to meet the right person. Someone who I know will always respect my decision, whether I decide to have children or not, and someone who no matter what we decide will always help me take care of my sister. If I decide not to have kids, I know I will need to sit down and have a conversation with my mom, because no matter what happens she has and will always continue to listen to me and offer me the best advice that she can. Even if she does end up disappointed at the end of that conversation, she would never judge me or ridicule me for the way I feel. Perhaps the most reassuring thing about this entire matter is that I know I will always have support for my decisions, even when deciding on something as life changing as motherhood.

For now, I take comfort in the fact that I do not have to make any decisions right now. The question of what will happen if I decide not to become a mother is one that does not have to be answered for some time. For now, I am my sister's caregiver and for now that's enough.

JENNIFER PALMER

REFLECTIONS

The lights of the dashboard echoed in the passenger door's window—red, white, and yellow dots hung suspended in the window across the night sky. The beacons atop the Golden Gate Bridge shone through the fog as the car sped down Highway 101.

"Where're we going?" Christina asked.

"It's a surprise," Adam said. When Christina glanced at him, his lips were bunched together, jaw set. After a moment, he added, "I'm sorry I was late." His hands tightened on the torn steering wheel.

"It's fine."

"No, it's not." Adam shook his head. "I've been planning this for weeks, but the shop got this rush order on a Mustang. Some guy needs it for that August car show in Reno. Why he waited till the end of July is beyond me . . ."

At least Adam had a job again. Working at the garage wasn't how he wanted to work with metal, but he had to get some money in the bank before he could work on his sculptures.

"It'll be fine," she said, placing her hand on his shoulder, but his shoulder remained tense. "Seriously, it'll be fine."

The next day was the second anniversary of their first date, and Christina knew Adam had been planning something, what with the way he kept checking to make sure she didn't have anything going on over the weekend.

After a few seconds, his shoulders lowered, without relaxing entirely. Christina rubbed his neck then turned to look out the back window.

"Wait," she said. "Pull off here, just for a bit."

Adam flipped the turn signal. The highway's noise faded behind them as they drove down the deserted road.

"Just park on the side," Christina said. He rolled onto the dry June grass and switched off the car.

As she climbed out of the sedan, a light breeze carried remnant sounds of the highway and tried to pick up her hair but did little more than shake its ends. She shut the car door, leaned against it. A few hundred feet in front of her, the land disappeared into the dark water of the bay. In the distance, the silhouette of San Francisco, lit by a multitude of electric pinpoints, peeked through the fog. Christina heard Adam's door open then close, felt his body rest lightly by her side.

The breeze carried sea salt scents and with them the ghosts of memories. Christina had spent childhood summer afternoons here with Jasmine and Valerie, playing with American Girl dolls while their mothers shared champagne at the picnic table. Nights Valerie borrowed her dad's Mercedes, and the three girls gossiped about prom dates and what might happen that night and what would happen in the months following the prom—where their college plans would take them.

College took Jasmine back East. Christina and Valerie stayed in the Bay Area, but Christina hadn't heard from Valerie since her sophomore year, when Christina was still wandering in the direction of law school.

She and Adam stood in silence. A yacht lazed across the bay, its own lights mere specks compared to the mass in the distance. Christina felt Adam's hand shift near his pocket, and her heart jumped.

"The whole city looks beautiful," she said, pushing herself away from the car and stepping toward the shore. "You can't even tell there are ugly places in it." She thought of their apartment on Leavenworth and Turk, where mold-spotted walls failed to block the nightly moans of the alcoholics next door.

"Yeah," Adam said.

"'Yeah'?" Christina said. "Really, that's it?" She glanced at his hand and saw it no longer hovered near his pocket.

"You're the poet, not me," Adam said. Christina snorted and looked away again.

"If I ever get my book published."

"Not if," Adam said. "When."

He stepped forward, and Christina tightened, but he just wrapped an arm around her waist.

"Are you ready to go?" he asked.

Christina exhaled the breath she didn't know she held.

"Yes."

They reentered the car and merged back onto the highway, leaving the lights behind.

※

They spent the night at a Hampton Inn, instead of a Motel 6 as Christina expected. They left the hotel the following morning as the sun crept across the dusty summer sky.

They were speeding down Sonoma Highway when steam began to pour through the cracks of the car hood. Adam swore and pulled off into the next parking lot, the one behind the sign reading, "B. R. Cohn Winery." Grapevines stretched into the yellow hills in the background as Adam popped the hood.

"It's a radiator hose," Adam said. Christina hummed and nodded as if she knew what that meant. Adam rifled through the toolbox.

"We're out of duct tape," he said. "I saw a gas station down the street. I'll walk there and get some."

"All right." Christina said, moving to join him, but Adam raised his arm.

"No, no, you stay here," he said. "It's too hot; you go inside."

Christina opened her mouth to argue, but the sweat gathering on her forehead convinced her otherwise.

※

"Good morning ma'am," the man behind the counter said when Christina walked through the door. "Is there anything I can assist you with?"

"I'm just looking, thanks," she said. She looked at his crisp button-down shirt and tailored pants then glanced down at her jeans. She shook her head and wandered toward the back of the shop.

She twisted her class ring around her finger. The three-year-old band of white gold still had the BA insignia carved onto the side, even though she graduated with a BFA instead. Her parents had refused to buy a new one, probably with the hopes she would return to political science instead of creative writing.

Christina eyed one of the emerald bottles. She wondered how the wine's bouquet compared to that of a bottle of Two Buck Chuck from Trader Joe's.

"Christina? Is that you?"

Christina turned, "Valerie?"

A lean woman in a tangerine, floor-length maxi dress strode forward, her heels clacking against the sandstone floor.

"How are you?" Valerie lifted her sunglasses to perch on her forehead, their white, plastic frames contrasting with her golden blonde hair. "It's been what, three years?"

"Yeah, it has."

"Crazy," Valerie said, shaking her head. "Why didn't you come to the reunion last month?"

Christina shrugged. Valerie rolled her eyes but smiled.

"Speaking of crazy, did you hear about Jasmine? She didn't finish at Vanderbilt. She dropped out to run off with some guy junior year." Valerie's eyes glinted as she smiled.

"No, I hadn't," Christina said. "I haven't really kept up with the old group."

"Clearly," Valerie laughed. "So, what have you been doing then?"

Christina opened her mouth, dabbed her bottom lip with her tongue.

"What do you mean?" she asked.

"What are you doing now? I heard you're in the city," Valerie said.

"Oh, yeah, I am," Christina said. "I'm working at a law firm, Morrison and Foerster."

"Wow." Valerie bobbed her head. "Yeah, I think my uncle used them for his company's merger. That's great. Good for you."

"Thanks."

Valerie face contorted, though, "Wait, I thought law school—"

A buzzing noise interrupted.

"Ah, sorry, hold on." Valerie dug through her oversized handbag before pulling her phone out and glancing at the number. "Ooh, I need to take this," she said. "I'll be right back, okay?"

Once Valerie was out of hearing range, Christina took a deep breath. At least she had a job. No, being a receptionist at a law firm was not where she saw herself when she entered college, but it was something. She imagined she would be the one driving a BMW instead of the beat-up Hyundai Excel Adam was in the process of fixing.

A hand touched her shoulder. "Hey," Adam said.

Christina took a step back. Adam had taken off his blue button-down and sweat soaked his white undershirt.

"Yeah, sorry," he said. He held up a silver roll of tape. "I got it. The fix should only take a few minutes."

"So it can be fixed?"

"Yeah, but we'll have to go straight back home and take it to the shop. The tape won't last long. I'm really sorry," he said.

"It'll be fine."

"Be back in a minute," he said. He pecked her on the lips and left.

Valerie reentered as Adam walked away from Christina. Her head twisted to look at him after he passed, and she wrinkled her nose.

"Who was that?" she asked.

Christina dabbed her bottom lip with her tongue again.

"A mechanic," she said. "I was driving this car up to Santa Rosa for a friend, and it broke down."

"Ah," Valerie replied. She looked at her phone. "Well, I need to go or I'm going to be late." She grabbed a wine bottle off the shelf at random and walked to the register. Christina glanced at the price tag on the shelf. Ninety-five dollars.

The man behind the counter rang up the bottle and placed it in a bag. Valerie gripped it by its neck.

"Call me, okay?" She flipped her sunglasses back down.

Christina nodded and watched as her old friend exited the winery, passed the sweat-drenched Adam, and climbed into a Mercedes before jetting out of the parking lot. She pursed her lips and turned away from the window.

Ten minutes later, she went outside.

"How's it coming?"

A grunt was the only reply she received from her boyfriend bent over the engine. She glanced around. Another couple walked toward the entrance, the woman's floppy sunhat perfectly askew. Christina's face burned at the sidelong glance the woman cast Adam's way.

"How long do you think it'll be?"

Adam looked up from the engine, sweat pouring down his face.

"As long as it takes, okay?" he snapped and buried his head once more in the engine compartment. Christina looked around once more.

"Hey, no need to—"

"No." Adam looked up from the engine again, duct tape dangling from one hand. "If I'm doing it, it's going to be done right. Or at least," he grumbled, ducking under once more, "as right as I can with this." He shook the tape blindly toward Christina.

Christina pursed her lips again but didn't respond. She sat on a rock a middle distance away as Adam finished up.

By the time Adam bought the radiator hose, replaced the old one, and showered, night had fallen. Christina sat in the windowsill, looking out at the street. An argument from next door filtered through the wall. Adam climbed into bed.

"Aren't you coming?" he asked, rubbing his eyes.

"In a minute."

Adam turned off the lamp, but Christina remained at the window with her legs pulled to her chest. She watched and waited as the lights reflected in her eyes extinguished one by one.

Christina stood at the front desk of the Emergency Room, out of breath from racing from the taxi, hardly aware of how much she had tipped the driver. She had rushed to the hospital when she received the call that Adam had had a run-in with a Camaro engine. The person on the phone had assured her that, yes, yes, he was still alive, but his arm had taken a chewing.

"I'm his girlfriend though!"

"I'm sorry, but policy is family members only," the receptionist replied. She smiled in what she must have thought was an expression of sympathy, but all Christina saw was patronization.

Another couple came up behind her, the woman's face pallid.

"We're here for Adam," the man said. Christina turned.

"Thank God," Christina said, and turned back to the receptionist. "Here're his parents. Can I see him now?"

After a short while that seemed to stretch for eternity, Christina and Mr. and Mrs. Levitt were escorted to the back.

"Oh, honey!" Mrs. Levitt cried out upon the sight of her son. Adam sat on the hospital bed with his arm in a sling, blood stains visible despite the garish green of the gauze.

"Mom, geez," Adam said as Mrs. Levitt descended upon him. "I'm twenty-five, get a grip."

Christina couldn't help but smile as Mrs. Levitt continued to fuss over her son.

After much berating, Adam went on to say how, no, he shouldn't be doing that kind of stuff alone in the shop, and yes, he would be more careful in the future. All the while, he kept looking over at Christina and rolled his eyes when his parents took a minute to talk to the nurse.

"So, what's up with you?" he asked Christina.

"You mean other than the heart attack?" She sat at the end of his bed and stroked his leg through the covers.

"I'll be fine," he said. "Don't worry about me."

"But I was worried," she said. "My mind jumped to these . . . to these awful—"

"Shh, shh, don't."

Adam leaned forward, planted a kiss on Christina's lips, and grimaced when he pulled back.

"If it hurts," she said, "you don't have—"

"Worth it."

\\ ❋ //

A couple of days later, Christina walked a familiar road from the streetcar station to her parents' home. Victorian houses lined the street while cars, no doubt tasked with schlepping tourists, drove by on the steep street.

She walked up to the facade and rang the doorbell. A significantly older woman answered the door.

"Christina!"

"Hi, Nana."

The two embraced, her grandmother holding on a little longer than Christina expected.

"Thomas is here too," Nana said. Christina blinked.

"Oh."

"Who is it, Mom?" a voice called from inside.

"Christina!" Nana answered. She turned to Christina. "Come in, come in."

"Actually, I . . . "

By then it was too late though; her grandmother had swatted her into the house. Another woman stood at the bottom of the oak stairs with the wrought iron railing.

"Hello," she called. Mrs. Martin did not move to embrace her daughter. "Look at that? Two children in one day."

"Yeah, Nana said Thomas was here too," Christina said.

"Yes, his plane arrived this morning."

A moment of silence passed as Christina's grandmother bustled around, tidying up the already perfectly arranged plates.

"So, you know that guy I told you and dad about?" Christina began. "Adam? The one I'm dating?"

Mrs. Martin nodded.

"Well, he had an accident the other day and landed in the hospital. He's fine, but his parents came down, so I saw them again. I realized, though, you and Dad haven't actually met him yet, have you?"

"No, we have not."

"Well, how about it then? How about me and Adam, you and Dad—we could make it a double date?"

As Christina waited, a man strode into the room, head ducked as he stared intently at the screen in his hand.

"Thomas!" Nana said. "Aren't you going to say hi to your sister?"

"Hey, little sis," he said, glancing up, then returning to his phone. "Listen, Mom, I've got to run; I need to be at the courthouse in twenty."

Mrs. Martin smiled, nodded.

"All right dear, go ahead. Dad and I will be here when you get back."

"Thanks," Thomas replied. He turned to leave, then stopped. "I'm sorry to bail on you Christina, but you know how it goes with work." He shrugged his shoulders, rolled his eyes.

"Yeah, sure."

Thomas grabbed his keys from the hutch and exited through the front door. Christina heard his Audi rev up and leave them as well.

"What is Thomas doing here?" she asked.

"His firm had a case with a client in San Francisco," Mrs. Martin replied. "Thomas thought he would come and visit while he's here on business."

She paused, before muttering, "At least he's doing somethi—"

"Can we not today, Mom?"

"Yes, Susan, not today," Nana interjected, "What did you say about your boyfriend, Christina? He was in an accident?"

"Yeah, he's not going to be able to work for a while."

"That's terrible." Nana turned to her daughter once more. "Go on, Susan, it sounds like you need to meet this young man. You and Landon."

Mrs. Martin said nothing at first, then pressed her lips.

"He's the mechanic, am I correct?"

"Yes, mother, and I had quite the shock when I received the call that he was in the hospital."

A moment passed in silence, and Mrs. Martin's lips twitched.

"I'll talk to your father about it."

"Thank you," Christina said. "I needed to pick up some dinner, and I wanted to drop by to ask you about that."

"You know you could have just called," Mrs. Martin replied.

"Susan, count your blessings," Nana said. She winked at Christina. "It was lovely seeing you, dear."

"You too, Nana," Christina replied with a smile. "Text me later, Mom?"

"I'll do that."

Nana reached Christina before she could leave and wrapped her in her arms.

"Love you."

"So, Adam, what exactly did you say you do again?"

Mr. Martin cut into his salmon with more aggression than Christina thought necessary. Heavy brocades covered the dining room in which they sat, their plates flanked by weighty silverware. Adam's arm sported a fluorescent green cast.

"He didn't, Dad," Christina answered.

"I'm a mechanic, sir," Adam said. "I work at Mike's Auto. In Sonoma." He attempted to wrangle a bite of chicken, but his cast prohibited such movement. The piece of meat kept sliding off his fork.

"Oh, so you work in Sonoma?" Mrs. Martin inquired. "Why are you living in San Francisco then?"

"For Christina's job." Adam turned to Christina, and she smiled at him. "Also, this is where we met, so it seemed like it fit."

"Adam's parents live here too, so there's that," Christina said.

"And what do your parents do?" Mrs. Martin asked.

"Well," Adam started as he took a bite of food. "My dad runs this shop on the beach, selling boats and stuff. My mom helps him with it. I guess that's where I got my thing for vehicles." He let out a little laugh.

"I see," Mr. Martin said.

"How about you?" Adam asked after a moment of silence. "What do you do?"

"I'm a lawyer," Mr. Martin replied. "My wife is a homemaker."

"Wow," Adam said and looked at Christina. "So, is that a thing in your family? Law?"

She swallowed her bite of beef tenderloin and replied, "Yeah, kind of."

"It was quite a surprise when she told us about the degree change," Mrs. Martin stated.

"Well yeah, sure, but the important thing is that she's doing her thing, right?"

No one said anything for a moment until Adam continued, "I mean, I don't want to work on cars forever, but if it's what I need to do to let her . . . ." He trailed off, but then waved his fork. "Then it's worth it."

"Well, it seems you need to find an alternative," Mrs. Martin replied delicately. She nibbled a spear of asparagus, then continued, "What with you not being able to work now because of your injury—"

"Mother," Christina growled.

The women didn't speak for the rest of the meal, while Mr. Martin and Adam talked about cars. A short while later, they wrapped things up between the two parties.

"I'm . . . happy to have met your parents," Adam said as he and Christina walked to his car.

"Yeah, sure," Christina replied, then sighed. "I'm sorry about that."

"Well, think of it this way—you met my parents in less-than-optimal circumstances. This is my way of making it up to you."

Christina laughed as she climbed into the driver's seat.

Four days later, Christina sat on the other side of her manager's mahogany desk, ears burning, hands clenched in her lap.

"You're firing me?" She heard the muffled whir of the photocopier and the brisk steps of business people through the office door, but her focus remained on the pinstriped-suited man in front of her.

"It's not personal," her boss said. His computer chirped with an email alert. "We simply don't have the resources to retain this many people." He clicked on the email and glanced over it.

"So that's it?" Christina asked, heat rising to her face. "I need this job. I can't—"

The man glanced up from his computer.

"It would be best if you leave now."

Christina grabbed the handful of personal items at her desk and managed to make it to the streetcar before the tears rolled down her cheeks.

She rustled through her purse looking for a tissue as the streetcar swayed back and forth. A wallet-sized photo of Adam fell out, the photo she had kept propped against her pencil holder at work. Christina wiped her eyes, picked the picture up.

The photo's quality did not do him justice. Its lighting made Adam's pale skin glow like a moonbeam and highlighted the old scar on his forearm, soon to be accompanied by another once the wound healed up. But the smile he wore outshone all the imperfections.

At the next stop, a high-school-age girl in a checkered hoodie and red headphones climbed onto the streetcar. She stumbled over to Christina as the vehicle lurched forward.

"Hey, is this the route to Fell Street?"

"Yes."

"Awesome."

The girl sat next to her and bobbed her head to the beat audible to Christina despite the headphones. She peered over at Adam's photo.

"Is that your brother?" she asked. Christina's eyebrows furrowed.

"No," Christina said. The thought repelled her, Adam as just a brother. "Why'd you think that?"

The girl shrugged.

"I dunno. Something about your eyes, his eyes."

Christina looked at the picture again. She couldn't see what this girl was talking about; her eyes held none of the gentleness of Adam's.

"No, he's my boyfriend."

"Nice," the girl said, nodding her head to the sway of the streetcar. She glanced at the picture again. "Lucky you."

Christina brushed her thumb across Adam's face. "Yeah."

When Christina walked into their apartment, Adam sat on the couch looking at something in his good hand. His head rose at her approach.

"Christina! What are you doing here? I mean . . . " He shook his head. "Why are you home early? Did something happen?"

"I got fired," she said, dropping her purse on the kitchen counter.

"What? Why?"

"Something about not enough money, but that's bull." She balled her hands into fists. "They've got plenty; I watched it going in and out every day."

Her grip collapsed, and she brought her hands to her face. "I don't know if I did something wrong, or something I said, or—"

"Hey, hey, shh." Adam wrapped Christina in a one-armed hug. "Don't think like that," he said.

After a few minutes, he took her hand in his.

"Have you had lunch yet?" he asked.

Christina sniffed, "No."

"I know what will make you feel better."

After an hour-long car ride north, they sat outside the Broadway Market, the mini-market on the corner of Leveroni Road and Broadway. The Sonoma scent washed over them, a mixture of sawdust and heat.

"Happy belated anniversary."

Adam placed a cherry Pepsi and a plastic-wrapped salami and sourdough sandwich on the picnic table. Christina smiled at the echo of their first date.

"Thanks," she said.

They unwrapped their sandwiches and chewed in silence. The air was noisy around them as cars sped and slowed over the pavement. A truck honked and sent a swarm of birds fleeing from their phone line perch.

"What was it you wrote that one time?" Adam asked. "'The summer sky rife with redbirds' song'?"

Christina smiled as she took another bite of salami.

"I can't believe you remember that," she said.

"'Course I do," Adam replied. "You read it at that open mic night."

Christina remembered the noisy crowd at the half-lit coffee shop where they first met.

"Why were you even there?" she asked.

"Joe was playing his guitar, remember?"

Christina shook her head and took a swig of Pepsi.

"No, I don't."

Adam laughed.

"It's okay," he said. "I don't remember what he played." He popped a chip into his mouth. "I was distracted by the poet in the lace top."

Christina looked down at her sandwich and smiled.

"I thought to myself," he continued. "'Damn, listen to that woman speak.'" He put down his bag of chips. "I'm glad I did."

"Stop it," she said, but smiled even wider. When Adam pulled something out of his back pocket. Christina's heart jumped.

"I wanted to do this earlier," he said. "But circumstances . . . "

Adam took a deep breath, and awkwardly lowered himself to one knee.

"Christina," he said, "Will you marry me?"

A quick intake of breath, and Christina's chin trembled. She dropped to her knees and buried her head in his chest.

"This afternoon," Christina said into her cellphone. She sat on her side of the bed, sheet draped loosely around her torso. A shaft of lamplight leaked across the spread. She rubbed her throat, sore from the number of calls she had made that night.

"Yes, Valerie," she continued, "The man you saw."

Adam stood in front of the dresser, changing into his boxers.

"Look, I need to go," she said. "I'll let you know when the plans are set up." As she hung up her phone, Adam came up to the bed and squeezed in beside her.

"'The man you saw'?" he asked, arching one eyebrow.

"I'll tell you later," Christina said. "Promise." She scooted to her right, the sides of their bodies touching from shoulder to hip.

"Speaking of telling," Adam said, interlacing the fingers of his left hand with her right, "Are you going to call your parents again?"

"Not tonight," Christina said. She had called three times already and left a message, but they had yet to reply. "If Valerie does what I think she'll do, they'll know soon enough."

Adam chuckled. They lay there for a minute, a comfortable warmth between their bodies.

"Good night," he said. He switched off the light. Christina adjusted her position so that her hand lay across the sheet over Adam's side. It felt so right there, so right.

It had to be right. It had to be right.

III
LETTING GO

MADLYNN HABER

ONE PERFECT MOMENT

For her birthday, I bought her a soft pink lunch bag. It is an unnaturally bright shade of pink with three Disney princesses on it. Belle, Aurora, and Cinderella. I bought the card that came with it and signed it, "with love from Tooie," our golden retriever. I often give gifts from our pets. Things I might not have chosen but I know will make someone happy, come from our dog. The two cats, Lassie and Lucky, often chip in on gifts together which tend to be more practical. On this occasion, their gift was a bright purple umbrella with yellow daisies on it. I gave her a charm, a journey pin, on a silver chain. The charm had a peridot stone on it. Her lime green birthstone. It was a special gift for her eighteenth birthday. Lime green is her favorite color. She's an adult now.

I pick her up this afternoon from her job as a day care program assistant, and as she sees me drive down the street, she begins jumping up and down in a goofy sort of way. Her pink lunch bag is bouncing with her, her puffy green jacket is open and flapping around her baggy brown pants with big pockets on the side and her dark green sweatshirt. Her hair is wafting out of her pony tail. I had to laugh watching her jump around full of smiles and silliness as I pull the car up in front of her.

"Where in the world did you come from?" I ask as she bounces into the car. She is an odd character. A young woman of her own creation. Her own distinct style. Not one of the pack. I feel a moment of unabashed acceptance. An instant of appreciation with recognition of the uniqueness of this daughter of mine.

For that moment, I let go of all the worries, mine and hers. I forget that she isn't going to college; she's working a minimum wage job with no future; she has no sweetheart, or even a best friend; her prescription for anti-anxiety medication needs to be refilled; there is mold growing behind her bed where she drops snacks and doesn't bother to clean up. In that moment, where she bounces into the car and we both laugh, for that instant, everything is just perfect.

LISA MOLINA

WHEN WE HELD HANDS

"You have your father's hands,"
I said when the nurse placed your
tiny waxy wet body into my arms.
Fingers thin and long.

Three years later, I held one of your hands
as you wailed at the shock of pain,
when a nurse pricked one of those fingers.
The blood soon revealing your body was full of leukemia cells.

I held your hands throughout the thirty-eight months of
chemotherapy, clumps of your hair falling into my hands as I
would wash it, until none was left.

I felt those tiny hands as fists banging on my chest because you
were so furious that this medicine that was going to make you
well made you feel so sick.

I felt those hands squeezing mine across the table
eight years later when the cancer returned.

"Mom, I don't want to die. Tell me I'm not going to die. Please! Tell me I
won't die."

I sat caressing your hands while four nurses and a doctor worked
furiously to revive you while you lay unconscious in septic
shock, nearly dying, remembering the day I first saw and held
them through a blur of tears.

And I held those skeleton-like hands two years later
when the cancer was now in your brain.
And the umbilical cord blood of an unknown savior child
was transplanted into your withering, nearly-dead body,
resurrecting you.

•

You're twenty-four now,
free of the grip of cancer.

We haven't held hands in many years.
But I look at them often, hoping you don't notice.
And I smile softly as I watch those beautiful, long-fingered
hands you inherited from your father, pulsate with
movement and life.

And I can still feel them holding mine.

JUDITH SANDERS

BUS RIDE THROUGH ROME WITH TWENTY-ONE-YEAR-OLD SON

I want to say, Look at that carved door, those begonias on that balcony,
that funny sign, how that woman gestures, even on her cell.

I want to lean in close, inhale the buttered-waffle smell of your hair,
and whisper over the bus's bang and rattle: Look at that street performer,

that fluted column, those nymphs cavorting on that fountain—
Look, look, how intricate it all is, how amusing, how splendid.

Long ago, I broke myself in two to give all this to the unknown person
you'd become. But that place is far away. We don't go there any more.

Soon we could swing through the market, suck on fresh peaches,
buy eggplants for dinner. I'll want to tell you to turn right, turn left.

But you have an excellent sense of direction. You know where
you are going. Look, I'll want to say, panting to keep up,
at the sycamores arching along the river.

But you'll be busy memorizing streets, the locations of ice cream shops.
The places you want to go are ahead. Here's my stop.
Here's where I get off.

MY FRIENDS' CHILDREN

The sweet little boys have beards
and girlfriends and broad shoulders.

They speak fluently.
Their mothers annoy them.

That young woman looks
like her mother forty years ago,

when everything was
as it always would be.

These young people have no idea
that they once didn't exist.

That they sprang from nothing.
It's a stranger trick

than levitating a lady
or pulling a rabbit from a hat.

If I had kept my eye on them,
would they have remained adorable?

Meanwhile, what happened to me?
I was just going along

and now my face is a prune
and I can't see without glasses.

Perhaps the grown children think,
When did she switch with Grandma?

No, I'm behind them,
and their heads don't rotate.

They see only what's in front:
Their own adorable babies

who will never outgrow
their strollers or teddy bears

or their mothers.

MK PUNKY

PRECIOUS BOY

When our son came home to Michigan for winter break
from the fancy college we'd sent him to in Illinois
his head now exploding with idea grenades
demolishing the scaffolding of lessons
his mom and I had dutifully taught him
as our parents had done for us
trying our best
to ready him for the world he'd soon inherit
he took care to acknowledge
my financial support of his scholarly aspirations
expressing deep appreciation and *mad* respect
before asking me
with concern painted on his face like too much makeup
how did I feel
spending almost my entire adult life
working on the factory assembly line
I told him I could imagine a million other jobs
I might have enjoyed more
less repetition and so forth
but the God's honest truth
every time I see a Chevy Tahoe
and some editions of the Equinox
I think to myself
I built that
sort of how I feel
every time I look at you
my precious boy

CAROL BARRETT

LOBSTER BISQUE

Bit of a splurge, Mom, but on sale, owing no doubt
to the expiration date in small print on the lid.
I was thinking of the protein in lobster, although
what glided down was the cream, thick as the split
pea soup you made from scratch with a ham bone.
I don't have time for such creative nourishment.
Suppose I could cook more and clean less, but
I have to keep watering the cacti you left us.
So prickly. Never would have bought them myself.
My daughter would shriek if I let go of anything
you touched, branching desert cacti and green
watering can standing in for your love and concern.

It was you who discovered the source of her asthma,
visits to doctors in three cities notwithstanding.
Given my late meeting one school night, she stayed over
with you, curled in your quilts and fluffy pillows,
freshly ironed cases, floral embroidery. Next morning
she could breathe again. You knew it was something
in our house closing off her airway. In the attic
we found black mold, where the bathroom fan
exhaust had been routed, all those hot showers.

She is doing fine, away at school with your salt
and pepper shakers. I keep watering your cacti,
wondering when she will have her own place
so I can shift all these planters. They do bloom
on occasion, spritely pinks and reds, chastening me
for my irritation, such a small burden really for your life
well-lived. I apologize for impatience. Next time
I will look for a different soup. You're right, this really
was an indulgence, barely worth the investment.
The accounting of memory, such an exacting science.

TERRI WATROUS BERRY

ON GUARD

She boiled all their nipples.
She boiled the bottles and the caps
plus the brush used to scrub
the bottles and the caps and the nipples.

There were long nights and high fevers,
hot little bodies under cool water rubs,
medicine minutely measured,
given round the clock, baby aspirin scored
midnights at twenty-four-hour pharmacies.

Bee stings poison ivy broken bones
hearts, ear-nose-throat infections
pinkeye. They had all their inoculations,
and she spent her summers counting
bobbing blond heads at the beach—
one two three, one two three,
one two three, ad infinitum.

She held tightly to their hands in public
places, discretely stood outside
countless men's room doors
when the boys were old enough
to pee alone, showed the girl how
to do it without touching the seat.

She taught them to cross the street,
to ride a bike, to drive a car, and
they have and they did and they do,
their circles ever-widening
beyond perked ears and straining
eyes, rarely does she get to count
them all at once anymore.

Twenty-odd years a vigilant sentry—
without a rest, with no relief—
blow out the porch lamp, mother, and
know that your watch has ended.

PURE CONDENSED OWL SHIT

Forgive me my children for I lied,
each day as you grew I lied to you.
It was I who filled your heads with
endless possibilities—yes it was I—who
looked into your wide blue eyes and lied.

You can do anything. (fiction)
You can . . . BE anything! (farce)
Life is warm and soft and sweet,
so are the people you'll meet,
love is waiting, love is kind—

lie, lie, lie, lie, lie.

I wanted you to believe these things,
I wanted to believe these things.
Now the real world comes to you as
quite a shock, just as it came
to me, just as it often still does.

MARK BLICKLEY

HAN'S SOLO

I've had this recurring Bridge Dream for nearly fifteen years. It first appeared one night after being exhausted by cram studying for my Bar Mitzvah. In this initial fantasy I was a swaddled infant left on the very beginning of a long and twisting walkway through a vibrant yet desolate forest. I was crying and there was blood from my bris seeping through the fabric covering my groin. We don't need to dig Freud up from his grave to figure out I was about to undergo a ritual of manhood, so I must've been thinking about the genital mutilation that first signaled my acceptance into the tribe. What's quite disturbing about this recurring dream as it appears today is that after fourteen years of experiencing it, I've only moved forward incrementally from the bloody infant that was first placed on this forest path, into a six-year-old boy that balks at moving forward. In the real world I'm about to turn twenty-eight.

My name's Han because my parents are both Star Wars freaks and the worship of this film series is the only real religion practiced in my household. They obviously were not the only disciples. When I was in Pre-K, there was another boy named Han as well as a girl named Leia.

What's strange about my abandoned boy at the bridge recurring dream is that it's always just a prologue to whatever else I'll be dreaming that night. This winding walkway always introduces whatever anxious or peaceful visions my brain has decided to focus on that night—-nightmare, erotic ecstasy, exciting adventures, idyllic beauty.

These days in my dream I am a first-grader who is really hesitant about moving forward, but I also see it as my feet turning into the classic ballet fourth position. My mother taught ballet for years so perhaps my foot position on the bridge is a nod to her. Once again I don't need to disinter Freud to figure out this bridge snakes into a representation of my life's journey. By the way, did you know that babies double their birth size by age five months? Yet in my recurring dream I remained a crying, bleeding infant for years——no physical growth, no emotional growth.

I'm a bit confused about relationships with women. My testosterone tells me to be more aggressive and not to feel so shy and unworthy. I'm always terrified of saying the wrong thing. In high school I didn't really have a girlfriend because I always hung out within this circle of friends that were both males and females. Most activities were communal, not individual dates. Recently I joined a dating app called Bumble. On Bumble only women can initiate first contact which I like because it reduces the stress of rejection, yet I've been registered on this app for five months and have yet to receive a single hit.

I'm presently undergoing E.M.D.R. (eye movement desensitization and reprocessing) therapy, which also includes hand tapping and listening to ambient sounds, like ocean waves, via headphones that seesaw these sounds from ear to ear to promote a kind of aural hypnosis. One of the side effects of this treatment is that it can cause vivid, realistic dreams, but my recurring dream happened years before I entered therapy. My therapist insists I keep a journal between sessions in order to maintain the session's progress she insists is occurring.

My shrink Martha works for the V.A. but please don't think I'm some sort of Veteran war hero suffering from PTSD. I never even enlisted in the War Against Christmas, yet I've never known a world without suicide bombings, school shootings and acts of terrorism that take place in my backyard, not in some distant land. Martha is also an ordained Lutheran pastor but she never mentions God in any of our sessions.

I tell Martha I'm so sick of reading/hearing reasons why Millennials can't grow up. My shrink calls it a "First World" problem not unique to young men my age. I am depressed and anxious all the time but don't know why. I am always smiling and laughing at jokes I don't think are funny so people won't discover how unhappy I am. I feel like I'm faking everything. Being an adult to me means not doing things you enjoy doing, yet that's nuts because my parents still act like kids at Star Wars Conventions.

Why am I so miserable? I had everything I was supposed to need while growing up——emotional and financial security, a good education and now I have a more than decent paying job. I do feel guilty that they are so many less fortunate than me and know it is unmanly to be so constantly sad. Every day there's somebody crying out what privileged assholes we Millennials are, so I always feel pressured to pretend I'm happy.

My shrink says I should spend less time always surrounding myself with people and more time being alone, even if it means being bored at first. But I can't relax by myself. I tried all different kinds of things, but I can't slow down my goddamn anxious thoughts. I've tried drugs, porn, video games and even different kinds of meditation—Zen Meditation with mindfulness on breathing and intentionally focusing on the moment. Then I did Metta meditation to focus on a loving kindness towards myself as well as empathy for other people. In my final workshop I studied Sufi meditation to try to achieve mystical union with a Supreme Being.

In every class and workshop I've taken, I seem to be the only one who can't obtain this metaphysical knowledge and peace. I would often comfort myself in class by thinking my fellow students are just bullshitting their enlightenment to try to make me feel like shit—-but thoughts like that defeat the entire purpose of meditation, which is to get to know myself and pull away from the outside world to focus on my inner world, instead of blaming everyone else for my failure. Do you understand how fucked up a person I am? Hell, I even get sad deleting old tweets because it feels like I'm flushing away a big part of who I was and who I am.

Last month Martha suggested I try using a weighted blanket that applies deep pressure touch. She says it simulates the feeling of being comforted, like a swaddled baby, and is supposed to help my insomnia and anxiety. So instead of fighting my anxieties like a real man, I retreat into acting like a fucking baby again, all tucked inside my crib beneath a blanket with thirty pounds of pellets sewn into it. So far it hasn't worked.

When I ask Martha how she arrives at the concept of what exactly my emotional age is, she turns the question back on me and asks what do I believe is my emotional age? I tell her I don't know anything except first my dick is snipped at birth and then as I advance in life, I have my balls constantly broken by social proclamations that I MUST BE SUCCESSFUL!

I worry I'll never live up to my own expectations. I grew up being told I could be anything I wanted to be, but I'm coming to the realization that I'm not as smart, talented or special as I thought I was and that fuels an obsession with having to succeed. My friends and I seem to be growing up poorer than our parents. My Mom and Dad can afford to go to Star Wars conventions all over the world but my important travel plans are still handcuffed by student loans.

I get incredibly stressed over not being able to find a WiFi spot, forgetting passwords to online accounts, the buffering sign when I'm streaming online—it's like taunting me that my life is going in circles, like the areola of a maternal tit. I stress when unable to find my TV remote just as my favorite Netflix show is starting.

Why am I unable to advance past the age of six in my recurring dream? Is it because I'm a victim of helicopter parenting? During my childhood my mom and dad hovered over every experience and problem I had growing up. Cell phones are the longest umbilical cords in the world. I was taught to be afraid of strangers, playing sports, sexual contact. Is that why they claim we *Millennials* act more like children than adults?

This outburst of self-pity is very tiring, so I'm going to disappear under my state of the art weighted blanket and hope tonight is the night it crushes my recurring dream of being a child stranded on a spooky bridge inside a dying, primeval forest. And if my heavy blankie is unable to extinguish the dream, perhaps when I wake up I will have at least gained a year of emotional age so I will be a seven-year-old boy on that walkway, just three quarters away from achieving my true age of twenty-eight.

DEBBIE PETERS

DELINQUENT ACCOUNT

> *I had an insufficient childhood.*
> Mary Oliver

Dear Adult Child,

Your personality has relapsed into emotional bankruptcy, causing us to return your latest failed attempt to transact an intimate relationship.

We wish we could forgive this mental overdraft as we have in the past, but new regulations require us to close all accounts suffering from an insufficient childhood.

Sincerely,

People, Places, and Things

THEA HEARD

TRANSGRESSIONS

I'm afraid to even make a grocery list anymore. This is beyond writer's block. It's like I have a savage spy inside my mind and all the words have gone into hiding.

"What right do *you* have to an opinion?" my only child Alistair asked me yesterday before opening the door to leave in a huff.

"Bye, Grammie," my granddaughter Alicia called as Alistair tugged her into the elevator and vigorously pushed the down button. Alicia waved; Alistair scowled.

How *am* I expected to keep the pronouns straight? I birthed a she, who became a he, and now, having given birth while bemoaning the temporary thinning of his mustache and goatee, wants to be called they. Because it's in. *Trending*. They says what *they* say, and thinks what *they* think and takes all those clichés as original, sui generis, theirs, *all* theirs. And rages if you disagree. It's a little thing, I know. And not. Something in me balks, but I could think of it as a contraction of the(-one-and-onl)y.

I was never a real fan of "they," always took it as a warning sign. My mother used it against me all the time. What will *they* think, Agnes, if your earrings don't match, if you wear something from the thrift shop to church, if you say what *you* really think? I learned to keep my mouth shut and let my real thoughts travel through my fingers into my pen. It was such a relief to have my words on the page heard, even if *they* were never spoken aloud, even if I was the only one with ears to hear.

That is why I have always tried to be so accepting and attentive to my daughter Alice's needs and preferences. I wanted her to feel heard. *Spoiled*, my mother said early and often when Alice was growing up. The rotten was never voiced, but it festered in the air. Both Alice and I could smell it. My mother just smiled that smile of hers that lived on the verge between knowing and malicious. The one she'd honed at church and PTA and the museum guild.

Which may be why I was never much of a joiner.

A reticence that also was open to interpretation. "You always act as if you're *above* everybody," Alice herself accused me when she was in school and I didn't volunteer to man booths at the school fairs or read a book instead of chatting with other mothers at the soccer field. She ignored all the dozens of cupcakes I baked, iced, and sprinkled to supply those booths, and the hours I spent loyally ferrying her to and from the soccer field. Those interminable afternoons I spent on the sidelines. What was I supposed to talk to them about? "Winning and losing aren't my favorite topics," I told her. "They wouldn't be interested in the poetry of Louise Gluck or Anna Akhmatova."

"*ME*," Alice said. "You could have talked about me."

As I did, incessantly, with my therapist, with her sperm donor (an old college friend who chose to remain anonymous—and safely distanced from *my* daughter's daily *sturm und drang*), with her teachers preschool through grade twelve, her counselors and therapists, and now her partner, Germaine.

Alice was *so* planned, so wanted—and she was born, I do not exaggerate, with a little sneer on her mouth—not that newborn grimace, something more insidious. I thought I had imagined it, but the nurse noticed too. "Looks like she's already having some serious questions about what she's getting into."

Megrims. When I read that word, it seemed to sum up the dilemma that was Alice. I used it in the first poem she inspired.

> *First Look*
>
> Minutes into this world,
> she has megrims, turns up
> her nose, turns down her mouth,
> and my own uterus convulses
> with doubt.

What *if* your first reaction to life is distaste—and your reaction to that sensation is galvanic? Alice's first expression was followed by six months of near-constant caterwauling. I called it colic, but it had nothing to do with food, just the bane of existence itself. I walked her day and night, drove her around in the car for hours playing Mozart, my own eyes tearing with fatigue, despair. I had brought this on myself. She hadn't asked to be brought into this world. Everyone I knew thought it was a bad idea, my own mother going as far as to call it a perimenopausal delusion.

But I was forty-five, no love in my life, and I knew it was up to me to create a life worth living. I think that phrase is trademarked. Certainly it is the title of a surfeit of movie and books. Alistair's partner Germaine says it is the ultimate goal of the form of therapy she practices.

For years I had thought that being a poet was sufficient. My art was my raison d'être—or, more probably, I felt it would naturally lead to more intimate forms of fulfillment. I never needed a dream life—or a dream child. I had Alice because I needed a flesh and blood, real and fallible person to be the object of my devotion. All those messy, sporadic love affairs with my professors or colleagues, or friends, or friends of friends left me feeling increasingly depleted. I wanted my world to add up. So I talked an old gay friend into jerking off in my bathroom, and used a turkey baster to bring Alice into this astonishing world. I wanted our life to be stable, so I went back for a basic teaching credential, enough of that hand-to-mouth adjunct teaching, and started to earn tenure and a retirement fund teaching language arts to high school students. You would have thought this would be good training for raising Alice—but even the worst of those adolescents were models of self-restraint and goal-oriented behavior compared to my once-upon-a-time daughter.

I'm being unkind; worse, inexact. Alice always had a goal. She wanted to do what she wanted to do exactly when and how she wanted to do it—and was ready to demolish anything or anyone who stood in her way. More than exasperating or infuriating, it was anguishing to watch her. Not to get her way hurt her with an intensity that defied all consolation, threw her into paroxysms of pure agony. I can't *bear* it, was her cri de coeur, thrashing on the floor, slamming doors. And yet, as soon as she reached her objective—that familiar moue of disgust soon followed.

And still I hoped. *Persisted.* Yet another trademarked word today.

I don't want to give the wrong impression. Alice/Alistair functions at a respectable level. She—I mean he—I mean they has a masters in gender studies and has channeled her—I mean his—I mean their idealism into LGBTQ activism. Oh dear, am I missing a few letters here? Right now, their focus is public education—beginning with their mother.

"People of your age and ilk," is how they often begin their diatribes. I think they mean recalcitrant, unevolved, undoctrinated, not necessarily doddering or demented.

None of this would matter except for Alicia, my three-year-old granddaughter. The most painful part of raising a child, particularly an only child with one parent, is that they know exactly where to sink their daggers to cause the most excruciating—but not fatal—pain. The kind that, against all common sense, keeps you coming back for more. I will do anything to stay connected with Alicia. Germaine too. Alistair né Alice knows this. Perfectly.

Germaine is everything that I might want in a daughter. I'd adopt her in a minute but her mother, Harriet, equally wonderful, would object. I'm sure she feels that her daughter deserves better, far better, than my demanding, nihilistic, chameleon child, but what mother wouldn't. Germaine insists—to her mother and my shared bewilderment—that she knows what she is in for and, furthermore, she has the tools to help both herself *and* Alistair. There are all kinds of wunderkinds . . .

Germaine is patient, measured, realistic, a touch fatalistic. In other words, she is more enabler than counter-balancer. I ache for Alicia, my beautiful, trusting, brown-eyed, gold-haired granddaughter—the product of an anonymous donor's sperm and her father's eggs. I *see* myself in that child, yes, but more I feel responsible for her fate. I know what she faces. She's totally subject to that formidable combination of centrifugal and centripetal forces that *are* the person who brought her into this world, those crazy rages that suck all the air our of a room and then fling you back against the wall. Who is going to protect her?

Or the one to follow? That was what Alistair had come to tell me today. They has ordered another sperm vial. "If Germaine doesn't use it, I will," they told me. "It might be better for me to do it. Then they will be full sisters."

And if they ever split, they will have sole custody. The prospect leaves me breathless.

It doesn't *fit* in a poem. None of it. The reality. The surreality. The emotions. All these capital letters and slip-sliding pronouns. The self-righteousness. It's like magic slime.

"Bye, Grammie." That's my true north. What that smile, those words release in me.

True North

The voice in the whirlwind
is a small girl's
assured of nothing

but the smile on my face—
and the power of the arm
that surrounds her.

"You can't let her," I tell Germaine when I call her a half-hour later, waiting until I'm sure they are not coming back.

"I can't stop them," Germaine says. "The only person whose actions I can control is me. On good days—" she adds with a laugh. "Even if I use the sperm, they can order more when it suits them."

"Do you think this is in Alicia's best interest?"

"Having a sister or brother?"

"Having Alistair—and all her variants—as a parent."

"No court would find neglect, Agnes."

"Because *you're* there. An island of sanity."

"No woman is an island—of sanity or its antithesis. It's a process, Agnes. Still evolving. A dialectic. Besides, I have no legal standing in their life. Alistair made that clear from the beginning. That is why marriage is out of the question. At least until they decides if they're done with child-bearing."

"Is," I corrected her compulsively.

"Agnes, I'm going to forget we ever had this conversation. I want you to as well. If Alistair gets even a hint of it, we're *both* out of the picture and where does that leave Alicia?"

I couldn't let it go.

"What's the glue?" I asked her. "Between the two of you."

"Honestly, I like the variety. I never know who I'll wake up beside, what fire I'll need to put out. They *all* need me, all their many, evolving selves. That's pretty addictive for a therapist." Germaine's laugh was loud and genuine, but it ended in a sob. "The truth is no one, absolutely no one in the world will ever need me as much as they does. We both know that. It allows *both* of us to feel powerful."

"And what about Alicia—and whoever follows?"

"They have front row seats. I assure you, it won't be boring."

Zensense

They draw their chairs into a circle
and slowly turn their heads right,

> left, until everyone is accounted for
> and, with a blink, the current charges
> through them all equally,
> no beginning, no end, their eyes fixed
> on the emptiness in their center.

I *have* thought of going to child protective services. But Germaine is right. What could I point to? Alicia isn't malnourished, maltreated. Does anyone really care that she was birthed by a bearded woman who insists we all refer to her in the plural? Should I begin, "My daughter has dissociative identity disorder that may be caused—and certainly is reinforced—by our current cultural obsession with the transmutations of gender—and pronouns?" In this regard, they is no crazier than the world around them, indeed they is its faithful mirror.

No, what I want to say is how can we let her, my one and only daughter, be solely responsible for another human being when she has never committed herself fully to life. I'm afraid, I have always been afraid, she will drown in whirlpools of her own making—and pull us all down with her, mother, daughter, lover, because even dying she will not be able to bear being abandoned.

> *Having the Last Word*
>
> *I've run out of lifesavers*
> *the small, sweet colorful ones*
> *we give to children*
> *and the large white ones*
> *threaded with ropes*
> *we throw to adults.*
> *I've given up hope.*
>
> *But not for myself.*
> *I can feel the earth beneath me*
> *how it fits itself to my tried*
> *and true feet, alerts me*
> *to the great gift of gravity.*
> *I'm not going anywhere.*
>
> *It's you I see out there*
> *so very alone, so bitter-*

ly thrashing and calling
their name, the one
who was never, ever enough.

I put down my pen, reread what I've written. Take a deep breath, then another one. It is so good to be heard. Even if I am the only one listening. As I begin to read through yet another time, their special tone sounds on my phone. I take a deep breath, close my eyes, open them, touch my screen. Read:

Mom, you know me. I'm sorry.

J. WEST

INTERIORS: TABLE, AS IS, WITH BLUE DOG

The Goodwill table needs a home. A mother and daughter muscle its weight up two flights of stairs, then pause in the hall, panting. The old oak surface bears multiple scars. Five stout legs look ready to send roots through the floor. As if in protest, a joist creaks. Today marks Sheila's third visit to her daughter's vintage apartment.

"Half a sec," Zoe says, jangling keys.

It's August, which ramps up the building's layered aroma: mildew, ammonia, forgotten mops, fast food cartons, discarded hopes.

With a flourish, Zoe opens the door, points to the east wall. "There, okay?"

Sheila stares at laundry draped over moving boxes. Scattered across the green shag carpet, tools mingle with knickknacks, dog toys, and unopened mail. No seating arrangement or focal point. No aisle to the window, where the fitful AC unit churns. "Shouldn't we clear—"

Zoe raps on the table. "Mom. *Mom*. I don't want you to move anything."

Sheila could not have heard that correctly. Kneeling to mask her maternal dismay, she re-ties a sneaker. The state of her bones these days makes her dread falling. "Just shoring up support for these unreliable feet," she says, simultaneously buying time for the tension to ease. "My P.T. keeps warning me to watch where I'm going."

"I mean it, Mom. Don't move *any*thing."

Sheila straightens, then steps into the room. Goodness, she thinks. Common sense alone justifies nudging aside that chair, at least a few inches.

"*Mom!*"

"I'll put everything back. I promise."

Even facing away from her daughter, she senses emotional static, like a downed power line after a storm. One hand drifts to her chest and settles there: An unnamed pressure throbs. Oh, she itches to shove that backpack aside, along with several teetering piles of books. Why won't Zoe consider disorder poses real perils for her mother. It would be so easy to trip, fracture an ankle.

Never mind. Simply note open spaces. Memorize route.

Once, years ago, kneeling together before Zoe's doll house, she'd guided the placement of a tiny dining set, piece by piece, mother and daughter inching toward shared visual harmony.

Sheila turns, smiling, deftly back-kicks a towel into a corner.

"Stop." Zoe's gaze locks like a vise. She keeps her voice low, even. "This isn't working. I need you to leave."

Sheila's jaw goes slack. She feels it sink, along with her heart. Chilled, she inhales deeply, takes the summer heat inside her mouth and holds it there. She needs to reply, but no words come.

Wait. She can still fix this . . .

"Mom, you should go now."

Zoe's adamance and Sheila's confidence collide. And something more, stirring underneath. It's always there, the trio of worries, on replay: the girl's raging teenage years; Sheila's mentally fragile kinfolk; her cousin's grisly death, self-inflicted. And Sheila, failing all of them.

She can't botch this.

"Please," she says, "will you help me understand what's wrong?"

The table divides them: She's on one side, Zoe on the other, her arms folded.

"Just. Go."

Sheila has never spoken to *her* mother this way—though she's wanted to. How dare Zoe dismiss her like this? Past hurts, tamped down, reignite: accusation, riding shotgun with shame. And, of course, guilt. No. Now is not the time. Sheila swallows her pleas, her questions, all her parental defenses. "Fine. If that's what you want."

She crawls under the stupid table, then stalks downstairs.

Once outside the building, Sheila rummages for car keys, pondering the sour stalemate over a Goodwill table. Helpless frustration blazes as she pulls away from the curb. Zoe had enlisted her aid, which Sheila was glad to give. Wasn't she? Well, not anymore. She brakes for the yellow light because her vision blurs, ambushed by tears. She'll never be the mom she has longed to be, the one her daughter needs.

The light turns red. Her fingers drum on the wheel. Maybe Zoe declares her independence by defying her mother's joy in creating beautiful spaces. Well, Zoe's a grownup. She can live as she wants. Flicking on her right blinker, Sheila makes the final turn toward home, asking herself if she really believes this, then why did she move the chair and towel? Simple. Orderly room, orderly mind.

An old line of gossip surfaces. A former friend once mocked Sheila's interiors: "Weird, every damn plant in the perfect place."

Sheila pulls into the driveway, switches off the ignition. She stares at her daughter's old bedroom window: green shutters, hot pink curtains. The engine ticks. Why can't the child compromise? Her leave-it-where-it-lies insistence seems abnormal. Honestly, sometimes she acts like Sheila's doomed cousin.

The headlights click off. She takes a breath. She's just tired, overreacting. This is nothing more than the classic parent-child standoff: "You're not the boss of me."

Unlocking the front door, she toes off her sneakers, heads for Zoe's old room, flops across the canopy bed. She needs help. Or a good laugh. Better yet, a do-over.

\\✻//

A memory clicks into view, fuzzy at first. Zoe's in grade school. Sheila heads to the grocery store with Sarge, their eighty-pound mutt. A juice can of leftover tempera paint from her preschool job sits beside her, wedged into the cup holder between the seats. She'll remove it later. First, the groceries.

"Stay," she commands, eyeballing the dog. Then she cracks the windows and locks the doors.

When she returns, all is silent. No lifted muzzle, no wagging tail. The windshield looks blurred. She steps closer. Paint splotches the dashboard and steering wheel. The seats are blue. The dog is blue. Smurf-blue. He must have stepped in the juice can and gone berserk, bounding from back to front, from footwell to dashboard.

"Bad dog," she cries. Behind the windshield, his head droops, matted ears molding to skull. "Look what you've done. Get in the back. Now!"

"Whatever he did," a male voice drawls, "he sure looks sorry."

Sheila spins around. Goateed and tanned, the bemused stranger epitomizes calm.

"Not sorry enough," she fumes.

"Surely things can't be that dire."

Is he placating her? She needs an ally, not some genteel attempt to diffuse her wrath. "Oh, you have to see this to believe it. No, I mean it, come over here and look at this."

Coerced closer, the man's brows rise.

So does her voice. "Blue paint *everywhere*. And you think he looks *sorry?*" She smacks the driver's side window. Moaning, Sarge oozes off the seat, leaving a long smear. She folds her arms. "How am I supposed to drive home? Tell me that."

Palms raised, he inches toward his convertible.

How dare he desert her! Around them, engines hum, shoppers slide in and out of their cars. A few stare. The man thumbs his key chain, unlocking the door.

"Wait," she shrills, "you haven't seen the back."

By now his car is purring. "Good luck," he calls.

She glares at Sarge. "Bad dog. *Bad*, BAD dog!"

He mashes his snout against the glass, his dark eyes liquid with remorse. Her rage peters out. She pulls tissues from her purse and wipes down the driver's seat. Gingerly, she eases into the car. Balanced atop the passenger seat, Sarge scooches her way, drooling.

"Back off," she growls.

Undeterred, he nudges her arm off the gear shift, tries to lay his dripping blue chin on her shoulder. "Don't. You. Dare."

Sheila sits up, pulling Zoe's old comforter around her shoulders. And here it comes, after all this time, her daughter long-grown, the dog, buried. Two stories intertwine.

That day in the parking lot with Sarge, she could have been Zoe policing her boundaries: "Stay right where I tell you."

Today at the apartment, curious, well-meaning, over-anxious—Sheila was the blue dog. Making a mess of things.

Should she ask her daughter's forgiveness? She's not sure. Zoe could have handled things better. Will Zoe say sorry? Perhaps. What a dubious strategy, these withheld apologies. Sheila shrugs, then throws off the comforter. Maybe she'll read up on mental illness, lay a few family ghosts. Her hand drifts to her breastbone and rests there. The dull ache remains—so many raveled edges over the years, never quite smoothed—despite her intellectualizing, despite the draining push-and-pull of emotions. There will always be hallways crammed with furniture, seemingly immovable. Perhaps these tensions can only be managed, never cured. Of course, she's still talking herself into all this, still tripping over her own expectations.

Maybe she no longer needs to furnish Zoe's future based on her own hopes.

After Sheila hoses down the dog, she grudgingly calls him indoors, forgetting the requisite wet-dog spin-cycle. Blue aftershocks spatter hall and stairs. Soggy paws track tinted puddles across the linoleum. She assesses the ruins: house, car, clothing. Emotions. Zoe's due home from school any minute. She kneels to scratch the dog's ear. "Sorry, pal."

He leans against her and sighs. They tussle awhile. Then, panting, they flop to the floor. He licks her hand, leaving a telltale blue streak.

JOAN GERSTEIN

DEAD WEIGHT

Phantoms buzz like mosquitos sucking blood
I'm being chased by ghosts in the dark
They weave webs overnight as spiders do
In numbered days   I'm caught in the past

carrying a card with holes punched
for every broken promise
joyless holiday   angry meal
Acid of criticism burns

I travel around the world
Live 3000 miles from abuse
Still furies fueled long ago
accompany my bruised soul

seep through cracks in my psyche
that desires a different form
All honors, accolades, smiles
can't disguise my core of sadness

I am not my mother
I stifled judgment   showered love
Yet we both became estranged from sons
Even six feet under, she weighs me down

SOME DAYS I SCARCELY THINK OF YOU

        since you ceased
speaking to us five years ago.
        You wrote that
you needed a six-month break
        from family
to pursue creative endeavors.
        I wonder
how one precludes the other.
        I've begun
writing again, creating mosaics,
        have more friends.
My dog wouldn't recognize you.
        You only played
with her once for a few minutes.
        The quilt I made
for you is on the guest bed, awaiting
        your presence.
Presents bought for you in foreign lands
        wait as well.
What do you tell people that ask about
        your parents?
Do you circumnavigate questions,
        change topics,
lie that we died in a fiery car crash,
        bless our souls?

HEATHER TOSTESON

CALL WAITING

Loving mothers hold out futures
for their children, so many
open doors. They take what they know
about us and keep blowing it up
into a vision they expect us to fulfill.
At what point does that innocent
hope and cherishing faith distort,
diminish, and condemn us
to failures not of our own making?
When do we refuse to assume
that yoke of disappointment
and with it all the good
intentions that built it?

When do mothers become equally
intransigent? When do we refuse
to be an excuse, or even
an explanation? I am breathless
with excess fluid they have pumped
into me after removing my uterus
and ovaries. Honestly, I wasn't sure
you would call to check on me
after surgery—a lapse I understood
would be driven by anxiety more
than indifference. But you did.
Three days later, just returned from hours
at the emergency room, the onset
of congestive heart failure, you call again,
but even when told, seem oblivious,
acting as if, as always, I am only there to hear.

I can't get my words out. My heart
can't take the weight of this third spacing.
I hang up.

You are years older now than I was
when I last made any decision for you.
What weighs on you most are the expanding
implications of your own choices. How long
has it taken me to stop reducing your life
to my own mistakes? How long will it take you
to do the same? Where does it begin?

The phone rings and rings. The sound
keeps expanding around me. I trust you
to keep calling.

NANCY WICK

HE DID IT HIS WAY

I had mixed feelings as I watched my son walk across the stage in his blue gown and mortarboard cap. He was graduating from high school, it was true, but hardly with honors. As I saw it, he had merely scraped by, doing as little as possible to get a passing grade. Worse, he seemed to have the attitude that if a subject didn't come easily to him, he could just ignore it, say he wasn't good at that, and move on. What was he going to do when he came up against challenges in the future? Give up? Admit defeat without even trying? The prospect scared me. Would he be one of those guys still living at home when he was forty?

"I think you should get a job when you graduate," I had told him during his senior year. "With your grades I don't think you could get into the university." I was hoping he'd push back on that, tell me he wanted to go to college, but he didn't.

"Yeah, my girlfriend's dad said he thought there might be something for me at his company," he said, not showing any hint that this wouldn't be fine with him.

"But how do you see your future, long term?"

He shrugged. "You know I want to work with computers."

"Well, you'll need a college degree to get ahead in that field."

"Bill Gates didn't get one." He was constantly citing that fact when we talked about school. Bill Gates had dropped out of Harvard to found Microsoft, and his resounding success was every tech nerd's dream.

"Yeah, well, Bill Gates went to an exclusive private high school, and that was long enough ago that the computer field was just opening up."

He sighed. "I'm only eighteen, Mom. I'll figure something out."

That was my son, always thinking the future would somehow take care of itself without any effort on his part. Although his high school years were the most trying for me, his casual attitude about school was not new. An early reader, he was placed in a special class for fast learners in first grade. But except for the social aspects of being with other kids, he never seemed to like school. From the time homework began to be assigned, he was "forgetting" to do it. The only school subject matter that had ever generated enthusiasm for him was computers, which he zeroed in on in middle school.

His attitude frustrated and saddened me. Why didn't he love learning as I did? I had read to him from an early age, and because he enjoyed it so much, I continued long after he could read for himself. When a piano-playing friend remarked about his ability to carry a tune as a preschooler, I signed him up to sing in a chorus and take keyboard lessons. I took him to concerts and plays, sharing with him my knowledge of and excitement about theater. He seemed to love all of this, telling me after he saw his first Shakespeare production at age eleven that theater was his favorite thing.

But he still sloughed off schoolwork, leading me to do everything I could to get him to take it seriously: requesting that teachers send home progress reports, hiring tutors, and taking away privileges when he came home with poor grades. Nothing made a difference. Given that both his stepfather and I had graduate degrees, I couldn't help thinking I'd done something wrong as a parent to have a son who didn't do his schoolwork. It never occurred to me that he was learning in other ways, that school wasn't everything.

"It's boring," he said, when I asked him why he disliked schoolwork.

"Sometimes in life you have to do things that are boring. You can't expect to always do exactly what you want."

That was not a message he was willing to accept. When I looked at things objectively, I saw that he did well at hands-on learning—something that wasn't in great supply in school. What he knew about computers was largely self-taught. He experimented with our home computer so much that we finally got an external drive for him to use so he wouldn't mess up our data; he taught himself to code with a technical handbook; by the time he was in high school he was taking computers apart and putting them back together again. No wonder he found it boring to sit in class listening to a teacher talk. But somehow, I didn't see this as his version of a love of learning.

The argument with my son contrasted sharply with what had happened between my mother and me at a similar time. Forced to drop out of high school to help support her own mother, my mother used what she had learned working at a bank to save and invest so that my sister and I could get the fiercely-desired college education she had been denied.

So I grew up knowing that of course I would go to college. And like my mother, I loved school, where I generally did well, though I was never a straight-A student. I respected my teachers, feared their power and always did my homework. In fact, doing my schoolwork was never a subject of discussion between my parents and me. I did it and they stayed out of it. I graduated in the top ten percent of my high school class.

Then I went to college, where the story became more complicated. Though I planned to become a journalist, I reveled in my liberal arts courses—which involved reading new and unfamiliar literature, learning about history that high school texts didn't cover and arguing over points raised by major philosophers. As a result, I started speaking a language my carpenter father and housewife mother didn't understand. I wanted to talk about what I was learning, but they didn't seem interested and had little to say. Or they scoffed at the "hoity-toity" classes, saying they were all very well, but wouldn't help me get a good job, which was in their view the only reason for going to college.

My mother sacrificed to provide me with an education, but it seemed to her that that very education was driving us apart because I now thought I was too good for her. I didn't think that, but I did feel that since my parents seemed to lack interest in all the new ideas I was encountering, they were in fact rejecting my emerging adult self. I came home bursting with all that was going on in my life, eager to share it, only to find that their sole topic of conversation was people in the family and the hometown. The result was long hours of boredom punctuated by desultory conversation or outright arguments.

It was a conundrum I was never able to penetrate, as I remained distant from my parents until their deaths when I was in my thirties. A college education had come between them and the adult me; I didn't want the same thing to happen to my son and me. I couldn't turn against him because he *didn't* want to go to college. And anyway, I couldn't transfer my desire for an education to him. I had to let go. But it was one thing to know what I had to do and another to actually do it. I was still blind to what he was seeking as he moved toward adulthood, as well as to what he already had.

He did get a job at his girlfriend's father's company, which did nothing to increase his interest in education. The company was floundering; he was almost the only one there who was up to date in his computer skills. As a result, he had a great deal of autonomy and was paid reasonably well. Even with the company's shaky bigger picture, he was content. I couldn't understand that. Why wasn't he thinking of/preparing for the future? It seemed to me he was just taking the easiest path.

He went to community college in his second year on the job, largely because his younger girlfriend went, and he did well. But she dumped him during spring quarter and he fell apart, his grades taking a nosedive with him. After that, there was a period of no school. He worked; he played computer games; that was his life. I thought about how college had opened up the world to me at his age; now he seemed to be retreating into a narrower and narrower space. Watching him, I couldn't stick to my goal of letting go and allowing him to figure things out. Our conversations on the subject followed a familiar pattern:

Me: "Have you thought about going back to school?"

Him: "I don't really have the money right now."

Me: "You know I'd help you with that."

Him: "Mom, I don't really want to go. I like working."

Me: "But do you want to stay at this company going nowhere forever? You'll need a degree to get ahead."

Him: (with a shrug) "I'm not ambitious. I don't want to be a boss."

Me: "I'm not talking about being a boss. I'm talking about getting to do more interesting work."

Him: "Maybe someday I'll want to go to school, but right now I don't. Just leave me alone, okay?"

I came away from these conversations feeling sad and a bit desperate. I believed he liked working because he liked getting paid with minimal effort, doing something he was already familiar with. That had to do with being risk averse. But surely it would get boring. Surely he would want more at some point. How could this young man, who I knew to be intelligent and creative, say no to a college education? He was depriving himself of all the richness college had to offer.

But I wasn't taking into consideration the fact that his childhood had been unlike mine in a small town in the 1950s and early 60s. He had grown up in an urban, culturally rich area with two parents who both worked at a large public university. He had had access to professional level theater and music events from an early age; he had gone to school with kids who weren't all white and middle class. Maybe some of what college offered me was already part of his life.

Still, on a more practical level, how was he—just a high school graduate—going to get anything but menial jobs? A college education, I thought, was still the key to work that paid well and had a future. How would he live on his own, much less support a family?

He lived with us for two years after high school, but finally in his third year he expressed an interest for his own place. We helped him with the deposit, and he moved to a one-bedroom apartment by himself. I was encouraged by this. It wasn't school, but at least it was a move toward independence. Maybe it would help him grow up.

Three years passed. He worked at the same struggling company. And then the inevitable happened: his boss sold the company, leaving him and all the other employees without a job. He got severance pay—enough to support him for maybe a year—but he made no visible efforts toward getting a job.

"Why don't you go back to community college?" I suggested one night when he came over for dinner. "You've got nothing else to do; it would help you qualify for better jobs."

He looked down, avoiding my eyes. "I don't really want to do that. I'd rather work."

"Are you applying for jobs?"

"Of course I am. I send out resumes all the time."

"Any interviews?"

His voice was tiny: "Not yet."

As far as I knew, his efforts were confined to submitting resumes electronically on general job sites, and I believed this was unlikely to bring any results. More risk aversion. With an effort I refrained from saying anything.

Time passed. I felt sick as I watched him use up his money without any prospect of his fortunes changing, but I knew I was powerless to do anything. Only he could get himself out of this predicament. He would have to make up his mind to do what needed to be done.

Finally, the day of reckoning arrived: He didn't have enough money to pay the rent. With deep misgivings I allowed him to move back home. Angry as I was at his inaction, I couldn't allow him to be homeless. I saw he was depressed; I worried about the lure of drugs, though he'd never shown any inclination in that direction. The old specter of him living with us at forty came back.

As it turned out, he was only with us for eighteen months. At first it was nice because we would come home from work to find he'd cooked dinner. He did his share of the housework too. But he was a night owl who liked to stay up until the wee hours playing video games, then sleep all morning while we were up trying to get things done. I couldn't see that he was doing anything about getting a job, and he continued to resist any suggestion that he go back to school. Finally I decided the situation couldn't go on. It was time to kick him out.

Not trusting myself to say everything I needed to say without breaking down, I wrote him a letter and left it on his bed. In it, I noted that he was twenty-six years old and it was time for him to make his own way. Living with us, I wrote, wasn't good for him or for us. I gave him a move-out deadline three months hence.

Time passed and he didn't react, so I asked him if he'd read the letter. He said yes and that he was working on some things. Then he walked away, clearly not wanting to talk about it.

I wondered what I would do if the deadline came and went and he was still with us, but fortunately, I didn't have to find out. A couple he knew agreed to let him live in their two-bedroom apartment temporarily. From there he moved in with another couple, with an agreement to help them paint their house in lieu of rent. But when the couple got pregnant and told him he would need to leave to make way for the baby, he finally felt forced to act. He signed up with a temp agency for computer geeks and almost immediately got a contract job. Then he found shared housing with a stranger looking for a roommate.

That was the beginning. It took him several years, but he worked his way into a staff position with benefits. Sometime after that, he met the woman who would become his wife.

Today he has a stable job, a stable marriage, and a young child. He still doesn't have a college degree, but here is what he does have: A wife with a master's degree with whom he can converse on equal terms; an abiding interest in theater that I nurtured, enabling us to share rich discussions about current films and TV; a boss who values him enough that he has brought him along on a couple of job changes. He is not wealthy, but he and his wife have been able to buy a house and provide for their child. He does not ask my husband and me for money.

I am happy that my worst fears about him did not materialize. I'm glad he seems content with his life. But I still haven't been able to fully let go of a nagging disappointment that he didn't get the degree I know would have opened doors for him. Over the years I saved $30,000 toward his education. I could give it to him for other uses, but so far I haven't. As he approaches his fortieth birthday, I'm relieved he isn't living in his childhood bedroom playing video games, but I'm still stubbornly hoping he'll want that college degree after all, my adult child. Maybe someday I'll give up and see that he is an adult adult who pursued his own kind of learning and reached his own kind of fulfillment. College isn't the only route to the good life.

PAULA BROWN

FINDING DAD

The heat of the room feels like a greenhouse, but there is nothing growing here. I drop my coat on the chair. He is lying on his left side, facing the wall with his back to the door, exactly the way he was last week when I visited. The smell of latex and industrial room freshener mixes with a lingering odor of human effluence. He doesn't hear me walk in. His hearing aids remain in the bedside stand where they were tucked away weeks ago. There seems to be no more need for hearing. His arms are bound in some type of white support gloves that reach up to the base of his arm pits.

My mouth opens with a quick inhale, and I realize I have been trying not to breathe. I walk around the bed. His eyes are closed. "Hey Dad." He is still breathing.

His eyes open. His face is blank. He is neither happy nor surprised to see me.

I begin our ritual one-sided conversation. My job is OK. The kids are OK. My husband is OK. The dogs are OK. I ask him what he has had to eat (he can't remember), and who has been by to visit (too hard to remember names). I wish I could just be happy to spend a few minutes with my dad, but our recent past hasn't been sweet. Not just ships passing in the night, we have been ships crashing into each other in a multitude of tumultuous seas.

He pressed me for more and more of my time, but I had a job and three kids to raise. He picked my kids apart. I didn't like his girlfriend. I wanted to help him empty his house and move into a retirement home. He refused to let go of the house or anything in it. I didn't know it was dementia when his anger no longer just seethed behind his gritting teeth but came out full force against me. We rolled through waves of his anger while his health steadily declined and he had to rely on my sister and me for everything: where to live, what to move, transportation to the doctors. His blatant distrust framed everything we did to help him.

Still, we had a history of sharing our love of sports. While he was living on his own, he would drive to my house on Sunday afternoons in the fall to eat pizza and watch the Vikings games. And we sat on my couch together, yelling and cheering through nine innings until Louis Gonzalez got the hit in the bottom of the ninth, and our Diamondbacks won the World Series. I called him every first Saturday afternoon in May to remind him to turn the channel and watch the Kentucky Derby. Year after year our hopes rose in unison through the Derby, the Preakness, and the Belmont Stakes, waiting for that Triple Crown winner that he never got to see. This day I tell him that the Vikings beat the Forty-Niners and the Lions in their last two games. Our team is finally winning but my dad is no longer watching.

He says, "I don't see much of your sister." I pause for a moment, thinking about her reaction if I pass along that remark.

"Dad, she's here every day."

His expression doesn't change. "That's good."

I look at his bound arms and the blankets. "Should I adjust your blankets? It's really warm in here."

"It feels good to me." He is always cold. His eyes are squinting, barely open. Now and then they close, and he appears to be dozing. He is still breathing.

Last week my sister asked him what he was thinking about all day while he was lying in bed. He said he was trying to keep track of things. What things? The buzzer for the nurse, his phone, and the remote control for the television.

Today he only stares at the wall, and the fingers at the ends of his mummified arms seem incapable of making or answering a phone call. He asks me where the buzzer is. It is pinned to his shirt. I show it to him.

What is this life that is no life? Where is my dad? How does this end? When he signed himself into this care home, he insisted that his status be *full code* so that his body would be resuscitated no matter what. Now I secretly hope that he will die peacefully in his sleep without anyone noticing, before someone can pull out a code cart and pound on his chest, breaking all his ribs.

Young parents have untold numbers of resources available to guide them through each stage of their child's life. It's a well-worn passage with signposts at every turn. No one plans for the roles to reverse with your own parents. Still draped in our status as son or daughter, we don't know when the day has arrived that we are supposed to take over. An accompanying lack of cooperation on our parents' part makes procrastination rule.

I don't know when it's time to leave. There is no time here. I hug him and tell him I love him, then walk out of the room. But instead of turning right toward the exit, I turn left and walk down the hall to the nurses' station. I greet the nurse standing at the desk, request the proper forms, and use my power of attorney to sign an order that changes his status to Do Not Resuscitate. The nurse looks at me, her head tilting, mouthing a sad smile. "I know. It's so hard to do."

She's wrong. It's not hard.

The next day the Vikings beat the Titans. They're leading their division. I pick up the phone . . . my dad needs to know . . . this could be our year . . . they could go all the way.

I can't call my dad anymore. Turn the channel, Dad.

PAUL SOHAR

MY CRUTCH

a curtain of words
a page torn from a dictionary
that's what I throw on the hospital bed

what is the opposite of orphan

widows and widowers go hand in hand
but a parent robbed of an only child has no label
no rubric no box to cross off on any form
not even on the death certificate

what is the opposite of gray
black or white

what is the opposite of melancholy
despair or serenity

what is the opposite of a wreath
a desert or a rose garden

the roof garden of the Met Museum
or the desert around Jericho
I'd take either if she too can come

what is the opposite of remembrance
pain or joy

the opposite of orphan is a lonely old
geezer sneaking into an empty cemetery
with a memory to lean on

what's going to break first
the question or the crutch

THE REAPER

panic attacks said the professional giving
a professional smirk
nothing but panic attacks

but she saw that monster coming
we'd seen enough scary movies together
Dracula, Frankenstein, and even the Reaper
Cammie saw his shadow coming with the blade
and it scared the hell out her
she was too afraid to talk about it
instead she went hrrrummmmrrhh and hrrrrmmmpp . . .
said she couldn't breathe

but you cannot say that without breathing
    we all said not knowing
she meant to say she was scared
and her panic attacks were not unprovoked

even her lungs were in a shock
the doc fed her more drugs for the brain
and I was getting a panic attack about all the meds

but no one saw the shadow of the black hood
and the blade that no meds can fend off

she was the only one who saw him coming
shadowing her—circling her—day and night

she kept smiling to stop seeing him
except when the shadow choked off her breath

THE CANDLE

mist engulfed the roads but we
made the trip to LI from NJ because
we knew you'd be there waiting like
you used to on the front porch of Q-House

mist engulfed your quiet hill today
no angels came down to say hello
not even raindrops
just the mist and you reflected in a stone

we lit a candle right next to it
and talked to you as softly as the mist
our words carried off by the flame
and your answers flickering in its glow

sorry we were late but
mist engulfed the roads and bridges
you remember what it's like on Belt Parkway
a long drive on a foggy day

mist engulfed our whole visit
and it got even thicker at the end
we couldn't leave the candle there
a mess in the family plot

but blowing it out was like
turning your life support system off
all over again

the mist got colder
and on the way back home
the roads seemed to lead nowhere

IV
GENERATIONS

GAYLE BELL

REFLECTIONS

Rush to get to my momma
Emergency room
I see an old-school brother
greet with horizon wide grins
hugs grateful of a minor distraction
a warm soul

I go see momma
Plumped kewpie smile
history is complicated
I pull her up in bed
how can flies be in a hospital?
"Momma, you must have oil on your ass
you keep slipping down the bed"

coax information out of jagged nurses
admonishing mom's desire
for a sneak out cig
that's why you're in this bed momma

I trundle momma home in a cab
I walk dazed toward the bus
see my renewed acquaintance
touch his shoulder and confess
"me and momma were so at odds
when I was younger,
who knew I'd be the dutiful daughter."

DOWN HOME BLUES

>My mom sells her homemade liquor a mixture of potatoes sugars, some citrus fruits
>bottled in bell jars set under the house
>"now don't smoke under there," she warns my stepfather

Down Home Blues is playing
in the afterhours joint
Shaky pool table, scratchy juke box
Mom, the part-time proprietress
with my 18-month-old baby
dressed in a diaper, T-shirt, and pink bows

>Papa packs food, diaper bag, blankets, and baby toys for next door excursion
>I fuss over my child with my uniform on *Now that baby will be just fine* Mom says

Mom shoos a couple of brothers away from the door *Take that weed mess away my grand baby is here*

>My baby is dancing on the pool table
>Momma smiles while holding her hand urging her customers to put some money in the jar talking about baby's new shoes

HOMEGOING

The media portrays someone's last breath
slowing beeps on the monitors
one long continuous beep
When they took my daughter off the machine
There was silence
my halted breath
She sighed
looking like she was having
the most beautiful dream

I stood over her
willing her to let go
letting her know we would be OK
I told her your grandmother's waiting
I pictured her running until
her granny laughed swooped her up

I hope that's what really happened
My hands like Rosary beads

On the train from Bakersfield
visit with my son
I stood in the observation car
from mountains to desert
A good description of my emotions

MELANIE REITZEL

BACK IN THE DAY

Five years before he died, my father suffered a stroke and yes, things like that are to be fearfully expected when someone is just two years shy of ninety, but I didn't want to believe it could happen to the once six-foot, five-inches tall WWII Marine who'd worked later as an advance man for Lowell Thomas—the roving broadcaster, journalist and movie maker you probably wouldn't know much about unless you are at least sixty and have seen Cinerama. My father, whose portrait as that young Marine, had to be removed from the photographer's window in downtown San Mateo because women kept coming into the shop and asking for his name and phone number. When working in Hollywood, he had dated the likes of Rita Moreno; Ingrid Bergman had winked at him once through the crowd at a party. Dad still talked about her as: "The one that got away," kicking himself for not crossing the room to follow up on that wink. He was the man Bing Crosby had waved to at the golf course: "How you hittin' 'em kid?" "Hard as I can, Coach," Dad had replied. He'd also played a few rounds with Hoagy Carmichael. In the early sixties he had been the advertising and sales director for Radio Nord, the original pirate radio station that broadcast from a three-masted schooner off the coast of Sweden—yeah, my dad the pirate.

The rest of us in the family, including me and my half-siblings—two brothers and a sister—from Dad's side with his second wife, don't have the stature or the cache our dad did, and we're pretty much OK with that. We know that if a stroke were to hit one of us, it would be one more thing on the list of *Crap like this is supposed to happen to people like us who are merely Dad's spawn and not the man himself.* This stroke was not supposed to happen to him but not even Dad could meet the odds. His name was even cooler than any of ours: Bok. Not Bob, Bok—ending on a sharp, declarative consonant. Top that. You can't. And seeing him in rehab, unable to do most of the basic tasks of daily living on his own was breaking my heart, but it helped knowing that Dad's mind was still pretty sharp.

My time to visit with Dad was late morning, between physical therapy and lunch. About an hour together was all he could manage due to fatigue and discomfort in his much-too-short hospital bed, but we'd cram in as much conversation as we could. When I'd arrive, he usually had something for me to see, something for me to move, before we got talking. That week it was: had I seen the newest picture of Jackson, his fifth male grandchild? He loved all his grandsons but had been disappointed that none of his four children had managed to have a girl. "What's the matter with this family? Have you all forgotten how to make girls? I can give you the recipe!" This was followed by would I please scoot the water pitcher closer, help him turn, straighten his blanket. "More than happy to Dad. How are you feeling?"

"This is the shits but there's this new little nurse's aide—wow!" Dad grinned as best he could—a lopsided post-stroke grin, but still a grin. Women had always motivated Dad. His speech therapist was encouraging him to talk and to practice words with lots of W's. Dad was obliging—the fact that the therapist was a young blonde was especially motivating to him. He was more than happy to chat her up. He'd work on his *W* list: "Winsome. Wonderful. Whoop-de-do."

As a nurse, I'd learned that stroke victims are often emotionally labile, switching moods quickly—tears come easily. Dad felt embarrassed whenever the tears would start, often seemingly out of nowhere. Losing most of the movement and strength on the left side of your body is something worth crying about. Expressing frustration and grief over that was normal and I didn't want to discount that event or even pretend it wasn't a loss. Sometimes we would both cry. But Dad could still laugh and spin a story and when we were done passing the Kleenex box back and forth, he'd sometimes tell me things he'd never told me before—like wanting to hire a private detective to snoop on a guy I'd dated right after my divorce. Dad said he was afraid he was after my money.

"What money?" I replied. "Oh, you mean the buck three-eighty I got stashed away?" And we'd both grin.

In the beginning of the relationship with Wyatt, my partner of the past fifteen years, Dad had been skeptical and protective once again. But I knew what card to play: "Dad, you know what? Wyatt was also in the Marines."

"Oh yeah? What did he do in the Marines? I was in the Military Police. You tell him I could have had him arrested."

"Wyatt ran payroll, Dad—he could have held your paycheck."

Thumbs up, from Dad, as best he could, crooked grin, and my guy passed muster.

Dad also asked me if I thought my ex-husband had been having an affair in the last difficult year of our marriage. He'd thought maybe he had been.

"I dunno—I did find his Craigslist M4W search in our hometown on my computer, so maybe he wanted to but didn't know how to square it with his beliefs."

"What beliefs would those be?" Dad asked raising his right eyebrow.

"That if he screwed around, someone was sure to find out. And he knew that if that someone was you, you'd kill him."

"You bet I would have. With *both* hands." Dad said as his right hand made a fist, and his left hand wavered a few inches over his thigh. Dad always watched my back.

My parents divorced when I was eighteen months old. They remained cordial and never was there a hint of rancor expressed to me by either of them. In fact, Dad told me of the time he came to pick me up for a weekend visit soon after my mother and stepfather had married, when I was four. "Your mother told me to come follow her into the bedroom." My eyes bulged. *Whoa, Mom,* I thought. *What were you up to?*

Dad continued: "She pulled open the top drawer of Steve's dresser and said: 'Meet your successor.'"

I knew immediately what Mom had been trying to show Dad—how different her second husband was from him, her first, who once lost his glasses, only to find them in the refrigerator. Her first: the vagabond Mr. Aquarius, a dozen jobs before he'd finished college, dozens since. His hands in ten projects at once, most of them scattered all over his desk. This vs. her second, my stepdad: Mr. Aries/Taurus cusp with a big dose of Virgo, for whom everything had a time, a place, and a purpose. Who'd sold steel by the ton since his twenties, who tracked his stocks on Friday nights, who shined his wingtips on Sunday nights, and who could probably lay his hand on any tool in his garage while blindfolded.

"What was in his drawer, Dad?"

"Little cardboard boxes and their lids on one side. They held his cufflinks, his tie clasps, a deck of cards and a fountain pen. And on the other side? His socks, Melanie—gees, they were cross-filed!"

We both laughed.

"Yeah," I nodded, still grinning, "That's Daddy Steve for you. That fountain pen? He was given that when he graduated from high school." Dad shook his head.

Dad and I could talk like this about my stepfather because years ago he had told me: "I was really pleased your mother married Steve. He's a stand-up guy and I knew that with all the traveling I had to do, he'd be the best possible stepfather for you, that he and your mom would make you a good home." That was my dad's heart for you.

Dad had lost a few inches in height over the years, as we all do as we age, but he certainly hadn't shrunk in anyone's affections. When I learned of Dad's stroke, the person I called after my two sons, was my mother. I'd called her four years earlier when I'd learned Dad had been diagnosed with lymphoma; she'd cried on the phone. He'd been clear ever since and we'd all started to relax a little. The holidays weren't spent looking anxiously into the new year, wondering how many more years we'd have with him. Up to the time of his stroke, he was still singing in his barbershop quartet, was running the talent show and the art shows at his senior residence. Whenever one of my sons was in town, he'd drive down from San Rafael to Wyatt's and my home in Pacifica or he'd drive into San Francisco, and we'd all meet for lunch. He loved the shrimp and crayfish boil we had out on the Sunset—it reminded him of eating crayfish in Sweden. He talked for weeks about the shells and corncobs scattered all over the butcher paper topped table, the sweet sticky residue from the shellfish broth all over his fingers. "Sure as hell not like anything they'd ever serve us at Alma Via," he'd said. "Beats the hell out of Monday's miserable meatloaf."

And then the stroke hit, and Mom was in tears again. I'd call her after every visit to update her and my stepdad, who always asked: "How's Bok doing?" All my parents: my mom, my stepdad, my two stepmothers—both of whom Dad had survived—had treated each other with kindness and respect. Like grownups should.

After my divorce, Mom and Dad talked together on the phone every so often, mutually fretting over my finances, my "prospects," where I would live, how their grandsons were taking the split. I had appreciated their concern but didn't want them to worry about me. I was relieved I'd had the nerve to call my marriage game on account of rain—because it was raining—and had enjoyed my year of what I called "serial frog dating" before meeting Wyatt. When Wyatt and I were happily settled together, I'd asked my youngest how his dad and new wife were doing, he replied: "Oh, Mom, jeez, you're both way happier."

I was glad, though, that Mom and Dad were talking and told them so. After one call, Dad reported: "Well, I've just had another chat with your mother, and we've decided not to have any more children."

After my divorce, my mother didn't give me dating advice; she'd done so decades earlier before I had gone off to college. Her dating and drinking advice could be summed up in seven words: "Scotch, straight—one—make one last all night." She figured if I learned to drink something strong and expensive, I'd only have one per date and wouldn't fall prey to mixed drinks and end up pregnant. Mixed drinks and pregnancy formed a one-to-one equation, according to Mom. *Not a worry when dating at fifty-eight, Mom.* I think she just held her breath, hoping I'd have as much luck with my next household associate as she'd had with Daddy Steve.

My father's post-divorce dating advice was also down-to-earth and practical and was dispensed one afternoon over the phone. "Dad, I'm meeting a guy for dinner tonight. It's my first date after thirty-plus years and I'm a little rusty. Got any advice for your oldest single daughter?"

"Yeah," he replied after skipping maybe just half a beat. "Don't fart." And then he added: "Your brothers and I have a bet going on which of my girls will get lucky first." Girls? I'm eligible for an AARP membership and my sister was only thirteen years younger, and my dad says "girls?" I love that. "Don't tell her," he ended with, "but my money's on you, kid." I'm not kidding, he really said that. And at fifty-eight, it was nice to still be his kid.

※

Dad was a talker and a writer who always had a line and a yarn. Several of his stories had been published in the local paper, which pleased him to no end. We talked about our writing and how, yes, sometimes we fudged the truth just a bit. On my last visit before his discharge back to Alma Via, he asked: "Did I ever tell you about the time Frank Sinatra hit on your mother?"

"No. What? Really?" My father's speech was still a bit slurred after the stroke, but it wasn't my hearing I was checking on, it was the Sinatra-Mom thing. Dad's eyes were lit up—I was loving this.

"Your mother and I were at a bar in Vegas and along comes Frank with his Rat Pack. One of them shoots me a tough-guy, get-lost-fella warning look, and Frank hits on your mother."

I wondered: *Did the stroke hit the truth center in Dad's brain? Was this a fabrication? Poor Dad. But he sure looks happy.*

"Go on," I said, and instead of leaning back in disbelief, I leaned in, eager to hear more. He was in top form when he told a story—truth or fiction.

"Now, both my second and third wife would have totally bought Frank's line. But oh, no, not your mother. She wasn't having any of it. She just waved Frank away."

Mom knew how to stand her ground. She told me about the time when she and my stepdad were at a cocktail party in San Francisco. We were living in the East Bay then and I guess Mom was feeling like a suburban housefrau in tennis shoes. As she told it, she was sipping on her martini, listening in on a nearby conversation. "Melanie, there was this long-legged, button-breasted, moist-mouthed, empty-headed model who was trying to impress this Italian banker with her Berlitz Italian. The model turned to me and said: 'So tell me, Dahling, are YOU bi-lin-gu-al?'"

Mom's response? "No, my dear, I'm bi-sex-u-al." In 2009, this wouldn't have raised an eyebrow. In 1956, it got her a kiss on her hand from the banker who said: "Madam, I salute you."

My mother was what they used to call "statuesque." She was five feet eleven inches in her stocking feet and her jealous friends called her "Big Jane." And she was gorgeous. By comparison, Ros Russell was a bobble-head dashboard doll. And if this Sinatra encounter had really happened, it would have been in 1946 or so. And if my future parents had been at a bar in Vegas, Mom would have been dressed to kill in high heels, a veiled cocktail hat (black, of course) and maybe over her shoulders, one of those swanky fox furs where the fox bites his own tail, his amber glass eyes daring you to challenge his right to drape the goddess's shoulders. Mom, the statuesque two-plus yards of her vs. five-foot seven Frank. In lifts, at best, he would have hit Mom at about Maidenform level. Now Frank was, by all reports, an ambitious man, but *Woo-wee, Frankie, trust me, you were not ready to take on The Formidable Jane.*

"Dad, that's amazing, and I'm not surprised Mom turned him down. I mean, come on—you sing way better than Sinatra." Dad grinned.

When my visit with Dad was over, I got in my car and hadn't hit 101 South before I was on the phone to Mom. I had to know. "So, Mom, Dad's floating this story that Sinatra hit on you in Vegas."

"Jesus H. Christ, Melanie. Your father." Uh oh, looks like Dad's been confabulating again. "First of all, it wasn't Vegas, it was the Cal-Neva, Tahoe."

I'm already laughing. Son of a gun.

"Second of all, it wasn't Sinatra—it was Lawford."

At this point, I was laughing so hard I nearly drove my car off the road onto the shoulder. There's a reason why the CHP tickets you on cell phone fact-check calls to your mother while you're driving—it's dangerous.

I'd always thought I'd picked up a certain wistful tone in Mom's voice whenever Peter Lawford's name came up on TV or radio. Now I know why. I remember him: he was a tall, dark, gorgeous specimen of a man with a beyond-classy British accent—the kind that makes you want to undo your blouse two buttons at a time. He was way more mom's type than Frank.

"Well, Mom," I said, once I'd steadied the car, "if Lawford and Sinatra were still alive, they'd both hit on you. But they'd both be outclassed." I could hear her grin.

When I told Dad about my call to Mom and said that according to her it hadn't been Vegas, but Tahoe and that it wasn't Sinatra, it was Lawford, he laughed off the vagaries of his storytelling and got to the point: "Melanie, your mother's always had great taste in men."

They don't make 'em like that anymore. They just don't. I remember when the term *Dame* meant something. When it was the perfect nod to the perfect combination of *Va Va Voom* and *Class*. Something about the era of veils on women's hats, cigarette holders, cocktails—not drinks, but cocktails. The days of broad-shouldered gentlemen in brimmed hats and freshly shined wingtip shoes, who tipped those hats when they passed a woman on the street. Men who honored their ex-wives, who looked out for their daughters—decades after it was necessary.

PATRICIA BARONE

THE FALL OF OUR ADOLESCENCE

All Thanksgiving dinners, one dinner:
turkey skin so tight, it strains out basted butter.
Truly, we are blessed in being born
children of these United States
in process, gifted with freedom
as long as it takes to grow up.

Mother, flanked
by aunts in the kitchen,
tells our brother: "It's time
you marry that girl!"
Seven siblings, reunited
at Aunt Claire's table,
we make it our own
singing show tunes
only for each other.

Crows peck fat nestlings out
before the branch breaks.
Our parents, tested
by war separation,
the death of a child
and work—
want us home
when we need a home.
We allow them anger
but grudge it.

OLD CHILDREN

We always want to be here
early, together with the wine,
uncorked to breathe.
We would be happy
except for confusion—
Mixed socks are one thing
but the good gray suit
Dad is tired of wearing?

The rucksacks
and the walking gear,
whose skis belong to the tallest,
and where our brother can bandage
his weak ankles, if they belonged
to our father before him?

Our sister insists her face is hers.
"This is what I am," she says,
"what I am becoming."
Stems and petals vein her cheeks,
a shell above each eye.
No one denies her nose is her own.

It's Christmas Eve, for candles, mass,
still we prefer to doze in chairs
or stoke the fires, half believing
our mother's and father's old stories.

ADULT CHILDREN: Patricia Barone

I should speak plainly, but
you know how it is with families.
After Christmas we try,
not low, the Coventry carol,
but high, Hark the Herald Angels,
many parts soaring,
and we break up,
old children who survive ungratefully,
laughing in a church.
The song that comes at last is good.

TIME'S ARROW

Monarchs flit among the milkweeds.
"The butterfly cycle's an example,"
says my son, "of time's arrow.
It only works in one direction."
I point to my white hair and laugh.
Already we see chrysalides,
expectant as painted buntings.

Lacking physics, unlike him, I argue
for a time machine that goes backward,
to an era before Corona interspersed
masks and distance when we meet.

When we aren't relaxing on Matt's pergola,
Surrounded by morning glory vines,
watching the dog worry
the edge of the yard for squirrels—
when it's winter, what will we do?

"I've been listening," I say, "to your father.
Despite his death and time's arrow,
he's proud of the way you built this deck."
"I've taken Dad inside me," Matt says.

LORI CLOSTER

SURVIVING FAMILY

"You'll notice a big change this time," my mother warned as she glanced into the rear-view mirror and changed lanes. She was maneuvering her silver Caddie through southbound traffic to Miami Beach, where my grandmother had been ensconced like a queen for half a century. Slouched beside her on the gray leather passenger seat, I felt pleasantly irresponsible without my children, in my father's care at my parents' canal-side home in Boca Raton. Tony and Angela, my mother had decreed, would be "too much" for Nana. I touched my sunburned cheek gingerly and loosened the seatbelt, which had tightened across the tender skin of my shoulder. My few hours of beach time since my arrival from ice-bound New Hampshire had been too much; I always forgot how easy it was to get scorched down here. Familiar exits blurred past—Pompano Beach, Fort Lauderdale, Hollywood, the evocatively named Ives Dairy Road—and my mother's words echoed in my mind.

Nana was a law unto herself. She'd come from money, but had somehow lost it. Later she'd divorced my grandfather, a scandal in her generation. Careful with cash to the point of frugality as a divorcee, she had aspired to and achieved the fundamentals of an Old European lifestyle: almost-daily trips to the market for fresh artichokes, cucumbers, and other veggies, designer shoes, and an impressive amount of global travel. She never bought a paper napkin; it was ivory linen all the way, which always gave me a surge of pure pleasure when viewed against the claret velvet chairs of her Mediterranean dining room set. Somehow she'd held onto her rent-controlled apartment with a private patio, right through the gay gentrification that transformed her neighborhood into a Caribbean kaleidoscope and made the Beach a destination. Aside from the lovely, progressive silvering of my grandmother's hair and the slight tremor she'd developed in her wrist, a visit to Nana in her lair resembled an annual drop into a rabbit hole in which only I myself, Alice-like, had changed in forty years.

Until now. The moment I saw my grandmother slouched over in her armchair, I knew my mother had been right to leave the kids behind. Tony is well-behaved, and at eight can entertain himself anywhere with a book or stack of Legos. But Angela, at six, can be a handful, asking a million questions and fingering everything in sight. Nana just moved her head a bit when we entered, while an exotic caregiver ostentatiously dusted knick-knacks on the cluttered credenza. Julia hailed from Barbados, I was told, and flashed me a gap-toothed smile during our brief introduction. I nodded, then turned eagerly to my grandmother.

"Mom? Here's Catie, all the way from New Hampshire," my mother chirped.

Nana peered forward, sharp-nosed. "Catie? My god, Melinda, why didn't you tell me she was coming? Look at you! What have you been doing with yourself!" As I bent to kiss her, she grabbed my hand and pulled me onto the footstool at her feet, her fingernails raking my flesh. The strength of her grip surprised me.

"Hi, Nana, not much. It's great to see you. I've been at Mom and Dad's, and—"

"My god, Catie, I'm old now, but at least my grandson still comes over. You know my grandson Daniel?" She leaned into my face, dark eyes glittering. The stubs of her few lower teeth were discolored and crooked, boulders askew in an angry sea of saliva.

I held my ground. "He's my cousin, Nana, remember? Of course I do."

"Well, he comes most weeks. My god is he handsome. One of the best-looking boys ever, even if he does take after—well, I won't say it."

Sigh. I'd forgotten the cardinal rule of a Beach visit: Nana didn't ask for, or want to hear, details of my life. The mere sight and feel of me, fingers and toes intact, seemed to satisfy her curiosity for another year. A corollary of this private truth: within minutes of my arrival, I wondered why I'd come. The entire conversation concerned other people—usually my cousin Danny, the longtime favorite, who's actually short, red-haired, and resembles a troll—but you forget it instantly with the force of his winning personality. That's love for you.

But today would be different, I'd decided. "Nana, I've got pictures of Tony and Angela. Do you want to see?" I pulled my cell phone from my purse and held it out to her.

She tilted her head while I scrolled through the images. "Very nice! The little one, with the curly dark hair—she's just like Stacy's daughter. Do you know Stacy?"

"Of course, she's my cousin too." The question wasn't senility. Just Nana. She would soon extol the praises of each of my southern cousins, apparently surprised I even knew of their existence. It's natural for her to prefer them, I told myself. They grew up nearby.

I knew the truth, though. Nana's conversations were the greenest shoots of a malevolent strain of favoritism that has twined through untold generations of my family's history. Decades of sowing and tending delicate seedlings of rivalry and resentment have borne a bounty crop of bitterness not just among her children—my mother and her sisters Gianna and Josephine seldom speak, though they still reside a block apart in their old neighborhood and both get along with their brother Lou—but among her seven grandchildren, too. She'd had eons to hone her skills, and her callous remarks were legendary in our family. The harvest from such a sowing was bound to be indigestible, and it was a wonder we didn't all hate each other. Of course, most of us had fled the state once we were grown; but how the ones who'd stayed had coped, I had no idea.

"Will anyone have a fruit cocktail?" Julia, the caregiver, spoke in a voice impossible to ignore. I told her no thanks, but she persisted. "Are you sure? We've got lots of fresh pineapple, orange juice, melon, coconut . . . all bought specially for you. Your grandmother can't eat fruit, her teeth are gone. You really should—"

"Fine." I gave in, ignoring the *we*, and tried to converse above the raucous rumblings of an antique blender in the kitchen. At last the drink arrived: a monstrous goblet overflowing with crushed ice, juice, pineapple, and who knew what else. Atop the entire concoction, incredibly, was one of those tiny paper umbrellas that invariably rip when opened. Julia had managed admirably, though. This one was pink and intact.

The whole thing was bound to upset my digestion. I can't tolerate citrus; it's way too acidic. Nana couldn't either, my mother had often said, thereby naming what might have been our sole common characteristic beyond our DNA. But this cocktail denoted such extravagance that I felt compelled to down the Kool-Aid, so as not to waste her money.

I took tiny sips. Nana leaned closer and closer, talking nonstop about a friend whose daughters had taken her on a cruise, and . . . *sip*. My grandmother's breath enveloped me, foul and fetid. I inched the stool back a couple of inches. *Sip, sip.* The friend's daughters had gotten sick. Now my insides churned. *Sip . . . sip . . .* Nausea gripped me, and I bent double, willing myself *not* to throw up on Nana's feet, not with that infernal, pushy woman grinning two feet away. Instead, I ducked off the footstool and scooted away, gesturing frantically to my mother to take my place.

Nana didn't notice.

"Yes, Mom. Yes, Mom. *Yes*, Mom, I *told* you already, remember?" My exhausted mother lowered herself onto the footstool, her irritation skittering like a mosquito along the high crown moldings. I moved away and inhaled slowly and deeply, willing my stomach to settle. Tiny souvenir plates and bric-a-brac from around the world covered the cool white walls, and I moved forward to inspect them, as I did each year. Nana had traveled a lot in her persona of the gay divorcee, and my childhood had been punctuated by scenic Kodacolor postcards emblazoned with "Hello from Albuquerque!" or "Greetings from Alaska!" that engendered no end of envy in my mother. "I didn't even know she'd gone away," she'd murmur as she turned the card over and studied Nana's bold, slanted script. Wanderlust may be inherited, but it must have skipped me; I am happiest in the bosom of my family, carrying out my responsibilities at home.

The tension in my mother's voice testified to her strained relationship with Nana. For years my grandmother would promise to give her some prized bit of family china or jewelry, or to take her on a cruise, then renege. Sometimes she'd give an item and later demand it be returned. "The boomerang strikes again," my father once reported with a chuckle. "Nana says she didn't really give her Spode tea set to Mom." That time the two women didn't speak for months, until Nana called and chatted away as if nothing had happened.

My mother spit nails every time she told that story. Not that she couldn't have bought her own Spode set; it was the principle of the thing.

On our return trip to Boca, I got an earful. The day help—meaning Julia—was stealing Nana blind, my mother said, but her hands were tied. Unlike the previous caregiver, Julia did take excellent care of my grandmother.

"What sort of stuff does she take?" I said, surprised. The woman hadn't struck me as a thief. "Jewelry?" Nana's collection of fine pieces was bound to be intact, as she didn't give things away. She lent.

My mother shook her head. "Nothing that serious, but the food bills are outrageous. I know she carries a lot of it home to her family. Last week she made a huge seafood paella, and the next day it was all gone. And there on the grocery bill were thirty dollars' worth of frozen shrimp and mussels! I know darn well my mother didn't eat a single one, she thinks shellfish are trash food and can't chew them anyway."

I pondered how many kids Julia might have at home. "Did you confront Julia?"

"Of course not. She'd quit! She's got us over a barrel, because it's almost impossible to find reliable help. And it's that or a nursing home for Nana—which I promised I'd never do. This way, even with the higher food bills, her money goes further." My mother sighed. "It could be worse, I suppose. The woman has two children, I hear one is disabled—" She frowned and was silent a moment. "But Nana—" Then she segued to the litany of resentments about Nana I'd heard my whole life, ranging from constant carping about trivia to unreasonable demands. Clearly, my grandmother gave her a run for her money. Why didn't my mother just tell her to take a hike? But if she hadn't by now, she probably never would.

There had to be some code of daughterhood I didn't understand.

At last she fell silent, and I gazed out the car window at the unrelenting edifices of enterprise off I-95, South Florida-style. As the eldest among her siblings, my mother bore the brunt of managing Nana's care, and her load would certainly lighten one day when my grandmother was gone. Come to think of it, I mused, their relationship wasn't all that different from my mother's and mine. Although we got along well enough on happy, pleasurable excursions—even now, for instance, when I wasn't the focus of her scrutiny—on a normal day, we rarely finished a conversation without striking sparks. Her flinty disapproval of my un-citified lifestyle (I married an organic farmer and raise sheep, whose fleeces I sell to a crafts co-op) underlay, as a substrate, the ebbs and flows of my life.

"You've got to finish your education," my parent intoned almost every week on the phone, plus much more on a variety of other subjects, right down to whether I wore my hair long or short. (Long. I pinned it into a bun, as did most other weavers I knew. I guess we were fond of strands.) Unlike Nana, though, my mother hadn't ever rescinded a gift she'd given me. In fact, she was an artist in the presents she gave, eyes aglow as she offered "something to open," beautifully wrapped, and explained the decisions that had gone into its purchase: what sort of artwork would show best in our entryway at home, how many placemats fit at our oak trestle table, whether Tony would prefer a construction set or a toy planetarium, or Angela a dollhouse or puzzle of the U.S. Presidents. These gifts, and the carefulness with which she chose them, represented my mother at her best. They covered a multitude of sins.

Unfortunately, those moments were rare and fleeting. From the passenger seat, I examined my mother covertly. Her palms on the leather-wrapped steering wheel, her reddened knuckles swollen with arthritis. Her skin lined from years of sunbathing, before the ozone layer was discovered to be disappearing; the expensive prescription sunglasses that hid her eyes. Those fine features contorted with rage sometimes, her mouth gone rigid. *I'm sure I love my mother,* I thought. *But why can't I feel it?* On my first day of kindergarten, I'd clutched her narrow hips and told my bemused teacher Mommy could *too* stay. I'd certainly been attached then . . . Now I swallowed hard and turned my attention outside the window again. A billboard flashed by, touting a giant jewelry exchange, and I snorted.

"What's wrong?" she said.

I hardly knew how to answer. Of all the confused, terrible, gnarly aspects of the visit to Nana, and even of this week with my parents, which tiny thread could I pull to unravel what had gone wrong between us? The lumpy, misshapen fabric of our lives was marked by criticism and pain, barring those pockets of warmth during gift-giving—but I doubted my mother was even aware of this. Emotional intelligence is not her forte.

"Why don't you put Nana in a nursing home?" I said instead.

She pressed her lips together and shook her head as she fluttered her beringed hand out the window to change lanes. "I promised."

Duty. Tears blurred my vision. How I hoped my relationship with my daughter would be better than this. Angela was still small, but the fabric of a life is woven thread by thread. I was determined to keep a close eye on our pattern, and avoid horrible mistakes before it was too late to correct them.

Re-entry from a trip to Florida always proved terrible, especially in the awful darkness that cloaks the Northeast at 4:30 each winter afternoon. Yet the snow along the streets of our village gleamed in the dusk with surreal beauty as our truck crunched along, and my husband's white teeth flashed attractively against his beard as he laughed at something I said. I'd missed snuggling with him before our hearth during my week away. But when at last we arrived home, all I wanted to do was wave a magic wand to get the kids in bed, look in on my sheep—especially Mousie, whose lungs had been ailing—and sink into my favorite paisley chair with a mug of cinnamon apple tea. A few days off to put up my feet and read weaving magazines would restore my equilibrium.

It didn't happen, of course. My ever-considerate spouse ordered a pizza that we picked up on the way home from the airport, but the rest of that first evening shredded my nerves. Angela, high-strung from the moment she'd entered the world squalling, was at her most disagreeable.

"I think she's relieved to be home. She missed this place," my husband said as our daughter cartwheeled around the messy living room. Housekeeping wasn't *his* forte. Already our daughter had destroyed her brother's newly begun Lego tower, and he'd retreated to his room in disgust.

Or Florida left her as tense as it did me. Mentally I geared myself for a siege. "Yes, Angela. No, Angela. Yes, I told you already, remember honey?" I'd say for a few days, in an uncanny echo of my mother, until my daughter settled in again. A tempting image flashed into my mind of heaping fresh wool onto her, the way kids bury themselves in piles of autumn leaves. She could still breathe, of course, and would shriek with laughter, and I'd have a few moments' peace from her incessant demands.

Talk about wool-gathering.

A month after our return to New Hampshire, Nana's doctors discovered a tumor on her spine. Six months later, to my shock, she died. Despite my mother's best intentions, ultimately Nana had to be moved, not to a nursing home, but to a private residence whose owners cared for just a few elderly. There was plenty of warning before the end, as Nana's biological systems failed one after another, but then she had a major stroke. When I pondered aloud whether to fly down to say goodbye, my mother surprised me. "She wouldn't know you, Catie. You might as well stay home." So I did, plagued by guilt but rationalizing that I'd see more relatives if I came for the funeral. Meanwhile, I phoned my mother daily for updates, in which my parent sounded surprisingly matter-of-fact. Nana was receiving the best possible care, and what would be, would be. I wasn't to worry.

\\✻//

All of Nana's posterity except Tony and Angela—children, grandchildren, the local great-grands—gathered at the funeral home, seated on rows of chairs opposite the ornate mahogany coffin where she lay in state. My mother and aunts sat carefully apart from each other, their clothes a study in shades of black. Their restless gazes moved over Nana's face and lifeless torso, as if in search of something they'd missed. Love, possibly. But she was regal, untouchable, her silver hair perfectly coiffed and her elegant nose more Roman than ever. Her handcrafted diamond cross—her prized piece of jewelry—nestled on her sunken chest against the pale blue-gray knit of her favorite St. Johns suit. Those waxy, folded hands would never again stuff an artichoke, fold a linen napkin, or dust a souvenir plate from Chile. Extravagant arrangements of lilies and roses flanked the coffin and tickled my throat, making me cough, and a famous Italian tenor whose name I ought to have known crooned some ancient Latin song, whose name I also should have known, through the sound system.

My mother had done Nana proud, fulfilling her daughterly duties impeccably. Taking a seat, I made a mental note to tell her so. Had it hit her yet, that the ordeal was over? Her stoic expression revealed nothing. I glanced at my aunts and flashed to the funeral scene in the old film *Charade*, where the big goon Scobie strides to the coffin of Audrey Hepburn's husband and jabs a needle into the corpse to be sure he's dead. From the identical, set expressions on my aunts' mouths, one of them might have done the same. Unless—I twisted in my seat. Yes. Uncle Lou lounged in the doorway, half-committed as always, chewing a toothpick.

That toothpick, firmly jabbed, could also do the job.

Oh, Nana.

A priest entered in full clerical garb, cleared his threat loudly, and delivered generic comments which included repeated mentions of "your beloved." Hysterical laughter threatened to bubble from within me. Did he mean Nana, whose children hadn't occupied the same room together in more than a decade? I peeked at my relatives, but everyone was listening intently. Fortunately. If they had showed any sign of amusement, I'd have lost it completely.

"And so, to your dear grandmother's surviving family . . ." the priest intoned, and at last it was over and the room buzzed with conversation. I hadn't seen some of my cousins in years and enjoyed our exchanges, in the ironic way one does while at a funeral. While I talked with my glamorous cousin Stacy, a regional TV personality, she glanced at the coffin where Nana lay stone quiet.

"She's finally at peace," Stacy said. I regarded her curiously. "All that anger," she added, confirming what I'd suspected: my local cousins had more to recover from than I did.

Our Aunt Jo overheard and moved toward us. "You know what your grandpa said about Nana?"

Stacy and I exchanged wary looks. "No," we said, not quite in unison.

"He said not to blame her for the way she was," our aunt said. "That we never saw the home she came from. Her brothers and father shouting at every meal, pounding their fists on the table . . . There was no love in that house, your grandpa said. He hated going there, not that he did it much. The old man disowned Nana when she married, you know. Cut her off without a cent."

So that's how she lost her money. My cousin's expression told me all this was news to her, too. She'd just opened her mouth to reply when someone tapped my shoulder: Danny, more somber than usual in a finely cut dark suit. The unruly red hair I remembered from childhood was clipped close to his head. "You look fantastic, Catie," he said. "I'm so glad you're here." He opened his arms wide, enveloped me in a hearty hug, and whispered in my ear. "Hang on, I've got to . . . Excuse me!" he called above the conversational hum. "May I have your attention?" He moved to the head of Nana's casket and clapped loudly twice. Which sounds obnoxious and controlling, but somehow wasn't.

"This probably isn't a typical funeral," he began when we were all quiet. "As you all know, we're not exactly a close family, some say thanks to Nana herself. Father McCallum here"—he nodded at the priest—"was stumped about what to say, when a few of us met with him. The usual sentiments just don't apply. And yet, you're here. It's not my place to thank you, but I'm really glad you came. It means there's a glimmer of hope for our family."

No one moved. Danny plowed on, intrepid. "I wasn't born yesterday, and know you all believe I was Nana's favorite grandchild. Well, who could blame her?" Someone snorted, and he gave his most engaging grin, revealing the dimple on his freckled left cheek. "But let's think about that for a moment. When you all visited Nana, she always talked about me." He grimaced. "Yeah, no secret there. You must have gotten real tired of it. Comparisons are odious, right? But here's the thing. Whenever *I* came, she talked about *you*. How proud she was of each of you." Ignoring the stirring in the room, he pulled a folded paper from his pocket, fitted a pair of reading glasses onto his blunt nose, and surveyed the room. "Maybe you'd like to know what she said about her grandchildren."

He began to read. "Stacy. 'Oh, my granddaughter Stacy is so successful, and she's on the Miami television all the time and takes wonderful care of those kids. She works hard and has all those famous people on her show, and I never miss a one.'" Danny peered over his glasses at Stacy, who appeared frozen in place. "Philip," he continued. "'You know my grandson Philip—he's an engineer, did I tell you? He was especially important after the hurricane in New Orleans, he helped rebuild the roads. Philip's company couldn't last a week without him . . .'"

Danny's voice had taken on Nana's intonations, and it felt as if she were speaking directly to us. "'Now Saffy, my son Lou's daughter, my god Saffy's beautiful, she married a stockbroker in Dallas and has those two beautiful children. And Ricky her brother, he's a successful lawyer, married to that beautiful girl Marcy from Nevada, she's a lawyer too. They're rich, you know, and may God bless them for it."

Someone snickered, breaking the tension in the room. Nana had been nominally religious at best—and yes, beautiful and successful were her two favorite words. I'd just never heard her use them about *me*. "Melissa, she's my youngest granddaughter, she works at the hospital at a very important job in the operating room," Danny went on. "She saves lives every day. And Lucas is a consultant you know, and he and his wife Joanne fly all over the world, so successful he is—"

He paused. "Last, but certainly not least," he said in his normal tone and smiled at me. Then, in Nana-voice: "My granddaughter Catie, she's a classy lady and lives up north and has her own business and those two wonderful children. You can tell they're from this family, they're so beautiful . . ."

Danny stopped reading, removed his glasses, and looked around. Letting it sink in. "I could go on. Nana said a lot about each one of you. You were practically all she talked about—the brains, beauty, and success of her whole family. Now, I can't say we didn't have our moments." He made a rueful moue, the dimple deepening. "Even with me, she could be . . . a challenge. But she loved every one of you. In her own way. I'll miss her terribly." His throat emitted an odd noise when he bent over the casket and kissed Nana's forehead. "Goodbye, Nana." He straightened abruptly, cleared his throat again, and strode from the room.

No one moved. Silence stretched tenuous filaments among us. From the doorway, my Uncle Lou let out a snort. By the time I turned, his staccato footsteps were receding down the hallway. Even as I wondered if he would overtake Danny and speak to him, I caught Stacy's eye. She wiped her cheeks with a carmine-tipped finger and moved toward me, fierce.

"'In her own way.' Fat lot of good that does," she said. "Would it have killed her to tell me she watched my show? But she was too damn contrary. The priest said it right. We survived."

Privately, I had to agree. Nana had favored Danny, and he'd clearly loved her too. But for the rest of us, especially those who lived nearby, the bile ran a deep, sulfurous yellow-green. Despite her shellacked newswoman façade, Stacy clearly carried wounds. I had my answer about how my southern kin had fared. I longed to hug my cousin, but didn't dare.

That evening, I fidgeted on the mile-long white sofa in my parents' home in Boca Raton while my mother sobbed. Given the thorn in her side Nana had been, I was nothing short of flabbergasted. In the face of such obviously genuine distress, I tried to put two and two together in an equation I'd never imagined. "She wanted to die in my arms, and she did!" my mother marveled. Tears furrowed her cheeks. "Ninety-four years old, and she waited 'til I got there."

"I thought you weren't close," I said tentatively. "You were always fighting."

My mother blew her nose on one of Nana's linen hankies. "It's—it was—hard to be at peace with Nana, she said and did such outrageous things. But she always had my back when I was a child. We were poor, you know, we lived on the south side of the city. But she scrimped on her own food, gave up her own lamb chops, so I could take the trolley to the rich section and then enrolled me in their school, even though we didn't live there. Who knows how she managed to persuade the district, it was completely against their rules. But it made all the difference." She paused and her next words carried the profundity of a prophet's. "If I'd stayed in the local elementary, I'd never have gone to college. There was no opportunity."

And I wouldn't be here. I shivered. "But wasn't she pretty tough on you? When you graduated second in your class at college, and she said, 'Why not first?'" I'd heard this a thousand times, but to mention it felt risky. My own decision to leave college after three semesters had caused such strife between my parents and me. For the first time, though, I began to comprehend why my mother had been so distraught. Might things have been different between us if she'd shared this story, instead of condemning my choice? Would Nana's caregiver Julia ever tell her children who'd paid for those frozen shrimp, if my mother's suspicions were correct?

"Nana was impossible," she affirmed. "But she loved me, in her own way. And when it comes right down to it—" My mother broke into fresh sobs.

The hair on my head and arms prickled. There was that phrase again. *In her own way.* Here it was. I leaned forward to catch her next words, hungry to unlock that most profound of all human mysteries: the ineffable bond between mother and child, the code of daughterhood I'd somehow missed, the *sine qua non* that separates us humans from the animals.

She brushed her tears away with the heel of her hand. Her next words laid bare her beating heart and tore the husk off my own.

"When it comes right down to it, a mother is a mother!"

I jerked away, almost falling off the sofa. *A mother is a mother . . . is a mother?* As I questioned silently, the gentle answer stole into the darkest folds of my mind. The gleam of truth, normally cloaked by darkness. Utterly, sadly, unsuspected.

Love. Not duty. Beneath the broken threads, the ugly knots, the sometimes-garish clash of tone and pattern, lay an abiding care, the warp and woof of an attachment looped onto a master loom. A love that was real, and would never fail. A love that would hold forth in time through generations.

Nana. My mother. Myself . . .

Angela.

RICHARD LEIS

PANGAEA PROXIMA

I.

My father was a supercontinent. He stood devastated craton, Vietnam War-forged, always minefield, always volcanic with rage, demanding from his wife and children the respect not received from country. Agent Orange obliterated the future terraces of his lungs, did not stop the yelling. "Up and at 'em," he bugled before dawn, and my brother and I were exercise- or chore-bound, bound to mess it up, forced to start over again, landscapes of welt and bruise. The general rages for and against his soldier's furthest extent. He beat us to make us men from the ground up. A supercontinent eventually marks itself with deep gouges, outlines the future shape of the broken world.

II.

      I broke apart. I feel all over I am off

a chipped block. There are no coincidences
in scars. Children look at the classroom globe,
see how continents nestle together, but before
the theory of plate tectonics, teachers would say
this was only coincidence. My siblings and I
could not escape on our own. We needed help
to break off. On a spinning globe, the puzzle
is not how continental drift occurs, but why

no one believed the children.

III.

My father was a supercontinent. Now he is nearly breathless. Soon his gasps for air will drive reunion or refusal, continued estrangement or collision. We deserve to witness his drowning. "Don't you cry," he would shout, "or I will give you something to cry about." I wonder if we will. The next supercontinent does not form until the former is unrecognizable. We prepare to dump his ashes.

PANTHALASSA

My mother is a superocean. She bore us. Bears us. Bears
our accusations in rain and rivulet to river. A wave, she
surrounds us. When our father could not bear to let us go,

when he towered volcanic in our path, she tidal and essential
freed us, though hers is a quiet body of waves and it works
its blue wonder into any gap found. Wave: she purchased

my bus ticket to Rochester. Wave: admonished my brother
"Run away for good this time." Wave: ignored my sister's
open window and absence nightly to rendezvous with

what my mother knew as "A better family elsewhere." Wave:
packed my other brother's vehicle with his thrown-out
belongings. She surrounds us. We cannot see beneath

us. We make her cry for her choices. She sank into abyss
so we could leave her behind, the surface waters, wave
after wave of goodbye, to these tides that do not let up.

JUNIPER TREE, BOY AND BIRD

My father warned me a man does not sing
for a living. He works hard, provides for his family,
raises strong sons, devoted daughters,
sits at the head of his table and
devours every drop of delicious meat
soup his wife prepares. Sing?
Only little birds sing.
Only sissies and fairies sing.

I was the son of a failed farmer,
the sensitive son of my mother
with the lovely voice. I took my songbook
under the juniper tree and sang until he heard me.
Then my father put me to work, or pretend work
with construction trucks. A man does not sing
for a living, he warned me. They shouted at me
to go to sleep when I resumed
my humming under blankets.

I pretended to join track and field;
instead took secret lessons in choir.
Lied about being a stagehand
building sets; instead, I was
getting roles, lead roles, singing roles.
Time passed too quickly, too slowly,
and if it gets better, that is on the other side
of getting a lot worse.

So much worse to be found out,
tossed out, to depend on friends'
better parents to get me through
my senior year. I sang beautifully:

> My father, he threw me,
> My mother, she let him,
> Out of the nest to the ground.
> I gathered my bones,
> Tied up in a song,
> And I flew far from the juniper tree.
> Tweet, tweet, a singer I will be!

Out in the world a week, a semester,
six years of training and auditions,
from smoke, flame, and fire rose
a beautiful bird. I sang gloriously:

> My father, he threw me,
> My mother, she let him,
> Out of the nest to the ground.
> I gathered my bones,
> Tied up in a song,
> And I flew far from the juniper tree.
> Tweet, tweet, a singer I will be!

But trauma hangs a gold chain
around your neck. The world
throws shoes. The millstone
does not crush your parents;
it crushes you. And in your head
your father warns you a man does not sing
for a living. I sang:

> My father, he threw me,
> My mother, she let him,
> Out of the nest to the ground.
> I gathered my bones,
> Tied up in a song,
> And I flew far from the juniper tree.
> Tweet, tweet, will I be a singer?

I sang and I sang, but for better or worse,
singing is a business like everything.
Some opportunities are smoke,
the competition is flame, and
forgetting to tend the fire left ash
in my mouth. Eventually I reasoned
a man is not meant to sing
for a living, no matter how
beautifully. No matter how
gloriously. Without gifts,
the little bird returned
a man, sat down at their table and
devoured every drop of delicious meat
soup his mom had prepared. Quietly.

SHERRY SHAHAN

LITTLE HOUSE IN THE REDWOODS

In 1959, Daddy drives a short-bed pickup.

I'm ten years old, barely a head above the door handle.

Weekends with him are patchy, an orange sherbet at Baskin-Robbins or lunch at My Brother's Barbeque, a restaurant with a big brown and white plastic cow on the roof.

Daddy scoots behind the wheel of his pickup, cigarette smoke making dragon shapes, while my brother Steve and me elbow each other for shotgun. "My turn!" The drive to meet our grandmother takes about an hour.

She tells us to call her Butch. "Everyone does." I love her right off because she stains her snowy puff of hair a scandalous red. She doesn't wear eye or face makeup but applies coral lipstick and stays in the lines without a mirror.

She painted her house herself, dipping her brush into rust-red to match the trunk of her redwood trees. A forest of green that never changes color, right in the middle of a city called Torrance. The branches are close together, throwing shadows at us. If I could've climbed to the top, I would've gotten an impressive nosebleed.

The house has simple furniture and smooth plastered sea-foam green walls. No alcohol or cigarettes allowed, but I bet she'd go to a PTA meeting if I asked. I never heard of a grandmother who lived by herself in a house she bought and paid for herself and painted herself.

Her kitchen cupboard has things I've never seen: blackstrap molasses, mineral oil, apple cider vinegar, witch hazel, henna. She lets me sniff jars of spice. If I were a spice what would I smell like? I settle on cinnamon because there isn't anything better than the smell of cinnamon, sugar, and butter bubbling on toast under the broiler.

Butch teaches me how to tie string around her stuffed cabbage rolls and stir grated carrots into wheat germ cookie dough. I want to close the windows when something is in the oven to keep the goodness inside.

Porcelain elephants gather on a shelf in the living room. "I've been collecting them for years," she says in an accent she'd carried from Massachusetts to California four decades earlier.

I kneel down. "Can I touch one?"

"Elephants are the smartest animals in the kingdom." She hands me one about four inches tall. "Their exceptionally large brains help them store information from the past."

I run my finger over its tiny white trunk and across its back. It has green eyes, like mine when I wear my olive mohair sweater.

"They never forget anything," she says. "Good or bad."

I reunite the elephant with its family.

Butch takes my hand and leads me through the kitchen. Beyond the sliding glass door a fishpond sits in the ground. The fish are bigger than a football—blackish or dull white with swirly pink splotches. Some are the same orange as the goldfish in small glass bowls at our school fair. I won one by landing a Ping-Pong ball in an empty bowl, a bit of luck.

The fish have whiskers and frown while staring at us through clear eyes. On these weekend visits she lets Steve and me sprinkle dried fish food over the water. Sometimes we tear up wilted lettuce. Pieces float like leaf boats before big sucking lips gobble them up. The fish slide all over each other when they see my shadow. Maybe they remember faces the way elephants do? I give them dog names: Spot, Max, Fluffy.

One lazy afternoon my grandmother says, "Did you know your dad built the pond? He dug a trench and mixed cement in a wheelbarrow. He painted the bottom blue and filled it from the garden hose."

I close my eyes, wondering what land I'll be in when I open them.

"See that pump?" she asks, so I have to peek. "It's an old motor rigged to keep the water clean."

"When did you do all that?" I ask him later when we're poking around the garage. It smells damp, like the first shovelful of dirt after it rains. I've never seen a wringer washing machine before.

"Back when I had the pool cleaning business." He sprinkles sand over a mosaic of oil leaked from her car. "Do you remember that? I used to set you on the counter so customers saw you first thing when they came in the door."

I want to say, *Goddammit Daddy, why didn't you build a pond in our backyard?*

But I don't yet swear in front of adults. "Why don't you go back to cleaning pools?" I pray for a Daddy who comes home from work with a lunch pail, ready to throw a ball around so the neighbors can see he's a good guy.

"Oh, honey." He taps his shirt pocket for his pack of cigarettes even though one burns between his fingers. "You need a store, equipment and supplies, and advertising so people can find you. All that takes money."

It makes me mad that he doesn't want to be better, because I haven't given up hope that Mom still loves him and a real job would steal her away from my stepfather. If only he'd *try*, he could take us to fancy dinners so she could show off her Cadillac and mink coat.

Daddy unhooks two rakes from nails on the garage wall and we go outside to scrape up pine needles. The smell of pine breathes in my face, sweet and sharply strong at the same time. We rake needles onto a piece of cardboard to dump in the oil drum incinerator.

He pauses, leaning against a tree. "Gotta go to the gas station and pick up a quart of oil for the Beetle."

I tug on his sleeve. "Can I go?"

"Sorry, honey, you need to stay with your brother."

Steve has been rubbing a stick against a rock until it's sharp enough to stab a squirrel—though he usually fires at stink bugs with his dime store six-shooter. *"Bang! Bang!"* His fringed cowboy shirt and holster look dumb. He needs something more like Steve McQueen in *Wanted Dead or Alive*.

"Hey, Steve! Wanna go to the gas station?"

"Sure!"

Daddy opens the door of his truck, tapping a fresh cigarette on the outside of the hollow pack. "Not this time, honey." He scoots in and slams the door on us.

I pitch my rake at the tailgate. "No fair!"

Wherever he's headed, I hope they only serve high-priced beer so he won't get too drunk and will run out of money and have to come back.

Steve and I spend the rest of the afternoon working on our fort in the tangled shrubs by the pond. He pulls weeds, and I weave them through twigs to make the walls stronger. Then he sits cross-legged, patiently holding a twig over the pond.

I almost like him during those long summer days, settling into slow lizard time while we play. "If you really want to fish you need a line and hook," I tell him. "You can dig worms for bait."

He squints real hard and aims his twig at me. "*Bang!*"

I grab it from him and break it in two. "You're stupid, you know that?"

Butch comes out with silverware knocking around in a mason jar for our mud pies and faded beach towels so our fort will have rugs. "Supper will be ready soon," she says, before going inside.

I watch her through the open kitchen window and breath in garlic and onion. I learn about exotic seasonings, the differences between tomatoes from a vine and those from the grocery store. Her tomatoes are little taste bud bombs.

Because my mom considers herself a modern parent, she only buys the most advertised frozen and canned foods. Swanson TV dinners fill the pullout bin in our freezer. Aluminum trays with compressed fried chicken, mashed potatoes, a slime-bomb vegetable, and some sugary dessert.

"Fish fry!" Butch calls to us.

Steve unfolds his legs and throws himself on the ground because he thinks she speared Max or Fluffy. I pin his arms and dangle drool over his face. He screams, squirming to get away.

The fish dinner doesn't come from a market. Our grandmother bought rock cod from a neighbor with a fishing boat. We clean our plates, never mentioning Daddy or his whereabouts.

Butch puts us to bed in his childhood room, an add-on just off the master. The step-down area is naked except for two twin beds shoved against walls. The bedspreads look new, like she bought them just for us. A turquoise background with orange and yellow boats bob when we jump from bed to bed. A shower curtain hangs over the closet instead of a door.

Butch tucks us in in the same bed, reading us poems that don't rhyme, written by poets with foreign names, from thin books that don't have to go back to the library. I can't wait to tell my fifth grade teacher that not all poems sound like "Mary Had a Little Lamb."

I picture him winking at me. "You should be in college."

As soon as Butch turns off the lights I ditch my brother because he kicks like a wild donkey when he sleeps. I line up my shoes just so by the other bed and crawl in. The room is too hot. It makes me sticky and thirsty.

"Wanna run away?" Steve asks through a yawn. "We could build a fort under the pier."

"Nah, who'd take care of Daddy?"

I can't keep the pillowcase cool no matter how many times I turn it. If I were at home I'd sneak into the bathroom and drink from the faucet, letting cold metal press into my cheek.

I wonder if Daddy got his unemployment check? Would he get extra drunk to have a supply of alcohol in his body to last him through the night? Or maybe he'd gotten into a good game of poker? Or was passed out on a stack of bottles behind a liquor store?

The only phone, on a kitchen wall, tosses out high-pitched screams. Branches creak against the roof. Gravel in the driveway, quiet. Then whining tires. A door slams. Something in the living room crashes. I scoot lower and tug little boats over my head. *Not the elephants!*

I hear my grandmother. "You're drunk." I imagine Daddy shrinking back like a little kid. "Go to bed and sleep it off."

*

The door to our room bangs open, and I hear Daddy swear and stumble down the stairs. Clothes rustle and stop breathing. Is he in the closet? Then something else. *Whooshing.* Pee? No. *Yes.* That's it. He's peeing in the closet. I smell it!

Then *thud*. Daddy lands across the foot of my bed, sinking the little boats and poisoning the turquoise water. I'm not sure what happened next. Either I fell asleep, or my mind created a space where I could hide.

*

It must be morning because the room is triangles of bright light. My brother is still asleep, tangled in his bedspread. Daddy is gone. I go straight to the bathroom to practice my *nothing's wrong* face in the mirror but can't get it right.

I pause in the living room, relieved to see the elephants standing unharmed. "Good morning," Butch says.

"Morning." I slide into my chair at the kitchen table while she fixes me toast with marmalade from oranges she squeezed herself and eggs-over-easy. "How'd you sleep honey?"

I pretend the yolks have the right amount of runny for toast dipping and think about elephants and how awful it must be to have a brain so big it remembers everything.

PAMELA BROTHERS DENYES

YOU MAY NOT KNOW...

For Susan and for Mother

Our mother knitted sweaters, using difficult circular needles at the neck.
Our mother was a wonderful hostess, always matching the napkins with the
    plates. Everyone wanted to be at Margaret's parties.
Our mother read books like a chain-smoker and played bridge like a master.
Our mother was steamrolled by the decision to leave you with your father
    and grandmother, but believed Nonni would care for you well.
Our mother was valedictorian of her class, then went to secretarial school
    because that was what poor smart girls did in the late thirties.
Our mother kept busy every minute of every day and compulsively made
    lists to be sure she got every large and little thing done.
Our mother was a weekend sun-worshipper, cooked to cocoa by August.
Our mother ate very little but smoked a lot, with gin in her Diet Fresca,
    and in everything else but coffee.
Our mother had her hair done after work every Friday, so she could feel
    acceptably beautiful on the weekend.
Our mother loved jazz and musical theater and took me to see the stars.
Our mother was an executive secretary with mad skills, and kept the books
    for the all-male Rotary Club in the sixties.
Our mother loved you and missed you horribly, lighting up with joy
    when a letter came in or a long-distance call from you.
Our mother had a biting, cruel tongue that could cut you to the quick.
Our mother had different costume jewelry for every outfit, scarves
    for every sweater, and adorned herself with the latest fashions.
Our mother had amber eyes, nearly the color of beer, and handsome legs.
Our mother sang around the piano with my dad and their friends, with her
    smoky alto voice. With any partner, she was a great dancer.
Our mother had cirrhosis at fifty and lived, then had butcher-knife
    dementia by fifty-two, probably earlier.

Our mother had constant burning leg pain, because she had phlebitis
> that kept her in the hospital for weeks after you were born.

Our mother had a philandering husband—my dad.
> I doubt her marriage sanctity, too.

Our mother read the daily newspaper cover to cover,
> completing the crosswords in ink.

Our mother's father pointed a gun at her beautiful seven-year-old head,
> threatening to kill her if our Nana left him.

Our mother had a psychiatrist and a tailor because life didn't fit her well.

Our mother made fabulous lemon meringue pies, with perfect crusts,
> but never ate them.

Our mother cursed, spat and told me she wished I'd never been born,
> as I drove her to the sanitarium one more time.

Our mother loved to meticulously decorate the outside of each
> Christmas gift, and every one had to be unique.

Our mother memorized "shaggy dog" jokes, the long ones with difficult
> punch lines, so she could entertain party guests.

Our mother was volatile like fire, calculating like a ruthless CEO,
> restless and constantly seeking approval like a seven-year-old.

I both loved our mother for being so beautiful and brilliant,
> and hated her for giving it all away to the things that destroyed her.

A.P. QUILT

INSTRUCTIONS ON HOW TO SURVIVE AN ALCOHOL-INFUSED BUTT REAMING

Though Mama can rip you a new one
on her own steam, she takes on a demonic demeanor
when she gets in her cups.
Every soap opera diva she's ever watched
comes to the fore—and worse!

If you know what is good for you,
you'll duck and run, provided
you see it coming. If you don't,
then man up, take it, tell her
you love her ten million times
until she gets tired of reaming your sorry ass.
Sorry is relative, of course.

Self-advocacy is out.
Trust me! Your best bet is to lay low,
agree with everything she says, apologize
profusely, and explain why you are even
there in the first place. You wanted to spend
time with her. You love her.
Let that be your mantra. The more she hears it,
The better off you'll be. If you want
the marathon treatment, tell her
anything she says is incorrect.

Whatever you do, don't mention her drinking.
She'll crawl up one side your behind, down
the other. No one *knows*, you see.

Catching on? Thought so. Remember,
this is not rocket science. She is right. You,
on the other hand, are wrong. If she accuses you
of owning ocean front property in the Heartland,
tell her you will cut her in on half. And, giving
her money is always good. She can't argue
with cash, and she will not return it!

There now. That wasn't so bad, was it?

KATE MEYER-CURREY

MOTHER'S DAY CARD: 'THANK YOU FOR THE THINGS YOU DO, SORRY FOR THE THINGS I DO'

You'd never guess what she endured
that watchful child, hiding within my
mother. Her guarded gaze keeps the
world firmly at arm's length. She still
flinches from hugs as if they are blows.
I know why. I do it too. Where she froze
I attack. Our battles were similar: we were
academic girls, bespectacled, too
erudite for our peers. School was hell,
apart from the learning. She was more
informed than her teacher, who asked
her to contribute less in class, as others
needed to speak. My mother's granite
stubbornness kept her silent for two
years, even when they relented and
begged her to talk, she would not.
I fought and argued instead. Not a
better way, but mine. If I failed, it was
of my own doing. She was not a
helicopter-mother. More like a sniper
who kept me always in her sights, not
that I was aware. My younger self
resented her approach and thought
she did not care, as I wept, swore and
blustered through depression and
anxiety. I know now she felt helpless
at every tearful phone call that gave
her sleepless nights. She kept those

cards close. As she did her feelings
of ambivalence for my father, whose
death left some chinks in her wall.
Our worst moment was when she
told me I was worse than him. A low
blow, as I told her then. Grief throws
those sucker-punches. We realised
Dad pulled me in and pushed her out.
Now I know my mother was in me all
the time, she is the backbone that
kept me standing straight, though it
buckled at times. Hers is the steely
gaze that sees through subterfuge.
Hers is the voice that speaks our
truth, in measured, clipped tones
with irony and detachment. Hers
is the laugh of appreciation at
shared jokes. Hers is the glint of
grey in our hair, the glimpse of
shared bones beneath our different
bodies and the subtle hints we were
somehow mother and daughter;
eyes that twitch with fatigue, shared
bingeing and dietary remorse, inherited
body shaming ("it's very tight") and
no-holds barred honesty; "you're not
my best friend, you're my daughter."
And there is the deep love she had for
me, her daughter, unguarded and freely
expressed; unconstrained by her
childhood's shattering damage.
She made me a warrior and she
tells me that I'm finally learning
the lesson she wanted me to
apply to my life: combine guile with
force. She's a lucid critic of my work
and her objectivity is my stance too.

I'm not sure if I'll show her this poem
as it is so heartfelt and she might say
it's too long. Probably. But my life
will always be too short without her.

DEBORAH SCHMEDEMANN

TITLE NINE DAUGHTER

"Oh. Of course. You look just like Mary."

This most recent time, just a few weeks ago, the comment came from the mother of the family that recently moved into the Chicago three-flat owned by my daughter Mary and her husband. I was delighted to meet this family and had just introduced myself as Mary's mother.

"Thanks," I responded. I wanted to say that as a matter of historical record it is *Mary* who looks like *me*. That is how people used to comment on our strong resemblance, when Mary was a child, a teenager.

How long has it been since the comment flipped? At least a decade, since she became fully adult. I do see the truth in what people say now: she is the vibrant version; I am the fading imitation.

For Mary's birthday this summer, I gave her a gift certificate to Title Nine, a company founded and operated by women, which sells clothes and gear for athletic women. Its catalogue features photos of women surfing, rock climbing, mountain biking; the captions provide the women's first names, occupations, hobbies, and zingy self-statements. These models not only look strong and energetic; they appear at ease and jazzed.

Mary could be a Title Nine model: "road cyclist, non-profit fundraiser, landlord, mother, craves fresh air." I gave Mary the gift certificate so she could pick up something for an upcoming trip biking and camping from Chicago to northern Michigan.

I like looking at the catalogue, seeing my daughter in the pictures. What I don't see is myself, even in my younger years.

We started out and grew up so differently. I was born with a small hole in my heart, blood slushing where it should not go, my heart working a bit too hard. The doctors urged my parents to keep me from over-working, so I was kept away from serious athletics. My slightly misaligned left knee is unstable, so certain sports have always been off-limits. I have had migraine headaches since I was a child. I have broken bones and been stitched closed, from head to foot. So I have navigated life thinking of my body as a fallible and finicky vessel to be managed with care.

Mary is blessed with a healthy heart in a trim torso; long, lean, well-aligned limbs; and only occasional headaches. She inherited natural athleticism from her father: stamina, strength, coordination, grace, nerve. As she grew, she competed in gymnastics, soccer, distance running, cross-country skiing, crew, triathlons. She made it through childhood unscathed: nary a sprain, break, stitch. No wonder she sees her body as a trusted, dependable asset.

As well, we are women of our times. I was born in 1956, Mary in 1984. Title IX, the federal statute paving the way for funding of women's athletics, was enacted in 1972. The culture was ripe for raising an athletic woman during Mary's youth—not so during mine.

I do give myself credit for one facet of Mary's athleticism. In matters non-athletic, I have a fair measure of resilience, a positive legacy of the sudden death of my mother Anna Mary when I was sixteen. This resilience helped me weather Harvard Law School and served me well in my career as a law professor. I see a version of my resilience in Mary's quiet self-confidence.

When I look back on that day—September 7, 2018—I sometimes wonder: what was I thinking about all day? My husband Craig and I (mostly residents of Minneapolis) were in Chicago that fall for Baby Watch Round Two.

Round One was in July of 2015. Early that spring, Mary had alerted us that she and her husband Adam had chosen a home birth supported by a doula and mid-wife team. I told her that I felt "nervous" about this plan. She sent me her research, which I read; I then was aware that she was a fine candidate for a home birth—and still nervous. I could not forget that I had delivered Mary and her sister only with medical intervention. As July approached, I resolutely deflected memories of their births and yanked to mind memories of capable Mary stretching, running, skiing, swimming . . . Craig and I were present with Mary and Adam when labor started at dinner and persisted late into the evening. We were not present for the midnight arrival of the doula and midwife just before Mary was ready to push out the baby, the discovery that the baby presented breech, the ambulance ride to the hospital, or the blessedly safe delivery by a highly experienced obstetrician—so quick that Adam missed being present. When I entered the hospital to meet my grandson Luke, I gave silent thanks for this hospital and this baby's safe birth.

Three years later, when Mary announced that they were planning a second home birth, my stomach clenched. She explained that the same team would assist, and they had made some adjustments, such as frequent ultrasounds to discern a possible breech presentation. I suggested that she and Adam call in their team earlier this time.

Early on September 7, Adam called to ask us to take Luke for the day. I gathered up Luke's day bag, scooted him out the door, and started answering his string of questions: "You are going to spend the day with me and Papaw. First we are going to have breakfast at our condo. Probably eggs and toast. Maybe go to the aquarium. It's a really big place with lots of fish." Did I notice then that Mary was pacing back and forth, hands pressed against her lower back, and that she wore a stretchy wide sash around her bulging belly? I think not. Only when I re-wound that day later did I remember this image.

The day passed in Luke-land: We spent most of it wandering around the Shedd Aquarium, trailing after Luke, watching him discover this fish and that, trying to answer his questions, lifting him up and kneeling beside him, feeding him lunch, wiping his fingers and face. We ran into his best gal-pal with the yellow curls, and the two of them raced around an exhibit while we chatted with her mother and kept watch. Back at our condo, we tucked him into our daybed for an afternoon nap, and I headed out to do something when the text came in.

"Peter Bowmann Arents, born 2:00 p.m., 9 pounds 8 ounces."

Hunh? Really? This afternoon? Oh, of course. That's why we had Luke today!

Mary and Adam wanted Luke to be the first to see Peter. I entered their home with unsuspecting Luke. He started to play with his toys in the living room, but I encouraged him to find Mommy and Daddy. Not interested. I set off merrily on this mission myself, and he joined in. He entered his parents' bedroom, went to his mother's side, and spotted the rosy golden-haired baby whose birth had just changed his life. He glowed: "My baby!"

I meandered into the kitchen to chat with the doula, who was sitting at the kitchen table and recording her notes on her computer. I introduced myself as Mary's mother. To make conversation, I asked, "So when did you arrive?"

"2:15." She chatted on.

I tried to listen, but my brain was stuck. "Oh."

I walked into the dining room and sat down. *2:15. Coulda been 2:15 this morning. But then she woulda been here when I came to get Luke. Do I remember seeing her? Nope. Maybe she was in the bathroom. But the whole time? Not likely. If it was 2:15 this afternoon, and Peter was born at 2:00 . . . But the doula is supposed to come first . . . Who the heck* was *here?* I felt queasy, as queasy as I was during my months of "morning sickness" while carrying Mary.

Only days later did I learn that the doula indeed arrived at 2:15 p.m.—which was before the midwife's arrival at 2:30 p.m. Peter's birth was an intimate affair, attended only by Mary, of course, and Adam, who caught Peter. Adam was coached over the phone by the doula (trained but not certified as a midwife), who was driving to their home as fast as she could in Chicago traffic. The midwife was also driving to their home but a significant distance away. When the doula arrived, she cut the cord and attended to Peter; when the midwife arrived, she attended to Mary.

Days later, I recalled the doula telling me that Mary and Peter—and Adam too—had come through their unplanned experience "with flying colors." Of course.

⁂

What *was* I thinking about all that day? Anything but Mary. To anyone else, it would have been obvious that Mary was in labor that day. But I was in my special mental state: subconscious suspension of attention. This state aligns my individual self with Mary's mother.

Having mothered Mary for thirty-plus years, I know that I have raised a Title Nine daughter. And having been me for three decades longer, I know I cannot place myself into her physique or her psyche; I cannot inhabit her way of being. So at those times when she is living on edges I dare not approach, my attention to her slips away. This way, I do not think about how she could possibly safely do what I cannot fathom doing—or worse, how I would go on if something were to happen to her. Only when she is back from those edges do I let myself think about her again.

❋

Tomorrow morning, Craig and I will load six-year-old Luke and nearly three-year-old Peter into our car and drive them to meet up with their paternal grandparents, who will take them on to Michigan. I do believe Mary and Adam will already be there—no doubt tuckered out, having biked there from Chicago over the past eight days.

How many miles have they logged? How has the weather been—pleasant, hot, rainy? Have their bikes held up okay? Were they riding on trails (I hope) or country roads or . . . ? Were they ever hurt or tired or frightened? I haven't the foggiest. Maybe I will ask Mary about the trip in a few weeks.

JOAN DOBBIE

MY MOTHER IS ALIVE

(This poem was written for my mother in 1984, when her life hung in the balance after a near fatal car crash.)

Some poets write
how their mothers are dead
who never really lived
anyway
except behind the ironing board
and in unfulfilled dreams—

Not me.
My mother is alive.

Floating on her back in blue water
she is monumental as mountains
on sky.

Other mothers drift
in white aprons
boneless as angels
in pitiful retrospect.

Not mine. Mine is rock hard.
Head on, two cars prove—
she is full of bones.
And a good deal of brain.
Swollen.
But—thank God—undamaged.

My mother sews like a factory.
Plays piano like an army.
Is a nurse, like a doctor.
A secretary, like the boss.

A lover of mushrooms
wild geese and waterfalls.
A connoisseur of North Country snow.

She can be a carpenter.
A seamstress. A politician.

My mother can knit an intricate sweater
& read a book at the same time.
Write a book. Design an afghan.

Organize a peace march.

At 72 she does JANE FONDA exercises
to keep herself strong.
And nobody beats her
in scrabble.

My mother speaks 5 languages
—fluently—
And Latin.
And Greek.

In fall she climbs trees
to pick crabapples
And bakes them into stroodles
And boils them into fruit soup.

Or she's working in the Dr's office
and the patients want her advice
as well as his.
Or she's teaching German in the high school.
Or she's traveling to South America.

Summers she swims her favorite river
to the island & back. Every day.
The breast stroke. The crawl.
She is slick as an otter on her back.

Dreaming under summer's blue dome.

Dreaming in the night under stars.

Dreaming this hard morning
on a different river. Today my mother is hurt.
She is drifting in a drugged stupor
on a river of pain.

Her high forehead is bloated
like a rank summer melon & life
tastes bitter in her mouth.
She cannot eat.

Under hospital sheets
my mother's body lies limp;
pitiful as an angel.
Her bones are all broken,
eyes swollen shut.

In her ears a roaring
like a waterfall.
Distant music of pain strums
electric against her overstressed nerves.

In her teens in Vienna she played
the accordion.
Wrote verses to sing at weddings
& parties. And all the boys
liked her with her flashing
green eyes.

She smoked cigarettes
with the best of them.
And danced into the night.

My mother was no angel.
But she knew how to live.

And then Hitler came & all Vienna
turned sour in her throat.
All dreams became nightmare
& the nightmare was no dream.

But my mother lived.
Crossed borders by batting her eyes
at the guard.
Crawled under barbed wire.
Death followed and roared
& howled in her eardrums.
But she clung to her spirit
in the white dizzy Alps.
And though everything hurt
she lived.

It's a family joke
how when she was born
all swollen and dark
in her little white bed

an uncle, condescending,
said, "Don't worry that she's ugly.
Maybe she'll be smart."

They named her "Angelika,"
"Angel."
And she was wild as
Cochise in the movies—

painted her face
& called herself
"Quimbo the Indian."

And only her guardian spirit
kept her alive
through a bone-breaking
childhood.

But she was smart, Herr Death.
And she kept faith
in her guardian spirit—
who kept faith in her.

And as for you, Herr Death,
this time in your "car accident" uniform,
you hit her but missed her
again.

And this nightmare
which is no dream
also will end
in her favor.

Already the x-rays
are changing their minds.
Her broken bones are healing themselves
in your face.

My mother will swim again.
Walk again.
Command the piano.

She will argue philosophy
in 5 languages.
Slaughter us all at scrabble.
And hold her grandson
on her lap—

whispering together
as they do.

And as soon as her eyes
are open again
my mother will read this poem
that I wrote for her.

She will know in this world
how much I respect her.
And love her.

And thank God.
And thank her.
And thank her true guardian spirit.

That my mother—
my strong unrepeatable mother—
is no angel.
My mother is alive.

PENELOPE STARR

TATTOO

The first time I met my daughter was a phone conversation when she was forty-four years old. A stranger introduced us.

My phone rang at 8 a.m. one November morning in 2009. I thought it was odd because most of my friends know that I am not a morning person. I didn't recognize the number that flashed on caller ID, but for some reason, I picked up.

A woman's voice asked me, "Are you the person who was once known as (she had my maiden name)?" and then quickly added, "You don't have to answer my questions."

"Yes, that is me," I said simply. I knew there was always a possibility I would get this call and had long ago decided what I would do if it came.

"Did you give birth to a baby girl on (she had my daughter's birth date) in a New York hospital?" and again the reminder, "You don't have to answer if you don't want to." My hand holding the phone shook, and I started to weep.

"Yes, I did. She can contact me if she wants to. Who are you?"

"My name is Carol, and I help people find their birth parents. Your daughter hired me to locate you."

"Thank you, Carol," I said, staring at the phone after we hung up. I gulped air, wondering if I had remembered to breathe during that three-minute conversation.

Lowering myself into a chair at the kitchen table, I eyed my teacup as if it were a foreign object and glanced out the window to make sure that the mountains were still solidly bathed in morning light in the distance. Nothing had changed, yet everything felt surreal.

At four o'clock that afternoon, the phone rang. I watched another unknown number flash across my screen. She couldn't be calling me so soon. I was afraid that I couldn't talk. I waited through three rings, knowing that the call would go to voicemail on the fourth. Then I grabbed the phone.

My boyfriend Bob and I were living in Chapala, Mexico, the winter of 1965, and I thought I was throwing up because of the food or water or whatever causes the turista. I didn't suspect that I could be expecting because he told me he was sterile. But, after not getting my period for two months, I thought something was up, so we borrowed a car and drove into Guadalajara to have a pregnancy test. No one in the doctor's office spoke English, and the only words I knew in Spanish were leche and cerveza, but they managed to convey that I was pregnant.

Back at the casita, Bob said, "It's not my kid. I told you that I couldn't have any. Who the hell have you been sleeping with?"

Bob and I had been fighting pretty much ever since we got on the bus in New York City a month before to make the six-day journey to Chapala. I thought he was lazy because all he wanted was to sit in the courtyard of his favorite bar sipping tequila with his American buddy Lorenzo talking art and revolution. He thought I was a pain in the ass because I wanted to sightsee and learn Spanish. The idea of getting away from him seemed like a really good idea.

"You bastard, I'm leaving," I said, pulling my father's WW2 canvas duffle bag out of the closet, grabbing for my shoes, dungarees, and a few souvenirs I wasn't going to leave behind.

"You can't go by yourself, especially in your condition. And where would you go?"

"So now you are concerned for my welfare." Maybe he genuinely cared for me, or maybe he just didn't want to be alone in a foreign country; I didn't know, and I didn't care.

"I'll marry you even if it's not mine."

"No thanks." Marry someone I didn't even like. No way. I was nineteen years old and wasn't about to get tethered.

The next morning, I dragged my bag to the town square and caught a bus to California. As I sank into the swaying of the second-class bus, my anger faded as uncertainty crept in. What was I going to do? Of course, I could always go home to my parents, but this trip was my first excursion in the world as an independent adult, and I hated to admit defeat.

When I got to Los Angeles, I discovered I could buy a plane ticket to San Francisco for only twelve dollars and save myself from the nauseating smell of the bus's chemical toilet. When I landed in San Francisco, I hailed a cab and asked the driver to deliver me to an inexpensive hotel in a safe neighborhood where I could pay weekly. He was a kindly man, somebody's father, and he must have sensed that I was freaked out. He took me to a charming but slightly run-down hotel and wished me well. I could afford a room for two weeks in this third-floor walk-up with a claw-footed bathtub and large windows overlooking the city.

I needed time to think. Maybe Bob wasn't the father. There was that one time that I had sex with my old boyfriend at the drive-in when he was home on leave and had to return to Vietnam in two days. But we were careful. It couldn't be him. No, Bob was the father, and I didn't want anything to do with him.

While looking for something to eat, I wandered into a used bookstore and bought a pile of twenty-five-cent novels. I calmed myself by reading in the tub for hours at a time until I grew stir crazy. After five or six books in as many days, I dried myself off, put on clothes, and ventured out.

I stumbled upon a huge protest against the war in Vietnam. Someone handed me a sign on a wooden stick saying End the War, and I joined in even though I wasn't very political. The passion and conviction radiating from these beautiful human beings were infectious, and when the rally concluded, I fell in with a small crowd of long-haired guys and girls. We went to a coffee house, and after hours of conversation, I revealed my predicament to my new friends.

For the next week, I visited their shabby apartments and shared meager meals with them, standing outside clubs to listen to the music we couldn't afford to hear inside. We made protest signs for the next march, sitting around a table in the basement of a progressive church. The church's young pastor called me aside and told me that baby and I could crash in the basement for free if I needed a place to live.

I decided to call my parents. I told them it was time for me to come home, and they sent me a plane ticket. When I got back to Long Island, all I had was pocket change and a secret.

The matchmaker told me that my daughter's name was Nancy. In the hospital, just before I signed the papers to terminate my parental rights, I had named her Elizabeth. Over the years, I had fleeting thoughts about Elizabeth, but now that person was gone, and Nancy was in her place. What do you say to a child that you relinquished? Is she going to be furious at me? Does she already hate me? Do I really want to deal with this now? Do I love her? Should I?

"Hello."

"Hello."

Longish awkward pause. I realized that it was my turn to say something. "This is so awkward."

"Yes," She didn't know what to say either.

"I'm really glad that you contacted me," I said. "I always thought that you would. I didn't want to initiate contact because I figured that you have your life, and I didn't want to interfere."

"I'm glad that you are willing to talk to me."

We were both in gratitude mode. I was crying, and I suspected she might be too, although I couldn't tell. I didn't know her. How to catch up on forty-four years? What do you share with your adult child in your first conversation? How far will this go? What are we to each other?

We shared statistics—location, family, time frames, just like getting to know someone on a first date. After fifteen minutes, I was exhausted from nervousness and giddy joy. I told her that I needed a break but wanted to continue the conversation another time. I think I heard a small sigh of relief from her end of the phone. We agreed that we would talk again the next day.

Jumbled conflicting thoughts consumed me. How do I know that she is really my daughter? Could it be a scam? Am I a horrible person for even thinking that? What sort of emotions, besides happiness and sadness should I be feeling right now? Confusion? Fear?

We had exchanged email addresses and sent photos of ourselves, so I gazed at Nancy's face when I called her back the next day. I desperately did not want to disappoint her. And I didn't want to be disappointed either. Our conversation was tentative, a cross between blurting out probing questions, "Who did you vote for in the last election," to the gentler, "What would you like to know." I was afraid I would shock her when I said, "I'm bisexual but have only had girlfriends for many years." She said, "I'm bisexual too! That explains a lot." By the end of the call, we had decided that she had to visit the next month.

I wanted my son to meet his older sister, and I needed his support, so I asked if he would come too. He arrived a few days early, and we went to the airport together.

～※～

The first time I was on an airplane was the trip back to New York to confront the dilemma I found myself in. Back then, you dressed to get on a plane, so I packed my jeans and put on my wrap-around skirt. I remember that the food was delicious, served on cunning little compartmentalized trays. I was doing my life in the same way—keeping some things barricaded from other things. But now, the rebellious girl was headed for a conflict with her loving but prudish family. My go-with-the-flow attitude was being pulled up short with the reality of bringing another being into the world.

To be sure that I wouldn't upset my family unnecessarily, I went to the family doctor to double-check my pregnancy status. When I got the results four days later, I called a family meeting with Mom, Dad, and my younger sister. Sitting them down in the living room in front of the fireplace, I said, "the rabbit died," a flip reference to pregnancy tests in the 1960s. My mother cried, my father gave me "The Look" of disappointment and disapproval, something that I dreaded more than his anger, and my sister was clueless.

In 1965 it was scandalous to be pregnant and not married. Shameful. Abortion was a vague option, either a dangerous back-alley procedure or a flight to Puerto Rico. Either way, it was illegal. The most popular option in the New York suburb I lived in was to go away quietly and have the baby in a home for unwed mothers while your parents told everyone you were staying with an aunt in the Midwest and, after you relinquish the baby, return to your life as if nothing had happened. Since my sister was still in high school, I thought I could protect her from gossip and judgment in our small town, so I agreed. She thought that I was being punished. Maybe I was.

I stayed home until I was showing, about six months gone, and then packed up for the best address I'll probably ever have, East 71st Street right off 5th Avenue, New York City. I think it was associated with the Episcopal church, but I have a possibly false memory of nuns in habits running the show. Maybe they just were stern women who acted like I thought nuns would act. Very judgmental. They tortured us in subtle ways; we had to walk up and down the four flights of stairs while they took the elevator, there was a room full of baby clothes when most of us were giving our babies up and, worst of all, salt-free food.

The home was a favorite charity of New York socialites (although my father paid plenty of money for me to be there), and Junior League women need a project. We were theirs. Once a week, two or three stylishly dressed volunteers would show up with department store bags of donated makeup. Sitting at tables on the top floor of our brownstone, they smeared foundation, rouge, and eyeliner on our puffy faces. And then we all played bridge. It passed the time, which seemed to drag on at a snail's pace the closer we got to our due dates.

The birth was hell. I was alone, and the nurses knew that I didn't put a father's name on the paperwork, which might explain why they were mean to me. "Don't be such a baby and stop yelling. You are scaring all the other mothers." The real mothers, the ones with husbands.

I had decided that I wouldn't hold the baby. I was afraid if I smelled her, I wouldn't go through with the adoption. So, I avoided the glass cage where they showed off the rows of babies in blue and pink. On the day I left the hospital she was still in her plastic bin, and I went by to say goodbye. Dark hair, tiny fingers, goodbye.

Every girl at the home went to weekly meetings with a therapist, and we could continue seeing her after "graduation" if we wanted to. I went for a few additional months until I felt satisfied that I had done the right thing. The counselor must have been pretty good because I never felt any guilt. Only shame and extremely vulnerable.

Seven years later, after many adventures, I had another child, but I did it in a socially acceptable order this time. First, I got married, then I got pregnant. When my husband and I split up nine months later, I became a single mother legitimately. Things were changing in 1972. Feminism was happening, at least in my world. I went back to college and learned that women have a right to control their bodies, that shaming is an act of domination, that I could design my own life. My secret seemed trivial, limiting, and ancient.

Sitting on a floor cushion surrounded by the women of my consciousness-raising group, I gazed around the room, tears sliding down my face, and confessed, "I had a baby out of wedlock." A few gasps, sad head noddings, and some reassuring pats on the back. I told them that I felt fortunate to have escaped the tyranny of marriage to a man I didn't love, and my sisters congratulated me on my bravery. Then we used it for a teaching moment. We talked about The Patriarchy, women's mandatory chastity, body image, the oppressiveness of secrets, taking back our power.

I felt liberated. And still a little scared, so I started to share the story with everyone I met. Not quite, "Hi, my name is Penny, and I had a bastard child," but close. It was still possible to shock people with that confession in those times, and I found that part quite enjoyable.

Some people reacted by telling me their horror stories about adoption. My neighbor, Shirley, told me about her daughter finding her and demanding money and an apology. Rob and his girlfriend went on a search for the child they had relinquished so they both could finish high school. When they found their son, he was in San Francisco, a gay man dying of AIDS. He was mad as hell at them and the world. Zoë told me that she finally visited her birth mother and siblings in Georgia after years of searching. Her romanticized fantasy of her real mom clashed with the reality of a worn-out bitter woman with seven other children who was resentful that her past was being stirred up. Zoë was heartbroken to know that she was the only child that was given away.

Although I had already decided not to do a search, each of these stories cemented my resolve to let well enough alone. I imagined that Elizabeth had been adopted by a lovely stable artistic family, having all the love she deserved, and I had saved her from being raised by a rambling risk-taking hippy.

My son kept me calm as the plane landed. "It will be fine, Mom, don't worry." We both stared at the monitor to get an advance glimpse of my daughter, his sister. He spotted her first.

"There she is."

"No, that can't be her, she doesn't look like her picture."

Do you hug someone you've never met before, even if they are your blood? Is it OK to sob in disbelief? I wondered if she had agonized over what to wear just like I did. I marveled at the identical smile that both of my children had. We did a lot of wordless grinning. There is no page in a book of etiquette for this situation. We all talked at the same time and apologized. Nancy didn't check a bag, so we went directly to my car, and she sat in the front seat next to me. The seat of honor.

"Is that a snake on your dashboard?" she asked me.

"Yes, a plastic snake." Oh no, I worried. Is she afraid of snakes?

"I have the same snake on my dashboard!"

"What! That's impossible." How could we both love snakes? Is it genetic?

Now, years later, I've finally stopped my emotional weeping when I tell people our story. We still marvel at the nature versus nurture experiment going on in our relationship. Nancy is very tidy. Nothing rests on her pristine countertops for very long before being put in its proper place. I do the same. Her house is filled with art. So is mine. She loves her children fiercely, and so do I.

I believe she was at a stage in her life when she was questioning her choices and searching for her true self when she made that phone call to me. Part of her journey was to find her roots, and part was to be honest about her sexual identity. She divorced her husband, and now she has a woman life-partner, as do I.

It took me a long time to believe that she was my daughter, even though she looks like me. Even though the DNA test came back positive. At first, I couldn't call her my daughter without the qualifiers of "My newly discovered daughter" or "My daughter that I did not raise." Adjusting to bringing her into my present and future was a process of relearning my past.

Last year she talked me into getting a tattoo, my first and her fifth or sixth. I loved the idea of having a permanent mark on my body (other than stretch marks) that declared our connection. We worked out the design via email, sending links to photos of tats we liked. We went back and forth, tweaking a little of this and stretching a bit of that, and finally came up with something we both agreed on. I made back-to-back appointments at a local tattoo parlor. The highly visible bracelets encircle our right wrists with swirly lines, two red stars, and some dots.

I thought of our matching tattoos as a symbol of our reunion and about me still being a wild child at age sixty-seven. When people asked me about it, that's how I answered, but on closer inspection, I realized that the two stars could signify my two children. The lines swirl but don't touch, which could symbolize distance and integration. One star has five dots, which could be Nancy's five children, and the other has one, Eli's child. It wasn't conscious, this decision to write my history on my arm, I allowed myself to find out what it meant after the fact.

V
REVISIONS

GARY YOUNG

"MY YOUNGEST SON CONSIDERS"

My youngest son considers the effect of imaginary numbers on imaginary numbers. His brother ponders the duality of abstraction and specificity, while I wrestle with the concept of essential nature. We are pilgrims. The branch of a willow bounces off its reflection on the surface of a canal. Mallards bob in a murky pond. A crow tears at the body of a mouse on the gray tile roof of a temple.

BETH CHRISTENSEN

INSOMNIA

They say that one of the worst things you can do for insomnia is to stay in bed, that if you get up and do something else, you might get sleepy. I don't really know if that's true, but most nights I get so desperate I'll believe almost any reasonable advice. Especially during those hours between *if I fall asleep now I might be able to make it through the day* and *if I fall asleep now I'll just feel worse when the alarm clock goes off*, I'm ready to try anything. Those are the hours when the harder I try to fall asleep, the less likely I am to do so. Those are the hours when even the silence is loud, when I find myself irritated by watching my husband Ben sleep, snoring, utterly unaware, and I have an intense urge to poke him with something sharp. Like I hate him for the way he falls asleep with no effort whatsoever—how can some people do that? Those are the hours when the numbers on the alarm clock seem as bright as Times Square, and I watch the long minutes pass by in red flashes. Those are the hours when I think of all the things I need to do that coming day but probably won't because I'll be too tired.

So, when it becomes obvious that I'm not going to fall asleep, I get up. I get out of bed carefully, moving gingerly away from my husband's sleep sounds and, pulling on my bathrobe if the house is chilly, I walk softly and quietly into the hallway. I don't wear slippers—I kind of like the feeling of my bare feet on the wood floors, cool and smooth, and I'm willing to take the risk that I might step on a wayward Lego block in the dark. When I pass my daughter Molly's room, I linger briefly, suspended in her sweet soft breathing and I have one of those parental moments, the kind in which my heart is so full of love and hope and fear that it literally aches. As I walk through the house, I am struck by how different it feels in these early pre-dawn hours from the daytime house. It's quiet except for the creaks that, I'm told, are caused by the house settling (whatever that means) and the hum of the air conditioner when it kicks on. I creep around as quietly as a burglar, and the cat looks at me with wide-open eyes as if I am one, maneuvering through the dark.

When I get to the living room, though, I don't turn on the light. The lights from the street cut clean and sharp through the big front window, with the big oak tree out front creating a pattern like old lace on the floor. I sit by the window and watch the sparse light in the eastern sky build, as deep indigo turns slowly purple then pink, and again it is morning and again I have not slept. As I wait for the coffee to brew, the traffic on my street gradually builds and the world is awake. Very soon my husband and daughter will make their way into the kitchen, tousled and ruddy and sleep-drunk, and I will try to resist resenting them for it.

I have always had insomnia, or at least for as long as I can remember. Even when I was a kid, I would lie still until the rest of the house was asleep, then I would pull out the book I had stashed under my mattress and tunnel under the covers with a flashlight. It was almost like I was afraid of missing out on something, or like something might be taken from me while I slept. I knew I needed to go to sleep, but I also knew that if I lay there still and quiet, sleep would not come. Instead, it seemed that the quieter I tried to be, the busier my head would become. Reading always quieted my busy nighttime mind, and eventually I would fall asleep on my book, and wake in the morning to find my flashlight batteries dead.

One thing I can say for insomnia, it can leave a person quite well-read. I collect used books from library book fairs, thrift stores, and Amazon, and most of what I have, I have read at least twice. Magazines, too—I read every article, recipe, miracle diet, and must-have haircut. I sometimes even paw through the previous week's newspapers, hoping to come upon some story I might have missed the first time around. Another favorite of mine is to use those long nighttime hours doing quiet chores, like balancing the checkbook or rearranging the bookcase, sometimes alphabetically by author and sometimes by genre. I have often thought that, if I could find an all-night library that needed help, it would be my perfect job.

One night, I decided to look over the previous year's tax returns, to see if maybe I had missed a deduction or two. It was worth a try but more importantly, it was a good way to pass the time. Reaching back into the cabinet where the tax returns were stored, however, my hand landed on an old shoe box secured with a decaying red rubber band. I recognized it as one of the boxes I had collected from my parents' house after my father, then my mother, had died a couple of years before. Honestly, I had never really looked inside the box. With all the things I had to do, caring for my parents as they went through their terminal decline, then funerals and lawyers and finally selling the house, I didn't have much time to go through the boxes. I couldn't imagine that there were any family pictures that were substantially different from the ones that I had always seen hanging in my parents' home or stuffed into photo albums, virtually all of which were now mine. I always thought I must have been the most thoroughly documented kid ever, and I figured that being an only child had a lot to do with that.

I have been hoping that I would have a second child soon, in large part to save my daughter from the all-consuming specialness of being an *only*. My parents, who had been older than most couples when they had me, had treated me like I was made of the most delicate crystal, both physically and emotionally. I had training wheels on my bike 'til I was almost ten, for crying out loud, and my mom pulled me out of soccer as soon as she saw the shin guards. "Those make you look like you're *expecting* a broken leg!" she exclaimed, and she whisked me off the field before I even had a chance to protest. A few weeks later, I was enrolled in the chess club. And the first time a boy crushed my heart, in seventh grade, it took some desperate begging and pleading to keep my father from humiliating the poor kid right there in the schoolyard.

Despite my certainty that the shoe box could not possibly contain anything I did not already know, one night when there was nothing new to read, nothing in need of organizing, and the house about as clean as a house can get, I got curious. I carried the box into the kitchen, laid it on the table and turned on the lights. I carefully tugged at the rubber band, but in its rotted condition it immediately snapped. Slowly (I was more than a little afraid that something with too many legs might crawl out of this box), I lifted the lid and found that the box was stuffed with letters and official-looking papers, and a few old photos. The pictures were all of me—from birth, it seemed, with the familiar unruly shock of dark hair that grew, Mohawk-style, along the top of my head and the fuzz that grew along the sides, and the big dark eyes that seemed like bottomless pools, and the always-inquisitive expression.

I smiled when I looked at my infant hair, especially when I thought about how much it resembled Molly's hair when she was a baby. My mother-in-law had told me that it was my daughter's hair that had been the cause of the indigestion that plagued my pregnancy, and I knew better than to question the scientific basis of her claim. My own mother spent countless hours trying to tame my daughter's unruly tresses and capture them into ridiculously big ribbons and bows, hoping to keep the hair at bay until she could snap a photo or two. She told me that she had done exactly the same thing with my own hair, even resorting to trying to plaster it down with gobs of Dippity-Do (a practice I forbade once my daughter came along). But the hair always won in the end, as if it were endowed with a will of its own, and the ribbon would dangle uselessly within a few minutes, forcing my mother to admit defeat. As silly as it all was, I knew that if I ever had a granddaughter, and she had her mother's hair, I would probably do the very same thing, and knowing that made me smile.

The photographs in the box were numerous and familiar, and the other papers in the box were my baptism certificate, vital statistics taken at my early pediatrician visits, and a couple of report cards from pre-kindergarten, where apparently I excelled at snack distribution and napping, but needed to improve in taking turns and putting away toys. These were not particularly surprising revelations, especially the napping thing. I know for sure that even back then, I was a nighttime insomniac and naps were as vital to me as oxygen.

I have tried every remedy imaginable for my insomnia, from pills to herbs, hypnosis, and aromatherapy. I even took a crack at acupuncture, in spite of my fear of needles. Nothing worked, at least not for very long. At one point, before I became pregnant with my daughter, I saw a therapist for a few times, in hopes of curing my insomnia. In one session, I began to cry, suddenly and inexplicably, deep heaving sobs that felt like grief. After that, I never went back to therapy. I was a little bit afraid that she would declare me crazy, and I simply would rather she didn't.

To my great surprise, once I got pregnant, at least for the first few months, I actually slept—really, genuinely slept. I have no idea how such a tiny creature growing inside me could make me so sleepy, but I luxuriated in the long nights of deep and peaceful slumber. Often, I would wake up with my hand on my belly, as if to thank her for this exquisite gift. Then I would go throw up.

Sometime around mid-pregnancy, I began to feel her moving inside me. It didn't feel like a kick, really, but like a butterfly beating its delicate wings in me. I wanted Ben to feel it too, and I would take his hand and place it on my belly, but of course he couldn't feel anything, not this early. That time was for my daughter and me alone, her communication to me by way of butterfly fluttering, and I came to cherish it.

Later, of course, came the real kicking, that girl of mine doing summersaults off my bladder and bouncing against my diaphragm. My nights of slumber were over, but it wasn't because of the kicks, not exactly. I would notice when she stopped moving, when I suppose she fell asleep, and I would try, really try, to leave her alone but I would get scared. What if something was wrong? What if she was strangling on her umbilical cord or something? I have no idea what I could have done about it if this were true, but I would poke at her until she stirred and kicked, and I would be satisfied, for a while at least.

As I rummaged deeper into the shoe box, I found my birth certificate, apparently the original one. When I needed it, in order to get my first driver's license, my mother had searched high and low and declared it lost. I had to go down to city hall and request a duplicate. The duplicate certificate had been new and crisp, while the one I found in the shoe box had a certain patina about it that made me feel older than thirty-six. But I liked looking at it; it felt good to look at the first document to ever confirm my existence. Across the top, in a fancy font, read "Certificate of Live Birth." It had the date of my birth on it, of course, and my parents' names and ages, and my weight of six pounds, two ounces and length of nineteen and one-half inches. It also stated that I was a twin. I don't remember how old I was when I learned that my twin sister had been stillborn. It seems to me that I always knew, and my parents never were very comfortable talking about it.

I almost didn't notice, in the dim light and my sleep-deprived state, that the name on the certificate was wrong. My name is Catherine, and this form said Caroline. I can probably count on one hand the number of times I ever heard my parents speak her name. It was puzzling because as far as I knew, my sister had been born dead and this was a certificate of *live* birth. I wondered if someone at the hospital or the city clerk's office or whoever was in charge of these kinds of things had made a mistake, or if my sister had drawn breath briefly after her birth. Given my parents' hesitancy to talk about her, I could have easily gotten that detail wrong.

Daylight came, and my husband and daughter arrived in the kitchen, so I closed the box and put it aside. I started scrambling the eggs and Ben came over to kiss me. "No sleep again?" he asked, but of course he knew the answer. I just shrugged and gave him that smile that I use to make it seem like no big deal. Molly put bread in the toaster—that was her job—and Ben poured coffee for himself and me, and juice for her. I looked at the family calendar on the fridge. It was going to be a busy day. A tiring, busy day.

While Ben packed Molly's lunch, I helped her get dressed. She was old enough to dress herself but she was easily distracted and if I left her to her own devices, I was very likely to find her conversing with her dolls, still in PJs, when it was almost time to go. And honestly, I enjoyed that morning ritual, helping her with shoes and buttons, brushing her hair—I realized that I was doing some of the "only child" stuff my own mother had done, but I did it anyway.

After dropping Molly off at school, I drove across town to pick up my Aunt Jen. She had a doctor's appointment, then a hair appointment. Ever since her own daughter moved out of town, I have been looking after my aunt. I don't mind it—I have always been very fond of my aunt, and I kind of miss doing those sorts of things for my own parents. I know she misses her sister—my mom—terribly, and I am the living link to her.

She was ready to go when I got there. She just about always is. We walked down the front steps of her house, with me holding her elbow in one of my hands, and my other arm around her waist. She tells me that she doesn't need any help, but I can see her creeping frailty and I want so much to protect her, so I just ask her to humor me. She is the closest thing I have to a mother now, and I want her to be safe.

Once we were both buckled in and I was about to start the car, I was unable to suppress a deep, long yawn. I looked at my aunt apologetically. "Didn't sleep very well last night," I said.

"You were never much of a sleeper," she replied. "Are you OK to drive?"

I managed not to laugh. Even with no sleep, I was a much better driver than she, with her failing vision and slow responses. Her daughter had made sure that she did not have access to a car before she moved away. My aunt had complained about losing her independence, but eventually adapted and was still able to get where she needed to go.

After the doctor's appointment, I dropped her off at the hair salon and went about my errands while she was there. After the bank, the supermarket, and a couple clients—I do bookkeeping for a few small businesses—she was just about done. Then we went to my house, as my aunt has supper with us every Tuesday evening. I was feeling very tired by the time we got home and I had unloaded the groceries, but I still had a big chunk of my day yet to go.

We settled into the living room. I opened my laptop to do a bit of work, and Aunt Jen watched the daytime talk shows, which she loved. But we both drifted off to sleep, and we didn't wake up until Molly came bounding in after getting off the school bus. She leapt into Aunt Jen's lap and launched into the chatter of a six-year-old with unlimited energy.

"Guess what? We're making kites *from scratch* at school and tonight I have to design what I want on the paper and then color it. Have you ever made a kite? I always used the kind you get at the store. I was thinking about a dragon, but I think a lot of kids are going to do dragons, so I need some ideas . . ." Molly went on as Aunt Jen smiled and kissed her on the forehead. She was obviously refreshed from her nap and went off with Molly to help her with her kite. I was glad that Molly had a grandmother figure in my aunt, and that my aunt took such pleasure in being that figure.

After supper, Aunt Jen helped me with the dishes despite my protests, as she always did. Molly was taking a bath and Ben was watching TV, so it was just the two of us in the kitchen. After the dishwasher was loaded and we wiped off the counters, Aunt Jen turned to me.

"I hope you don't mind, but I looked through that old shoebox while Molly was coloring her kite," she said.

"No, of course not," I replied. "I think I have a copy of just about every picture in there, so if there are any you want for yourself, please take them."

Aunt Jen nodded. She looked like she may have been lost in a memory for a moment, but then snapped back to the present and started talking about her plans for Thanksgiving. It was still two months away, but she loved the holiday and knew that her daughter, along with her husband and children, would be coming. After Aunt Jen tucked Molly in and promised to watch her fly her new kite as soon as possible, Ben drove her home.

The days between that Tuesday and the next flowed in their usual rhythm. Somewhere in there, Molly's class held a bake sale to which I contributed brownies that were only slightly burnt, Ben had an overnight trip for work, and I balanced work, housework, and tending to Molly all while hungering for sleep every night and getting just enough to survive on. When Tuesday came around again, I picked up Aunt Jen as usual, but she didn't have any doctor or hair appointments, so we went to lunch at a little diner that had been there for as long as I could remember. Aunt Jen told me that it had been there since she was a kid, and some of her best memories of my mom, who was ten years older than she, were those rare times when she would take her there for ice cream sodas. Aunt Jen remembered how special it felt to spend time with her big sister, who usually didn't want her kid sister tagging along.

"Cathy," she said after we had ordered our sandwiches, "is there anything you want to ask me about the shoe box? I mean, anything you found in the shoe box?"

It took me a moment to realize what she was talking about. "Oh, not really. I mean, I found Caroline's birth certificate. As I always understood it, she was stillborn. But I guess she died soon after birth? I've never found any pictures of her, so she must not have lived very long."

"Actually, most of the pictures in that box were of her. You two were identical."

"But Aunt Jen, some of those pictures were of an older baby—like five or six months old. Those have to be of me," I replied, wondering if my aunt was beginning to have problems with memory.

Aunt Jen opened her purse and retrieved an envelope. "You deserve to know this," she said as she carefully removed an old, slightly creased photograph from it. She placed the picture on the table and slid it toward me. I picked it up.

The picture was of two babies, side by side in a crib. They both had that unruly hair and dark eyes. They were looking at each other, their foreheads touching, and they were laughing. Their toothless mouths were wide open in this apparent hilarity. They were both me.

My heart was racing as I struggled to make sense of this picture, and Aunt Jen slid another one across the table to me. In this one, the two babies were lying on their stomachs, again side by side with their faces turned toward each other, but this time they were asleep. One of the babies had her arm around the other. I looked up at Aunt Jen, whose kind eyes were rimmed with tears.

"I wanted your mother to tell you. I thought it would be best for you and for her. But she was adamant. She just refused to tell you, or to talk about it with anyone, not even me," she said softly. "The doctors said it was crib death, and that there was nothing anyone could have done to prevent it. You woke your parents that night crying, screaming really, but when they got to her it was too late. You still had your arm around her when they came into your room."

"No," I said, once I found my voice. "You don't put babies down on their stomachs. They have to sleep on their back or on their side," I said this as if saying it could undo the past and disprove what my aunt was telling me.

"Not back then. We didn't know that back then," she said.

I sat in stunned silence for a moment, and I'm sure my aunt wondered if she had done the right thing by telling me that, for a few months, I had a living, breathing sister. And that sister had died in my arms while I slept.

"You started fighting sleep as soon as she died," my aunt said. "It was always hard for your mom and dad to get you to sleep. And once they did manage to get you to sleep, you would wake up crying when they tried to put you down in your crib. I told your mother that I thought you missed Caroline, but she told me that you were too young to miss her, and that you would be better off never knowing that she was ever alive. I got my hands on these right before she destroyed every other picture of the two of you together. I'm surprised she even kept Caroline's birth certificate."

I made my way in a daze through the rest of that Tuesday's routines. I thought about my mother, keeping this painful secret from me, thinking she was protecting me. I tried to imagine what it must have been like for her to lose a baby. I managed to get through Molly's antics and dinner and all the rest of that evening, but when Ben drove Aunt Jen home I got into the shower and the tears came like water rushing from a broken dam, and sobs generated deep in my chest made their way out, and I cried like that until I was thoroughly spent.

When we got in bed that night, I moved close to Ben. I had not yet told him what I had learned. I'm not sure I would have known, at that moment, what to say or how to say it. Instead, I wrapped my arms around him and put my head on his shoulder.

"Just let me hold you, OK? I need to hold you and not let go."

And finally, I fell asleep.

MK PUNKY

EGO DEATH

When I managed momentarily to vanquish my swollen ego
impaling it on a saber of honesty
the *I* who was about to be nevermore allowed himself
a final review of the constituent parts comprising his whole
and this guy realized
many of what you would call his *worst* qualities
      if you were to operate in the judgment paradigm
could be traced directly to
his mother
whereas many of what you would call his *best* qualities
could also be traced directly to
his mother

Cataloging complete and new knowledge stored for freshness
shortly before the crusade against myself commenced
I called my mother and reminded her
I loved her

PROUD MAMA

When I saw that viral video
of an unidentified Federal law enforcement officer
beating with his baton a Navy veteran
who stoically absorbs the blows
I had mixed feelings
since on one hand I have nothing but respect for our military
but on the other hand the brave policeman
confronting violent anarchists and moms in Portland
happens to be my oldest son
who I raised right
with good Christian American values
worth defending

Watching my boy just doing his job
amid other fine young men doing their job
protecting government property and what have you
I realized the fellow working beside my son
the one you see spraying a chemical irritant on the veteran's face
while my baby chops at his knees
that officer also has a mom
who loves her child
and did her best to make him an honorable man

If I knew her name I'd tell her
it's OK to cry when you watch this thing for the 100th time
even though you're not sure if the tears are from maternal pride
or something else altogether

AROONEY

ELEGY FOR DARLEEN

The sense of falling,
that's how my mother must feel,
or like she's already fallen.
And then comes the flailing
at all of us, mostly my brother
and I. Nearly done, at 91,
and I want to ask if she's
able to hear the sounds
all around her now,
the distant, the interior?
But knowing the answer I skip it.

           1
A South African doctor called
last evening to say you
hadn't filled out the forms,
that you can only remember
the past, nothing from today,
and that you'll need to go
somewhere, that is, somewhere
else, where you've made it abundantly
clear you don't want to go.
They say you don't have a choice,
you can't stay in the patio home
you paid for and reversed years ago.

2

Calling out,
I often hear you calling out
my name as you sink,
as you grasp and
flail, as the water rises
above, above your head.
Dear Mother,
I want to write,
should I send you
all my money, that's
what you've asked, fly there
today, leave my students?
We took a field trip to the
art museum this morning, the
kind of thing you might like
to do, and the traffic on the
Grand Trunk was already stop and go.
A young student crossed the aisle
and sat down next to me,
to be out of the Sun, she said,
and immediately inserted
buds in her ears, then
after a moment
offered them to me.
Who is it? I asked.
The Grateful Dead
she said, and I said,
No, thanks. She insisted,
though, so I took them.
Box of Rain was playing,
terrible song, and as I listened
she asked how I liked it.
With my hands I made the sign
for two thumbs up.

3

The faculty around me,
across the aisle and behind,
weave and mumble
with their mouths slack, and
I want to join them,
but next to me the student
sings, dances in her seat,
and in my glance I see
the tiny hairs on her dark
face and cheeks illuminated
by the window light.
To her I want to say
someday it will be you, dear,
who struggles at the end, you,
dear, who will become paranoid,
angry, delusional, who
at the drop of a hat will
flail her family, you,
my student, who will not
be loved, who will love
no one but yourself, you
who will make a mess
of things in your last days.
And then I want to turn to her fully,
put my hand on hers, say something wise,
but I'm afraid I'll begin to weep,
not for her, but for myself,
my mother's son,
who feels the drift, the collapse,
who senses the inevitable.

MY FATHER TURNING

The turning began not last year,
not the year before,
but one day at the table
when we played a parlor game
and I could see your eyes,
your mind wandering.
Going where?
To the time on Long Island, maybe,
with Nana,
Clete and Jerry,
and Aunt Joan.
To Germany
with my high-cheeked mother
and brothers, Danny still alive.
Or later, after she was gone, to the days
at the officers' club,
the tedious officers' club,
and the women who wanted
to marry.
To the horse tracks in New Mexico,
Denver, and San Francisco, with the priests
who bet and drank
and removed their collars.
In the ragtop as we moved
from post to post,
late at night,
listening to country,
you singing on bennies.
Or to Iran, with the Shah
and Dr. Nejad.
Did you travel to India again

where you took Gen and the girls
and they came back talking like Brits?
Were you picturing yourself
in bowler hat, Hawaiian lei,
and Paddy's Day smile, glass
always in hand,
not able to shake
the scourge?
You were passionate about something
weren't you, besides that?
There was love, yes?
Sperm for sure.
And in that turning, drifting
eye, like a lighthouse in
your brain, off-on
off-on,
across the land it
shined,
illuminating your posturing,
melancholy clan, their
mouths agape, as if
young birds
beneath a balcony,
waiting
for just a little more.

LAMENT OF A LATED ORPHAN

1.

Mother, now that you're gone
I have no one to ask about
the mysteries of family life,
like the hole in Uncle Clete's throat,
Joan's house burning down,
or the split.
But I'd wanted to know
about Danny's demise from the cord,
the creaking moments after,
and how you managed to breathe
for even a second.

In my childish eye
I see him convulsing,
in the living room
in Frankfurt,
our father being heroic,
but that's not what happened, is it?
On the return, aboard the ship,
him in the hold, us in the cabin,
did you weep and tear
at your hair, your flesh,
search the seas
for the soul of your boy,
your plump blond boy,
your floating boy?

2.

Father, I always wondered,
after the split, would you have
preferred we not live with you?
It often felt as if we were interrupting
your time at the officers' club.
You were a generous guy,
people often said that,
but it was hard for you, I know,
to share yourself with us.

Once, when I came to visit you in the hospital,
do you remember,
when you cut yourself near your groin,
and the nurses came and the operation
had to be postponed?
I thought you might die then,
sitting on the toilet,
bleeding alone,
or during the by-pass later on.
But it only served to mark
the beginning of your demise,
which, at 70, I often think about myself.

3.

Mother and Father I miss you,
but I'm not sure why.
We gave each other up for adoption,
but were never taken in
by a kindly couple,
like Superman
and the Kents.

ON SEEING MY MOTHER IN THE FRANKFURT AIRPORT

Once in the Frankfurt airport
I saw my mother asleep on a bench.
She appeared to be dead with her arms
folded across her chest,
a black leather coat
draped over her legs.
But for a dead woman
she looked pretty good–
bright red lips,
make-up,
jewelry,
bosom,
a third husband beside her
reading the paper.
And she did die
just a few years later.
Mom was—
how to say this—
something else,
if you couldn't guess it.
In fact that probably wasn't her
on the bench.
I was just there a few minutes
to change planes from India
and was tempted to say something anyway
to whoever it was:
Mom, how are you?
Mom, where you headed?
Mom, is that your latest?

But I didn't,
and then,
of course,
there was my flight.

JAN CALLNER

OKAY, GOD

Dear God i

Okay, God. This is it. The hospital cacophony evaporates when I slip through the chapel doors at St. Joseph's Medical Center. The room is empty, the wooden pews beckon, the silence in the chapel as deafening as the tumult outside. Sliding into one of the long benches, I pull down the kneeler, lean forward on my knees, and fold my hands in prayer. *I hope you're listening, God, 'cause this is the big one. I'm cashing in. Cashing in on every Sunday mass, the years of Catechism, the Novenas; cashing in on all those confessions and thousands of Hail Marys.*

The antiseptic medical smell is replaced by the faint whiff of lit candles emanating from the altar. Should I light a candle?

Words drone in my head—on a continual loop, *Dear God, please . . .* my eyes alternate closed and open, left and right. If only my left eye is shut, I can see the statue of Saint Joseph on the right side of the altar. Saint Joseph is the patron saint of workers. Dad is a worker, or he was. He worked for The Ford Motor Company. Maybe that will help. I add, *Saint Joseph, please help Dad. Saint Joseph, please help Dad.* If I close my right eye, I can see the statue of the Virgin Mary on the other side. Mary in her blue robe. I wonder if she had clothes of any different color. I always see her in blue. It suits her, I think.

Dad and I both made a Novena to Mary a few years ago; maybe she can put in a good word. "Please, Mary, intercede for Dad," I say out loud, the sound of my voice cracking in the silent room. Aloud, maybe she could hear it better. Both eyes close, and I'm back to, *Dear God, please . . .* I hold myself still so as not to interfere with the strength of the prayer.

I'm a good prayer, focused, intense, creative.

"Whatever you ask in Jesus' name, you will receive." Those are the words I inherited from the nuns when I was twelve. They, those all-knowing women, said it could only be used for something extremely important. I have been hoarding it for seven years. I don't know what could be more important than this.

Dear God, please let Dad's brain surgery go okay. Please make him better . . . in Jesus' name. Yesterday afternoon, I walked into my dorm room to see a folded piece of paper on the floor. The note read: "Your mom called. A friend of your dad's will pick you up to take you and your sister home. Your father is having brain surgery in the morning. Friend's name is Joe Eagleye, and his daughter is a student here. She'll be with him. Be ready at five o'clock." The message was signed by my floor's resident advisor. It took a few minutes for the words to stop bouncing around and settle themselves on the page. I looked at my watch, 2 p.m. We had three hours. My sister, a freshman at the University of Cincinnati where I am a sophomore, lives in a different building. I clutched the note, slipped into the phone booth at the end of the hall, and closed the door to dial her extension. A young woman answered, "Just a sec, I'll get her."

"Hey Lily, I have some bad news. It's about Dad." She started to cry when I read the message. Crying is contagious, not contagious like yawning is, but when it's your little sister, the lump in your throat is hard to swallow. I cut her short. "Meet you out front in a few hours."

Dad has been sick for a while now, but I had no idea brain surgery might be in the immediate future. He's had severe headaches for years. We could tell it was a bad one when we saw him lying on the couch with a cold washcloth over his eyes.

The four-hour drive from Cincinnati, Ohio, to Avon—the bottom of the state to the top—was quiet, and the sick feeling in my stomach was not from hunger. Mr. Eagleye drove, and his daughter sat with him in the front. He didn't talk much. What little he said told me he valued Dad's friendship. I had never met him or his daughter, but I was grateful he could deliver us home. Lily huddled next to me in the back seat, sniffling quietly. We were close sisters, not only in age—fourteen months apart—but as siblings; we enjoyed each other's company and hardly ever argued. Dad's health had been declining the past year when Lily still lived at home. I didn't witness it closely since I was away at college. Our older sister, May, attended nursing school and lived in an apartment near the hospital.

The last time Dad and I were together, just the two of us, we'd taken a ski trip near the New York border in February—only a year and a half ago. Small ski resorts were springing up all over—wherever there was a hill and a chance of snow. If he had free time, Dad hit the slopes. If someone could go with him, that was even better. It was President's Day, 1967, and there was no school. I joined him. We drove northeast to Pennsylvania.

The two of us skied all day. As we floated on the chair lift toward the summit for one last run, the mechanism stopped, leaving us suspended halfway up the mountain. Twenty feet in the air, we waited for it to start up again. It didn't. We seized the opportunity to gaze out over the mountain range and watch the skiers underneath the lift schuss down the hills. The temperature began to drop, and the wind picked up.

"Pull your scarf up over your face, Jan." Dad did the same. We didn't think we might die up there or anything, and it was exciting, but as it got colder, the excitement quotient decreased. After fifteen minutes, we spied a cherry picker rumbling up the slope to pluck us to safety. It stopped right under our chair. The driver raised the bucket and motioned for us to get in. There was only room for one.

"You go first, Jan." My fingers were frozen, but I managed to scramble in. "Wait for me," Dad said. "I'll be right with you." The bucket lowered to the ground, and I hopped out. It was scary to look up and see Dad swinging over my head in the open chair. He climbed into the bucket, and the cherry picker brought him to my side before moving on. Relieved to have our skis on the packed snow and not dangling in mid-air, we skied down the mountain from our rescue point.

The lifts shut down, for real this time, and the sound of motors and pulleys gave way to the quietness of a snowy mountain. We trekked to the car through the crunchy snow and loaded all our gear. The gray clouds hung low in the sky, kissing the sun goodbye.

"Do you think you can drive?" Dad asked as he closed the trunk.

"He probably has one of his headaches," I thought." Or maybe he wants to give me driving experience."

I had my license, had it over a year. I could drive. With my contact lenses in all day, and glasses forgotten at home, my eyes were on fire, but I said, "Sure," and got into the driver's seat. Twenty minutes later, I pulled over.

"Dad, I don't think I can make it."

"Okay. I'll take over." I took my contacts out and sat in the passenger seat watching the blurry landscape along the road. He drove the entire three hours

home.

\\❀//

Dear God ii

Dear God, please let . . . I'm fervently praying when I hear a knock on the chapel door.

A nurse sticks her head in. "Your father is in recovery. The doctor would like to speak to the family." I snap out of my self-induced hypnosis. Recovery? That's a good thing, right? Doesn't that mean he's recover*ing*? I follow in a prayer fog as she leads me to the elevator and past the nurses' station where nuns in white and orderlies in blue congregate. I resist the temptation to ask the nuns if they know about the magic prayer I had been invoking.

The surgeon's office is on the second floor. Mom, Lily, and May are already there. I stand at the doorway. Mom's face looks thinner than it did this morning, and her mouth is a straight line. When Mr. Eagleye dropped us off last night, she had met us at the front door and thanked him. The three of us, all exhausted, went to bed. The house felt empty without Dad in it.

This morning on the way to the hospital, Mom told Lily and me that his doctors didn't know what else to do, so they scheduled this exploratory surgery. One of them had previously diagnosed him with depression and had tried shock treatments, but that wasn't working.

"And the other day, he set the kitchen on fire. He forgot about the frying pan on the burner. He isn't working anymore. Ford Motor let him go."

He made too many mistakes, she explained, dangerous mistakes since he was an electrical worker. He bore the imprint of a burn on his finger in the shape of his wedding ring, the result of a misconnected wire. Workers aren't supposed to wear jewelry, but Dad hated to go without his wedding ring. I wonder if he wore it when the doctor administered the electric shock treatments.

In the surgeon's office, my sisters sit far apart from each other. May is in nursing school at this very hospital. She's wearing her uniform and looks to me like she might understand something about what is happening. Lily is sitting in a corner quietly, as far away from May as possible—not surprising—I recall all the fights they had as we were growing up. Mom makes room for me on the loveseat.

The doctor explains, "We drilled three exploratory holes in Anthony's skull. We wanted to see what his physical brain actually looked like." He pauses and takes a deep breath. "What we saw does not look healthy. The organ is quite shriveled. We don't know how he is even functioning."

We just stare at him, four pairs of eyes not blinking. There is nothing wrong with my hearing, but what he just said doesn't make sense. I mentally review his words, "We drilled these holes, looked inside, decided there was nothing we could do—we stopped." This was my Dad he was talking about. The one who was able to drive us home from our ski trip less than two years ago. The one who helped me figure out my college applications. The dad who convinced me to apply for a Ford Foundation Scholarship. It's 1968, and he is only forty-nine years old, for Pete's sake. The doctor cannot be telling the truth.

Finally, Mom asks, "Could this have anything to do with the fact that his parents were first cousins? And that their parents were also first cousins?"

What? Says the scream inside my head. "That's news to me," I say aloud.

The doctor squirms, looking uncomfortable. "I don't know. It is possible."

"Could it have anything to do with the fact that he was completely paralyzed after the war and was told he could never work again?" (I knew *that* story.)

"I don't know. I don't know what happened to him in the war."

"Could it have anything to do with the fact that he's had debilitating headaches for the past fifteen years?" (I was acutely aware of his headaches.)

The doctor shuffles his papers. "I'm so sorry. I don't know the answers to any of those questions. Anthony has a degenerative brain disease. It might be a condition that is starting to get a lot of attention. It's called Oppenheimer's."

Oppenheimer's? Wasn't that the person who created the atom bomb? Over twenty years ago? Why would that be a disease? What does the atom bomb guy have to do with my dad's brain? Then I realized I had misheard this word. It was Alzheimer's. The doctor said Alzheimer's, not Oppenheimer's. He was telling us he thought Dad might have Alzheimer's.

"How will this affect my children? They're not going to turn out like my husband's sisters, are they? There is definitely something wrong with them."

Wow, Mom, I think. *That's intense.*

"Well, we don't know much; research is just starting. But since you're not Italian, like your husband, or even Mediterranean, a completely different bloodline has been introduced. My opinion is that your three girls should be okay." The doctor puts his shuffled papers into a folder. He gets up and leaves us sitting stunned in his office.

Okay, God. This is cruel. I prayed so hard. No one could have prayed harder. I did everything right. Tell me, what is this "power of prayer" stuff? Which prayer is it that has power, and what are the prerequisites for its success? You might have let me in on that part of it.

I was angry and not afraid to give God a good talking to. Not only was I angry with God, but furious with myself for being so gullible. Or maybe I didn't say the words correctly, or perhaps I heard wrong. Maybe it wasn't, "Hocus pocus, dominocus, in Jesus' name," but instead "Zippity do dah, zippity day, in His name." Any one of those might have worked just as well.

※

Dear God iii

Dad comes home the next day, his head wrapped in a big bandage. Our health insurance won't cover this "Alzheimer's" condition, so the doctors diagnose it as Parkinson's. They give him doses of the Parkinson's drug L dopa. "It won't hurt him," they say. *It won't help either,* I think.

Lily and I stay home from school through the end of the week. We sit at the dining table and play "Go Fish." Dad keeps calling me Nancy, his youngest sister's name. At dinner one night, out of nowhere, he says, "If they had just let Patton go ahead with his plan, the war would have been over six months earlier." We don't know how to respond. I *never* heard Dad talk about the war.

We finish the meal, and Lily and I clean up. Mom takes care of Dad. Then I head downstairs to the basement. Halfway down, I stop and sit on a step to look through the jalousie window overlooking Mom's sewing room. How many times had I done that? Come home from school, sat and watched her take a piece of fabric, turn it into a skirt, or a blouse, or a suit for one of us while we talked about the day. Mom has always said I'm the one of her three daughters she can best talk to.

I reach the bottom of the stairs and see that my piano still stands against the wall in the family room. The small round swivel stool looks lonely. How many hours have I spent playing and singing in that space? Left of the piano is the bar Dad built, and behind the bar, a mural of a lake and pine trees, all blues and greens. I was surprised and impressed when he painted that mural.

As far as I knew, he'd never painted anything. But then, he built this whole basement too. Because of his skill and creativity, we had all this extra space to spread out: a rec room, a full bathroom, a study room for homework, the sewing and laundry room, and his beloved workshop. Above his workbench, he added cupboards for storage.

I know that what I'm looking for is in the cupboard directly above the heavy-duty vise-grip attached to the bench. I used to flatten pennies in that vice grip just for fun. Now I hang onto it and stretch to open the door. Inside, Dad's horn case is the first thing I see, but behind that, where it had always been, is the brown rectangular box. It's still in the same place my father put it all those years ago when he said I was too young to know what was inside.

He said I was too young. I was eight years old and sat playing the piano when I heard a strange sound. I could see Dad's workshop from my piano stool, and I swiveled around. One of the cupboards was open, and Dad stood in front of it with an instrument to his mouth. I never saw that before! I hopped off my stool and skipped to his side.

"What are you doing? Is this a trumpet?" I stood looking up at him.

"It's a cornet. I used to be able to play it," he said.

"Really? I didn't know that! Why can't you play it now?"

"Well, I lost my lip." He replied.

"Um, Dad, you still have your lips. I can see them."

He smiled. But when he smiled his lips didn't always look natural. It was like he had to make them smile.

"That's just an expression," he said. "Losing your lip to a horn player means you can't tighten your lips enough to get the right vibration on your mouthpiece."

"Oh."

"And if you can't get the right vibration, you can't play the horn."

"Oh."

"So, I can't play the horn anymore." He paused. "I'm thinking of taking piano lessons like you. My fingers still work!"

"Oh!"

He put the instrument back in its case. I looked up into the cupboard and saw something else far back on the shelf.

"What's that?" I pointed over my head.

He glanced up too and then reached to bring down a brown cardboard box. "It's full of things from when I was in the service," he said.

"Can I see?"

After a couple seconds of silence, "No, you're too young. Maybe in a few years."

"Hmm," I stuck my lower lip out in an eight-year-old pout, "Okay."

Even though I could see no dust, Dad wiped the box and the horn case with a soft cloth and replaced them carefully in the cupboard.

My father didn't talk a lot. It made me feel special that he had taken that much time to speak to me about his horn. I would have to wait to see what he kept in the box till he was ready to show me. Dad's word was the last one — always; we didn't dare cross him.

※

Dear God iv

I'm not eight years old anymore. I'm nineteen and I'm in college. I move Dad's horn case out of the way, put both hands around the box, pull it down, and set it on the workbench. I wonder: Am I old enough now? Do I need his permission?

With one hand on each side of the top, it lifts smoothly up and off. The first thing I see is the bright red, black, and white of a Nazi flag. My mouth fills with saliva like it does when you're about to throw up. I breathe in slowly a couple of times to quiet the nausea. Under the carefully folded flag lies a small pile of Nazi coins. Next, Dad's discharge papers, some ribbons, and medals: campaign medals, a sharpshooter medal, U.S. Army Corp of Engineers, and more. Under all of this, a stack of pictures—a dozen or so black and white Kodak pictures of naked bodies lying on flatbed trucks. I squeeze my eyes a couple of times to clear them so I can see. The last one is of a gate with an iron banner that reads, "Arbeit Macht Frei." I recognize it as the gate of Auschwitz, the notorious internment camp in Poland.

Beneath that pile of horror, in a small dark green box, sits a Bronze Star.

※

I don't feel old enough. I want to be a little girl again. I want him to tell me I couldn't know the contents. I don't want to know that he picked up a

Nazi flag from a real concentration camp. I don't want to know that he saw bodies, once live people, piled one on top of another in a grotesque sculpture. I knew Dad had been in the war, but this was tangible, personal evidence: a sharpshooter medal—meant he shot a gun—a flag and coins that Nazis once touched. What did that mean? Everything looks cloudy again. I blink to clear my eyes then replace the contents exactly as they had been. I don't want to touch the pictures, but I have no choice. I hold my breath as if that might erase the images from my memory. It doesn't. I return the box to the shelf behind his horn. In a gesture reminiscent of my father, I take it out again and wipe it off carefully, just like he had done all those years ago. I "close the lights" as he would say and climb the stairs to the kitchen.

Back upstairs, Dad is already in bed. Mom is in our tiny living room, semi-reclined on the Victorian sofa she loves so much. I ask her how he is feeling and then tell her I opened the box.

"Why does he have those pictures?" She doesn't act surprised at my discovery.

"Your father was one of the first American troops into Auschwitz," she says, "after Russia liberated the camp. Eisenhower directed American G.I.s to take pictures, so he did. The General thought the world should know what really happened — to never forget."

I think to myself, *Well, it worked. I know one person who will never forget. Make that two, Dad—and me for sure.*

"I'm so tired — we can talk tomorrow."

"Okay. Goodnight, Mom." I go to my bedroom, lie down, and try to sleep.

But my memories are spinning, resisting sleep. I think of the night I babysat for a family down the street and was terrorized by loud banging noises erupting around the house. Panicked, I called Dad. He was at the front door within minutes, baseball bat in his hand and one of my mischievous friends in the other. I think about the ski trip when I couldn't drive, and Dad took over.

I remember him trying to play his horn with a lost lip. And the image of the box in the cellar with its grotesque contents is now indelibly etched into my brain.

Mom and Dad are asleep in their room, Dad with his damaged head in bandages, but sleeping peacefully. I hope.

I close my eyes and try to think of nothing.

LAURA GLAVES

THE PRICE WAS TOO HIGH

I awoke this morning
with my heart breaking for you,
my father.

I understand it all now:
your pain concealed beneath
your silence,
your wine,
your cloud of cigarette smoke.

My mind rolls back
to the fall of 41
when boys were groomed
to fight a world war.

Four years in the jungle,
hot streams of sweat
pour under camouflage,
while plotting and running,
while shooting and hiding.

The stench of blood
and dismembered bodies
defy reason.

Flames ravage fields and villages,
day after day,
an unfathomable hell.

Comrades arrive,
survive or die.
They were brave and stoic
or maybe they were just pretending.

You return home in 45
to relief and cheers,
to hugs and tears.

You return to a town
once known, now foreign
in its disquieting peace.

Malaria strikes like an intruder
from a mosquito-filled jungle.
Your rigors rattle the headboard
against the bedroom wall.

A feverish sweat streams down your face
like the tears you never cried.

Now the year is 77.
I'm 12 years old.
You've been home for 32 years.

I ask about the war.
You respond with a blank stare.
Mom answers on your behalf.
She describes snipers in trees,
with loaded rifles ready to fire.

Then she tells of swarms of flies,
too thick to remove
from your pineapple and Spam,
so you ate them.

ADULT CHILDREN: Laura Glaves

Enough stories for a curious child
with a watchful eye.

I discover a drawer filled with
photos of Japanese soldiers
and of New Guinea natives
with saggy breasts.

I know all your hiding places
for those tall green bottles
you call your medicine.

I spy on you
from behind cracked doors
and watch you transform
into someone
I no longer recognize.

You mutter piercing epithets
under your breath
at imaginary foes.

My security crumbled
with every staggered step you took
and with every thunderous fall,
a pool of blood formed
on the green kitchen floor.

Your glassy eyes
failed to see me.
Your vacant stares
bore holes through me.

Your trauma
became my trauma
as our silence and secrets
sickened our souls.

We won the war
and saved the world
from tyranny,
but in a daughter's eyes,
the price was too high.

The price was too high.

MELVIN STERNE

THE REST OF THE STORY

My father was a *jack-of-all-trades-and-master-of-none*. A man who could get things done. It didn't much matter what. Carpentry. Roofing. Cement. Pipe. He could run wire and lay bricks or tile or carpet. He did welding. He could push a dozer or fly a crane. I've seen him pick apples, flip burgers, dig ditches, cut grass, milk goats, tend bar, and sell encyclopedias door-to-door. But he was most himself when whatever the job was, it was *his* job. No forms to fill out, no hoops to jump. A project to finish with a fat payday.

He wasn't big and he wasn't good-looking. He was wiry and strong. Sinewy is a good word for it. Scraggly, they say out west. But he carried himself bigger than he looked, and people noticed. Some liked it. Some didn't. He was careless with his hair and about shaving. He wouldn't dress up. He'd say, "I'm a Levi's-and-T-shirt kind of a guy." But he could talk. He meant what he said, and said what he meant. That confidence got him work.

But his schemes—no matter how good they looked on paper—never paid out like they should. It wasn't for lack of trying. He was up before dawn and home after midnight. Most of the year I didn't see dad except Sunday afternoons. In retrospect, I wonder about that. There was always something. A blown gizmo. A truck repair. A medical bill. A fire. A flood. Taxes. Insurance due. One of those "god-dammits" people complain about. *Life's a bitch and then you die. I'm gone go get a beer.*

Summertime, when I was out of school, if he was into one of those gigs, I might go with him, helping out the best I could, and watching in wonder when he did things that I thought couldn't be done. Like the afternoon in New Mexico I watched my father lever a thousand-pound cottonwood stump up a makeshift ramp and into the back of his pickup truck. My father might have weighed one-fifty.

My mother, God bless her, wasn't much good at taking care of me. She was depressed because she drank, and she drank because she was depressed.

Dad could take care of himself, but there were plenty of times she couldn't take care of herself, let alone me. And when that happened there were neighbors, or friends, or relatives someplace. Or else I was on my own. And when she was home and my father was home, they fought. So maybe that was why I looked forward to time alone with my dad.

And maybe my mother was on a bender that day, or maybe dad took me along for no reason at all. But she was off someplace, and dad had a job down by Las Cruces clearing a patch of land. So he took me with him, and I was glad. I was thirteen and riding in a truck to work. I wore my oldest jeans and my newest boots.

My father had rules and made sure I knew them. *Take care of your tools and they'll take care of you. Measure twice, cut once. Do it right or do it over. Work now, play later. You only got one name and one reputation, don't blow it. Take pride in your work.* He did things *by the book* and he expected me (and anybody working for him) to do the same. And he kept a schedule. Breakfast at five. Coffee at ten. Lunch at noon. But at three-thirty—without fail—it was afternoon break by the radio. At three-thirty-five Paul Harvey was on, and his program *The Rest of the Story*. Paul Harvey was like the voice of God to my father.

Nobody talked when Paul Harvey was on. It was like church. We listened in rapt reverence to that smooth, mid-American, eloquence—a voice both throaty and nasally at the same time. It was a friendly voice, but a voice of authority. You didn't argue with Paul Harvey. The old man used to say, "Paul Harvey could sell ice to Eskimos."

And I still remember the story we listened to that day, riding in the truck in the hot New Mexico sun. It was about George Westinghouse and his feud with Thomas Edison. The point of the story was that George Westinghouse gambled everything he owned that alternating current was the power of the future, and it turned out that way, and George Westinghouse got very rich for believing in himself. It was a good story. But when it was over, dad slapped the radio off with a bloody hand and said, "Bull *shit*."

My father wasn't educated, but he wasn't stupid, either. I've seen him take a pencil and sketch a blueprint on cardboard and explain the layout to an engineer—symbols and all. And he could do math. Add. Subtract. Multiply. Divide. Volume. Trigonometry. I've seen him convert degrees of angle to feet of radius all in his head. He knew the weight of brick and tile and mortar from memory. And iron. And shingles. He knew how much a good two-by-four could bear. He knew voltage and amperage, and what gauge of wire they required. Dad never finished high school.

When I asked him how he learned all that, he said, "More'n one kinda school." And maybe that was why he insisted that I earn my diploma. "College is good," he'd say. "You make more money at a air-condition desk than you will bus'in' your ass in the field."

Dad knew a little about almost everything. I credit that to reading. Anything would do. A novel. A newspaper. A sports magazine. A history book. He couldn't sit still, and if there was nothing else to do, he'd whip out a book from someplace and pick up where he left off. And maybe that's why he liked Paul Harvey so much. One day the talk was about electricity, and the next it was about the iceberg that sank the Titanic. The day after that it was Hank Aaron, or the Beatles. Andrew Jackson. A pope. A gangster. There was some of everything. Sometimes dad would listen and then talk to me more about what we'd heard. But that day, outside of Las Cruces, as we headed north towards Ruidoso and home, dad snapped off the radio and said, "Bull *shit.*" A minute later, he said, "I ever tell you about my brother?"

I knew Uncle Lenny. I'd spent a few weeks with him and Aunt Heidi back in Memphis. A couple of times. That's where dad was from. Uncle Lenny's name came up when mom was fucked-up and there was talk about me going someplace. I didn't think much of it. A tall, bald uncle. A short, fat aunt. Three annoying younger cousins: Denise, Danny, and Annie. A big house and a bad rash I got from some ivy in the woods.

We were driving with our shirts off and the windows down. It was hot, and the sun fired up the truck and burned my eyes to squinting. The rushing air felt good on my chest, my arms. We were drinking cold cans of Coors. His bloody right hand was wrapped in his T-shirt. He punched me in the shoulder with that hand. The hand was so bad he was steering and holding his beer with his left. "Big fuckin' war hero, my brother. Lost a leg in World War II. When we was growin' up, our dad meant to send us to college. He drove a truck. 'You go to college,' he'd say. 'Be somebody.' But when the war came, Lenny enlisted. Dad pitched a fit. I was maybe your age. Gas got tight, money got tight. Dad got sick and died. I hadda quit school and work. When Lenny come home, I figured he needed college more 'n me, what with his leg and all. And they had this thing—the GI Bill—that helped pay for it. I chipped in. I did what I could. My brother the war hero."

The stump crushed dad's hand. We drove to the site that morning. Dad had been hired to clear it. A strip mall, maybe, or a little subdivision. Like a lot of things he did, there was something shady about the deal. Probably didn't have the necessary permits. Or title. Something. He'd demolished an old house, a barn, some sheds. A few concrete block outbuildings. Hauled off a dozen tons of junk. He'd leveled the ground with a bulldozer. But there was this big cottonwood tree down by the river. Really big, an ancient tree. It was three, maybe four feet across at the base. Dad didn't want to take it out. He liked the tree, but for some reason, the tree had to go. So dad cut it down, sawed up the limbs, split the trunk. Sold it off for firewood. But there was still this stump with all the root tangle. It was our last day. He had already hauled the bulldozer back to the rental lot. No sense paying for the extra day, right? We were going to muscle that stump into the truck by hand.

Dad had these two guys helping—Marco and Mario. But the guys didn't show. Drunk? Arrested? Skipped town? Who knew? We'd got there early and dad fussed around "tidying up." But when it was clear that we were on our own, he'd pulled out the chainsaw and went to work on the roots. It was dirty work—and dangerous. The root mass spit gravel and sawdust, and every time he hit a rock the chainsaw bucked on him. It put him in a bad mood. There was no talking to him when he got like that. Let him work it off. And he cut most of the morning, and I raked the mess up and shoveled it into the truck, and then we drove to the dump and threw it all out. That was the root tangle, but what to do with the stump?

The old man spied a stack of pallets. They were pretty busted up and mostly useless, but he sorted out four that weren't too bad, and we loaded them into the truck and drove back to the site. We stacked two pallets near the stump and broke two up, and the old man used the boards to make a kind of ramp. And then the two of us levered and rolled that old stump up the ramp and onto the pallets. That got the stump up about a third of the height of the truck bed.

We took lunch and the old man eyed the thing for a while. Then we got shovels and dug a trench deep enough to drop the truck another foot when he backed into it, but not so deep that we couldn't drive out. And it would help hold the truck still, the old man said. And he backed the truck into the trench and we took another break.

It was hot and the old man was pissed at Marco and Mario. He was more pissed that he hadn't bought beer on the way back from the dump. I was thirteen and feeling the glory of aching muscles and dirt and sweat. We sat on the pallets with our backs against the stump, and there wasn't any shade, and the truck door was open and the radio was on, and there was this song, "Mammas, Don't Let Your Babies Grow Up to Be Cowboys" by Willie Nelson and Waylon Jennings. It was all the rage right then. And when the song was over dad went down by the river to take a piss, and he was gone a while. When he came back he was sweating, and he wiped his face on an old red mechanics rag he hung off his back pocket.

It hadn't been too bad rolling the stump up the ramp. The two of us levered together in tandem. Then I braced and held while the old man changed his angle, and he braced and held while I changed mine, and then we'd muscle the stump up a few more inches. And we worked it like that all the way onto the pallet. But now things got dicey. The ramp now ran from the pallet to the truck, not from the ground to the pallet. The ground was stable, but the pallets were rickety as hell, and the truck—with its springs—wasn't much better. We nailed the pallets together, and the ramp, but the stump weighed so much it felt like it might break through or tip over. And we couldn't stand on the pallets. We had to work from the side, and that made it harder to push. And the angle was steeper, and the stump wasn't all round. It had flat spots, and one side was bigger than the other, so it wouldn't roll straight.

Twice we got the stump almost in, only to have it slide back on us. The first time it nearly pinned me to the pallet. That would have been bad. The second time it almost slid off. How dad held it I'll never know. After that he went around to the toolbox and found the tire jack, but it was busted and he cussed and threw it away and looked up at the sun for a while. Then he took a scrap of two-by-four and sawed a couple of wedges. We'd heft the stump up the ramp a few inches and catch it with a wedge to keep it from rocking back. And it was going pretty good until the old man went to wedge the stump and missed, and the whole thing rolled over his hand and slid all the way back to the pallet. I swear I heard bones crunch. The old man got quiet. He looked at his hand for a minute and said, "Come 'ere."

We changed sides then. He went around where I'd been—on the right—and took the lever on his left shoulder and we started again. I had the only wedge. Dad only had one good hand. But he put his shoulder to that stump and got his legs under him, and we got the stump to the tailgate and rammed it in.

When it was done the old man wiped his face again and said, "That was a bitch." We threw the pallets and boards into the truck. Dad peeled off his shirt and wrapped his bloody hand with it and then we drove off. Dad found a truck stop and bought a twelve-pack of Coors and a bottle of aspirin. I had to open them for him, and after he took a slug dad pointed at the beer and said, "Take one."

I said, "I'm thirteen."

He said, "You did a man's fuckin' job. Have a man's fuckin' drink."

That was the first beer I ever drank. And on the way home, we listened to Paul Harvey and dad said, "I ever tell you about my brother? My brother," he said, "got his leg blowed off someplace in Africa. Tunisia I think it was. He was a captain in the army. The Germans counter-attacked, and there were some tanks. They were in a bad fix. He told his men to fall back, but he stayed behind and took out one of the tanks by himself. When The men saw what he was up to, they came back for him. And when they came back, some of the other men from some of the other units stood their ground, too. So instead of retreating, they stayed and fought. They stopped the Germans. My brother came home a hero.

"So he went to college, and I came out west to work. I sent money when I could. But there was more men than work after the war. And everybody wanted to put the veterans to work, and I hadn't been in the army. It wasn't easy getting by. And I tell you something, son. You can believe whatever you want, but that don't make it so. *Belief* never made nobody rich. Paul Harvey got that one flat-out wrong."

A few days later, one of those "god-dammits" came along. The old man never got the money he was owed for that job. I don't know what happened. It was like that. He left for some job in California, and shortly after that he was out of work and in the hospital, his hand infected, calling home for money to pay the bill. My mother drove me to Albuquerque and put me on a plane to Memphis, and I lived the next five years with Uncle Lenny. I never saw my father again.

I thought my mother was going to California to tend to dad, but it didn't happen like that. I guess there was some man or another, and she figured she's give it a go with him, and when that didn't work out, she shot herself. Or he shot her, one. And my old man never came back either, though there were some letters, and few phone calls the odd holiday or birthday.

Uncle Lenny wasn't so bad. He was personnel director for a Memphis bank. He and Aunt Heidi had a big split-level house. And my cousins were nicer to me than I remembered—especially after word came about my mother. Denise had her own room. Danny and Annie were still little enough to share a room. But when I moved in, Denise and Annie took one room, and Danny and I took the other. Bunk beds.

It's no fun being the cowbird in the nest. The older, adopted brother. I always felt different and in-the-way. And Memphis never felt like home. But Uncle Lenny and Aunt Heidi were fair to me. They encouraged me to do well in school, and asked me questions about college. What did I like? What did I want to be?

Right up until the day I heard the bones break in my father's hand, I wanted to be just like him. But grunting a thousand-pound hunk of wood up make-shift ramp scared the shit out of me. I loved my father, but suddenly I didn't want to be like him. I wondered, what else was there?

Uncle Lenny was tall and soft all over. Not fat, just flabby and soft. He had an office. It was air conditioned. I saw it. He wore suits to work. He drove a Lincoln. He walked with a limp. You could tell he missed the leg below the right knee. He never talked about it.

One day, my junior year in high school, Uncle Lenny took me to work with him. It was Family Day at the bank. He introduced me to everybody and showed me around. There was a banquet lunch at this swanky restaurant, and the bank president came by our table and shook my hand. Riding home that afternoon, Uncle Lenny switched the radio on. Paul Harvey. I hadn't listened to Paul Harvey in years.

The story was about an inmate on death row, but really it was about a Broadway musical, *Annie*, that was all the rage. More specifically, it was about a dog. The dog had been in the pound, about to be put to sleep, when he was rescued to perform in the play. Of course, Paul Harvey didn't tell us that the "inmate" on "death row" was a dog. That was the "rest of the story." But it was a good story. I asked Uncle Lenny, "How come you never talk about my father?"

Lenny shrugged. "What do you want to know?"

"What did he want to do when he was a boy?"

Uncle Lenny looked at me for a long time, then said, "What did your father tell you about growing up?"

"He never talked about it," I said. "He said your dad wanted you both to go to college, but you joined the army and lost your leg. And because grandpa died, there wasn't enough money for dad to go to college, so he went out west to work."

Uncle Lenny's eyes got big. "He said *what*?"

I repeated the story.

Uncle Lenny chewed his lip and stared hard at me. Finally he said, "*I* wasn't a war hero. Your *dad* was. And your grandfather didn't die until long after the war. And I had the GI Bill. College didn't cost much."

"But . . . how did you lose your leg?"

"How did your dad say I lost my leg?"

"In the war. Tunisia."

"I never went to Tunisia. I lost my leg at Alconbury, outside of London. I was a warehouse tech. I was driving a forklift and it tipped over on me. Your father was the war hero."

"Dad?"

"Yes. Your father."

"I knew he was in Korea, but I didn't know he was no hero. He told me he was a mechanic."

"And he was," Uncle Lenny said. "And a good one. But when the North attacked, every man who could carry a rifle was on the line—including your father. He was in Pusan where they stopped the North Korean attack. He got a medal. Your father is the hero."

"But what about college?" I said. "What about your father dying? Dad told me he quit school to work. He said he sent money to help you go to college."

Uncle Lenny shook his head. "Your dad couldn't go to college. He went to jail for stealing a car. That's why he never finished high school. There was plenty of money to send him." Uncle Lenny sighed. "Your dad was a great kid to grow up with. Full of energy. A big ball of fun. Non-stop. That was your dad. We used to play football, baseball, ride our bikes, go hike in the woods. We'd fish some. Swim. But after I joined the service, something changed in him. I don't know what it was. Maybe it was his friends—the company he kept. He couldn't stay out of trouble. Even after I came home. *Especially* after I came home.

"Your dad went to prison in 1948. He shot a man. Didn't kill him, but the judge had had enough. And dad—our dad, your grandpa—begged the judge to lock him up. Maybe he thought jail would do your dad some good. But hearing that pissed your dad off. A year later they paroled your father on the condition that he join the army. That's how he got to Korea. Your grandfather died while your dad was overseas. There was an inheritance. Your dad could have gone to college someplace. He could have done something. But he took his money to the racetrack. He thought he could be a bigshot. And you know what? For a while, he was. A big ball of fun. And maybe that was the problem. All that money. But there's more than one thing you can get addicted to. Success. Women. Drugs. Thrills. Your dad made some money, but this isn't Vegas. This is Tennessee, and that kind of stuff isn't legal here. People don't like it. Eventually, it caught up to him. Your dad left Tennessee because if they'd put him in prison a third time, he might never have got out."

We turned off the main road and onto the lane where we lived. Uncle Lenny pulled over before we got to the house. He lowered his voice. "Your dad ever talk to you about drugs?"

"No."

He nodded and shut his eyes. "He drank in high school. That wasn't so bad, lots of kids drink in high school. But later on, in the army maybe, or just after, it was amphetamines. Speed. Maybe some dope, too. That was the second time your dad went to prison. Your father could have done a lot of things. Hell, he could have done *anything*. He was smart. Except for one thing. He had this problem." Lenny shrugged. "That's why your dad went west. Didn't hear from him until you were born. Didn't even know he was married. He never saw your grandfather again. Wouldn't talk to him on the phone. For a few years there, I thought your dad had cleaned up. He said he did, but I guess he didn't." Uncle Lenny pulled out and drove us home.

I didn't know much about drugs back then, but I learned soon enough. I graduated from high school and joined the Peace Corps. No army for me, but I spent two years in the Sudan.

While I was gone, I got word that they'd found my father dead of an overdose. Looking back, I realized that even when we were together, there was always a distance between us. He had a way of disappearing. An errand. A piss break. Something. He'd go away mad and come back jumping.

When I came home, Uncle Lenny met me at the airport. That night, over dinner, he told me that when I figured out what I wanted to do, he'd pay for me to go to college.

"You'd send me to college?" I said. "Why?"

He said, "Why wouldn't I? My father—your grandfather—he'd have sent your dad to college if he'd ever come clean. I'd have sent him, if he'd asked. But he never did. I'll send you, if you want." He looked at me with something like hope in his eyes. "If you will."

Today I work in pharmaceuticals. My degree is in chemistry, but my job is a salesman. Most of my customers are farmers and the drugs I peddle are for chickens and cows and pigs. And dad was right. I make more money behind a desk than I could ever make in the trades. A lot more—though money isn't everything.

I often wonder about my father. I can understand why a man might not own up to being in prison, or doing drugs, but why would a man not confess to being a hero? But maybe he wasn't. I haven't seen any write-ups. He didn't leave a medal behind. There were no pictures.

Or maybe he wasn't the hero. Maybe dad knew what was up with my mother and this other man. Maybe he lied about the money he said he didn't get. Maybe he wasted it on drugs or some other scam. Or maybe *she* got it and didn't tell him. Maybe he knew that it was the end of the line for our family. Maybe that war hero business was his way of telling me that things were going to be okay with Uncle Lenny. Maybe that was his way of sending me off, or of letting me go.

Or maybe the whole thing was Uncle Lenny's way of helping me feel less bad about my dad. Maybe Lenny really *was* the war hero. I don't know. What's it take to be a hero? To roll a thousand-pound stump up a makeshift ramp? Or to plod to a dull job every day to support a family with dignity?

I suppose I could write the army and somebody would know. But then again, think about some conversation you had. A conversation with someone you love. How much can you really remember? You talk all day and remember fifty words. And what will that conversation look like five years from now? Or ten? Or twenty? Are our family histories reliable?

At the end of that day, long ago in New Mexico, I looked in the mirror and saw the sweat, the grime, the blood-smudge on my shoulder where my father punched me with his bloody hand. I think I knew then that I didn't want to be my father—even in the moment that I best remember being with him. And I feel both good and guilty about that. My father's blood pumps in my veins. His DNA drives my cells. His words ring in my ear. *Measure twice, cut once. Do it right or do it over. Work first, play later. You only have one name and one reputation, so don't blow it. Take pride in your work.* My father's words got me through college the same way they got him through whatever impossible job lay before him. I owe my father for that. The same as I owe

Uncle Lenny for his kindness and generosity.

I am and I am not my father. My father doesn't have to be a hero for me to love him. I can love him for what he was—a small man who could roll a thousand-pound stump up a makeshift ramp. A man who knew a little bit about almost everything. A big ball of fun. And I recognize in him what I don't want to be, either. An addict. A dealer. A gambler. A thief.

I still remember that story about George Westinghouse. Funny how my father and I both listened to it and came away with different conclusions. It wasn't bullshit. Paul Harvey was right. At the end of the day, we are what we make of ourselves. We get to choose what we have faith in—which dreams to believe. If you ask for miracles, act like you expect them to happen. And maybe that one small thing is, in itself, what separates me from my father; the thing that allows me to succeed, and the thing that, missing, condemned my father to failure.

My mother died in 1978. My father died in 1985. Paul Harvey died in 2009. Uncle Lenny in 2010, and Aunt Heidi in 2015. Today I have two kids with college degrees. And if my grandkids want to go, there'll be money for them, too. *And now you know the rest of the story.*

LAURENCE SNYDAL

DADDY

These big blunt men, my uncles, now
They offer food and drink. They tell
Me stories of my dad, how well
He lived, the songs he sang and how
He sang them. He braked trains. He wore
A banker's vest and chain. He taught.
He was a businessman and bought
Good wool from crafty farmers. More,
They thought him Jewish. He was dark
And people called him Siggy though
His name was Sigurdur. I know
Him as a photo, as a mark
Left on my face and life. He died
When I was three, too young to love
This man my uncles tell me of.
I don't remember if I cried.

MY FATHER'S MANTEL CLOCK

Electric circles, no analog tics,
Gothic brass hands within a walnut case,
Snug in its niche above the fireplace,
Cycling an ancient system based on six.

He won this clock in 1929.
He died before I knew him. Now at times
I hear him speaking in between my rhymes,
And can't distinguish his low voice from mine.

He died of cancer, 1942,
And all I know of him is what I've heard.
Did he give me a hug, a whispered word?
I have no memories I know are true.

I have the walnut clock won by my dad
And 40 years of time he never had.

MARK TARALLO

FOUR FATHERS

I.

Ralph got drunk, alone, the night before his father's heart surgery. The next morning his car wouldn't start. He lifted the hood, a pointless exercise, and stared at the engine through the fog of his hangover, thinking of his father.

His friend Tim gave him a lift to the hospital. Tim was in-between jobs, and had a lot of time on his hands. When they entered Hackensack Hospital, the smell of it—sharp, sterile, auguring pain—turned Ralph's already churning stomach. He found a floor diagram; it hurt his head just to look at it. Still, he tried, and puzzled over it with Tim standing behind him.

A voice came, familiar.

"Ralph! We're over here! Hello Tim!"

Down the empty corridor, he saw his mother's wave: hand fluttering, palm down, like the wing of a seagull.

"Hi Ma. Any word?" Ralph said when they joined her.

"They said he should be out at about one, so he'll probably be in there for another hour," she said. She was thin and slightly stooped, but her voice was loud. She wore bright clothing. Again, Ralph regretted his hangover.

"They have to do three bypasses, you know, so it takes awhile," she said. "But the good news is, he got Streeka."

"Who?"

"We found out late last night," she said. "Dr. Almo was supposed to do the surgery, but we wanted Streeka. He's the expert—he did Arthur Ashe, the tennis player, Arthur Ashe—but we were too embarrassed to say it. So of course your father blames it on me. He says to Streeka yesterday, he says, 'Ya know, Dr. Streeka, my wife will be disappointed . . . she's heard so much about your reputation.'

"So Streeka just says, 'we'll talk.' So last night I was just about to leave the room and Streeka calls, and he says—he's all business, that Streeka, all business—he says, 'Yes, I spoke with Dr. Almo. I will be performing the operation tomorrow at 8 a.m.'"

"That's good, Ma," Ralph said. "He must be the best they have. He's the guy from New York, right?"

"Oh sure, Columbia Presbyterian, very well-known," she said. She looked at Tim and smiled. "Did you guys eat lunch yet? There's a cafeteria downstairs. Why don't you go down there for a sandwich?"

She started rummaging aggressively through her purse.

"No, Ma, I got money," Ralph said. "Tim, c'mon. Let me buy you lunch. Least I can do, for the ride."

"The cafeteria is lovely," Mrs. Stallo said. She ran both hands along an imaginary display. "Buffet style, you know, with all the food out. You can take whatever you want."

"I'll meet you in a bit in the waiting room," Ralph said to her. "Anyway, Ma, how are you doing?"

"Me?" she said, surprised. "Oh, yeah, I'm okay. I have a good feeling about this. He went in with a good attitude. He knew he hadda have it done."

She touched her forefinger to the side of her head and nodded. "Your frame of mind is very important with things like this. What you think is gonna happen."

II.

"Has your dad had heart problems before?" Tim asked. He slipped a pointed straw into a small carton of apple juice.

"Nothing major," Ralph said. He put down his sandwich and looked at the blank cafeteria wall. "I mean, not that I know of. He didn't talk too much about that stuff. And I'm not home that much these days. I probably should visit more."

Tim didn't respond. Ralph felt obliged to continue.

"It's like, we get along fine, we just weren't that tight for some reason when I was growing up. I had nothing against him. That's just the way it was," Ralph said.

"At least you had nothing against him," Tim said. "My dad's given me a lot to be against."

"Yeah, you told me about some of that. Some bad scenes when you were young, right?" Ralph looked at Tim with expectant eyes, trying to silently coax his friend into a story that would veer the conversation away from his own father.

"It's hard to get past them because some are still so clear in my head," Tim said. "I might have told you about the time I left home and hitchhiked for a month?"

"I'm not sure," Ralph said.

"I can still remember, it's totally clear, the day I got back," Tim said. "I had gotten tired of hitchhiking and called my folks and apologized, and my dad wired me money to fly back home. He met me at the airport, totally stone-faced, no hug, no nothing. And then total silence in the car driving home. Not one word to me, for an hour. Total silence."

Ralph nodded, eyes fixed.

"We get home, step into the house," Tim said, "and then he grabs me by the back of my collar and drags me into my room. Still not saying a word.

"When we get in my room, he gives me a hard push and then lets go, and I stumble forward a few steps. So I start to turn around and it's like, everything's happening in slow motion now. So I finish turning around, and I see that he has his fist cocked back to hit me."

Tim paused, his large fist cocked back like his father's.

"Now, I expected to see that—I knew he wanted to hit me—but the thing that totally surprised me was his face. It was beet red, man, like fire engine red, like the face of a maniac. Like he really wanted to kill me. I saw that, and I totally froze."

"Now, when I was sixteen I was about as big as I am now, so we were both about the same size and probably about equal in strength back then. Maybe he was a little stronger, but I was pretty close."

Tim started speaking faster, arms and hands illustrating the action.

"So he throws the punch, but it wasn't a direct hit. It grazed the side of my face, and that broke me out of my shock, and we start wrestling, and I got him in a headlock. Now I had his head locked tight with my left arm, and I coulda started beatin' on him with my right. I mean, I had clear shots at his face. But I was like, 'this is my dad, man, I can't hit my dad.' So I let him go, and I just stand there, like it was all over.

"He hits me with a quick right cross, which knocks me back on my bed. It was a really clean shot, and for a few seconds I was just seeing stars, I mean, like, literally—they were blue and yellow and they were spinning around."

Tim looked down at his tray, then continued, his voice lower. "So the stars stop spinning and go away, and I can see my dad standing there in the doorway. I mean, in my head I can totally still see him right there, just standing there, breathing hard, still fire red, looking down at me. And then he says, in this really hateful voice, 'I'm embarrassed to death to have to hit my own kid.'"

"Jesus," Ralph said.

Tim stared at his tray. No one spoke for a few seconds.

"That's rough, man," Ralph said quietly. "How is it now?"

"Well, it's not as bad as that anymore, but, I still sometimes have these, like, fear flashbacks when I'm with my dad." He leaned back in his seat, as if trying to extricate himself from certain feelings. "I decided to bring it up last Thanksgiving. He's getting up there now, he's almost seventy, so I figured I'd better try. I don't know how much longer he'll be around."

Ralph felt his stomach twinge.

"How'd it go?" Ralph said.

"I had it planned out," Tim said. "I knew what chair I wanted him to sit in, because I felt more comfortable with him in the corner. So one day I was visiting and I said to him, 'hey, why don't you sit in this chair, I want to tell you something.' He knew something was up, but he didn't know what.

"So I said, 'Listen, I want to talk to you about the problems you caused me in the past because you were so big on authority. I'm not trying to get you back, but I'm trying to get past this cause it still causes me problems. I think you owe me an apology.'"

"What'd he say?"

Tim looked down again, his voice barely audible.

"I was ashamed of myself, man. I broke down." He looked up at Ralph and his face showed self-contempt. "I mean, the last thing I wanted to do was cry in front of my dad."

"Yeah, but . . ."

"Ahhh, it's . . . whatever. No use talking about it. So anyway, this operation, it's pretty standard, right?"

It took Ralph a second to shift.

"Yeah, I mean, I guess there's always risk with a heart bypass, but they told him there's a ninety-seven percent success rate," Ralph said.

"That's pretty good," Tim said. He shifted in his chair, chuckled. "I don't know, I guess my problem is, in situations like this, my mind always gets fixed on the three percent."

III.

They finished lunch, and then Tim left the hospital. Ralph went upstairs and tried to find the right waiting room.

He wandered through the second floor, dazed. Each hallway looked the same. His mind kept coming back to Tim and Tim's father—both the fight and Tim's attempt to talk things over, years after the fact. Both events were so unlike anything Ralph ever experienced with his own father. Dramatic, like scenes from a movie.

Ralph tried to think of how it had been with his own father. In truth, there didn't seem that much to think about. What was it supposed to be like? How were you supposed to feel about your father?

He thought about another friend, Glenn, a grad school dropout who moved back in with his parents, and Glenn's father, a food labeling consultant named Norman Knopf. Glenn called him "Big Norm." Glenn always had a different comment every time Ralph dropped him off at his house. "I'd invite you in," Glenn might say, "but Big Norm may be in his skivvies. I'd hate to subject you to that." Once, when Glenn's father was chatting with an attractive neighbor: "Look out—Big Norm's making his move," Glenn said.

Ralph used to wonder if Glenn called his father that to his face, until one night Glenn finally invited him in. His father, in boxers and an A-frame undershirt, was drinking a beer.

"Big Norm, drinking a brewski!" Glenn said. "I want to party with you, cowboy." His father did not seem annoyed at this; he smiled and he and Glenn exchanged glances, as if they shared a secret.

Ralph saw a blue sign, CARDIAC OPERATIONS WAITING AREA, hanging over a doorway on the right. Inside, his mother sat at the end of a couch, inspecting the backs of her hands.

Across the room, a younger woman sat silently. She looked serious, with square eyeglasses and long, straight, unstyled auburn hair. The room offered no comfort whatsoever: boxy chairs and hard couches lined the perimeter. A small television with the volume turned off hung tilted from the ceiling, like a flashing eye.

"Hi Ma."

Startled, Mrs. Stallo looked up. "Oh hi! How was lunch? Did you guys get a sandwich?"

"Yeah. Tim just left, he had to go."

The woman in the back stood up. "Let me get that out of the way for you," she said, walking toward her coat, which lay on the couch. "I was sitting there before but I moved to see the television. My father is not supposed to come out before one, so I thought it would help me fill up the time. But nothing's on."

"Yes, sure. My husband comes out at one also," Mrs. Stallo said. "From a triple heart bypass," she added.

The woman looked at Mrs. Stallo for a few seconds without speaking.

"Did he go in at eight?" the woman said.

"Yes, that's right. 8 a.m."

"With Dr. Streeka?" the woman asked.

"Yes, that's right, with Dr. Streeka," said Mrs. Stallo, brightening at the familiar name. "How about your . . . father?"

"At eight also, with Dr. Almo," she said. "I think Streeka switched from my father to do your husband." She paused. "Is your husband having open heart surgery?"

"Oh, no no, it's a triple bypass, but not open heart. They said the heart was okay, but the valves were clogged," she said. "They have to bypass all the valves. How about your father?"

"He's having open-heart. He had a major heart attack, and there was major heart damage. They told him he's lucky to be alive." She paused. "The success rate isn't as high as I'd like it to be. There's always more risk involved when they open the heart."

"Oh, sure," Mrs. Stallo said. "With my husband they told us the success rate is ninety-seven percent, because there wasn't heart damage. Ninety-seven percent," she repeated crisply, nodding.

She suddenly realized this was the wrong thing to say. "But I think all the doctors here are just terrific, so I'm sure your father is in good hands," she said.

The woman sighed. "I hope," she said. "They told my father it was fifty-fifty." She looked away, lowered her voice. "You would think Streeka would do my dad, since he's in worse shape, but oh well."

Above on the soundless television were unreal-looking soap opera actors and actresses, with faces running through litanies of emotions.

"Ma, do you know what time it is?" Ralph said softly.

"Twelve thirty."

"I'm think I'm gonna take a walk. I'll be back soon."

"I'll walk with you to the fountain," she said. "I need a drink."

When they were a few steps past the doorway, Mrs. Stallo turned to Ralph and said in an animated whisper, "Did you hear what that woman said? Streeka switched from her father! He didn't tell us that!" Her expression was wide-eyed and questioning, as if she had glimpsed something dark and shadowy. "She must have been mad when she heard that. Ohhhhh, I bet she was mad."

"Well I'm sure Almo's good too," Ralph said. "They must have some reason for switching."

"Isn't that something?" she said. Her voice held an appreciation for mystery. "You can never figure out these doctors. Why they do things."

IV.

In the hallway, Ralph's mother stopped at the fountain. Ralph kept walking.

His mind kept returning to his father. Almost always, they got along. He could say that to others and it wasn't a lie. But it wasn't right to think that here. Not with his father under the knife. This place deserved the truth. No half-truths.

What was it really like? General admiration for his father as a child. (There had been that, right? Ralph thought to himself. It was hard to remember. The memories were watery, weak.)

Minor resentment of his father as a teenager, thinking he was a drag, but no serious rebellion, just offering as little information about his life as possible.

Away at college, obligatory weekly calls: his father eager to talk, devouring any news Ralph gave him, but Ralph still in the teenage stance of withholding, giving him the bare minimum, just the surface details of his life.

And now, at thirty-one, not much had changed, except the calls were less frequent, less regular.

But what was it really like?

A growing feeling of overwhelming difference. I'm his son, there is some resemblance and I picked up some of his mannerisms, but that's all, Ralph thought. We're very different inside. So distance is inevitable. We get along and I have nothing against him, except possibly the fact that I picked up some of his weaknesses, his character deficiencies. But that wasn't intentional and I can't resent him for that. I shouldn't resent him for that. But it's just not within myself to make a stronger connection. There would have to be more in common for that. It doesn't feel right. And that's just the way it turned out. It is what it is.

Strange that I'm his son, Ralph thought. The strangeness was like a cruel joke someone played on them both, to take two people so different and bind them by blood. So neither could feel comfortable. Like being handcuffed to a stranger.

When Ralph returned to the waiting room and sat down, his mother gave a quick hi, then continued listening to the woman wearing square glasses.

"I mean," the woman said, "this is a man whose father dropped dead of a heart attack and he still smokes, gets no exercise, and eats all kinds of fatty, greasy foods." Her voice was looser now, more intimate, with a controlled exasperation. It didn't quite match her appearance.

"And it's like talking to a wall when you try to tell him," the woman said. "And he absolutely despises doctors. They practically had to drag him to the hospital when he had the heart attack. He hasn't had a check-up in forty years."

"Mmmmmm," Mrs. Stallo said sympathetically. "He must be very strong, to live that kind of lifestyle and survive a heart attack. Very strong."

"Yeah, they said to me, 'It could be worse. It could be a heart transplant.' Hah!" she laughed high and ironic, "that's pretty bad, if that's the only thing it's worse than."

Ralph watched her as she shook her head slowly, the trace of a rueful smile on her face. His heart, spilling with waiting-room feeling, started to fix on her. Framed by her unstyled hair, her face was handsome, and behind her square glasses her eyes shone with perception. Her ring finger was bare. She wore plain jeans and a plain gray sweatshirt. Confident enough to ignore fashion, Ralph thought: reflects strength of character. A very noble woman.

He noticed that her jeans, some generic brand which looked a little cheap, were just tight enough to suggest firm thighs and a narrow waist. His arousal translated quickly into guilt, which was in turn eclipsed by a strong and admiring affection. He tried to imagine himself comforting her, stroking her hair as her head rested on his shoulder. This seemed outside the bounds of realism, even in a dream. Sitting side by side, lightly holding hands but with a few inches of space between them—that seemed more credible.

The woman sighed. "Well, I'm glad he got this far," she said to Mrs. Stallo. "It's almost one o'clock. No news is good news. I don't want to see Almo coming in here telling me that he died on the table."

Mrs. Stallo nodded. "It's a good sign," she said.

The words "almost one o'clock" and "died on the table" sank like rocks in Ralph's stomach. He felt afraid, and the banality of room itself—the ugly functional furniture, the television looking down, the sickening sterile smell—became more oppressive.

He struggled up from his seat.

"Ma, I'm gonna get another drink," he said, and shuffled out of the room.

V.

Ralph got a long drink from the fountain in the hall and then went to the men's room. From the stall he heard two men talking at the sinks.

"What's the word, bird?"

"Rough shift, my man. Right rough. Lotta clean-ups. Some nasty-ass fucked up a toilet."

"Dang! Dag nasty."

"Probably that dude in 713. The squeaky wheelchair."

"Oh man. He's one mean mother. He cursed me out the other day."

"All I know is, that fucker better die, like, real soon. Know what I'm sayin?"

"Serious."

Ralph returned to the corridor, annoyed and anxious. How could they talk like that? Where's the respect? And then his mind came back to Tim's comment about the three percent and he became frightened. Now the three percent didn't seem so small, in this place where death was casually accepted.

The thought made him feel sick. In the corridor a nurse in white uniform and Reeboks passed in brisk stride, pushing a covered tray. Her crisp movements and the clattering of the small wheels heightened Ralph's disorientation but he started walking quickly after her, hoping that quick movements would make him feel more centered.

He strode through the hallway and tried not to think about his father but thoughts were racing around his head: *Tim's father shunned him, even beat him for Christ's sake, and still Tim tried to make amends with his dad. And what did you do? Tim had a huge wall to surmount, but still he tried to reach out. Compared with that you had a three-inch hurdle to get over—your own self-absorbed, self-indulgent feelings of alienation. And you couldn't even get past that.*

Ralph kept walking. The brisk nurse turned off into a room and he gained on an older couple walking slow and resigned down the middle of the hallway. Ralph shot past them, turned the corner, and kept moving, with no idea of where he was going.

The thoughts would not stop. You didn't even try. You didn't even try. You know damn well he always treated you like a prince, and all he really wanted was to be part of your life in some way. Not to dictate it but to share it, at least a part of it.

It was always about yourself.

The last thought triggered a fresh wave of the hospital smell that engulfed Ralph's senses like swamp water and made him stagger, his stomach reeling.

He stopped, took a deep breath, and started walking faster, racing through the corridors with the dread of a lost child, trying to find the waiting room. Every new turn held the unfamiliar; the blandness was menacing now.

He turned another corner, tired but not slowed, and found himself almost upon a small man who had been walking with his head down. Just before they collided, Ralph saw the sign above and past the man, on the left: CARDIAC OPERATIONS WAITING AREA.

In the waiting room his mother sat quietly.

"Any word?" Ralph said breathlessly.

"Nothing yet. Oh, did you run? You're out of breath. Where did you go? You're sweating! Do you feel OK? Do you have a temperature?"

"I'm okay," he said, sinking into a chair.

"It's a few minutes after one. I'm gettin' a little worried," she said. "I was OK until now, but now that it's after one . . . I hope he comes out soon. It was supposed to take five hours. I hope they didn't have any problems. Oh, God."

Ralph thought what he should have said—"don't worry Ma, I'm sure this is normal"—but he couldn't utter the words. He sat there hunched, head down, sweating, in a state that was something like prayer, an atheist's version of prayer.

He tried to rally some hope within himself by drawing on whatever good he could think of—Tim's desire for reconciliation with his father, the courage of the woman in the waiting room, the kindness of his mother. But this mental appeal was difficult to sustain, and he felt himself facing judgment, and asking for mercy.

VI.

After a few minutes, a voice came from the doorway.

"Stallo family? Is anyone from the . . . "

"Yes?" Mrs. Stallo rose quickly from her chair, alert. "How is he, Dr. Streeka?"

Dr. Streeka, dressed in loose green hospital shirt and pants with a white surgical mask hanging from his neck, stood with his forearms raised in front of him, elbows pointing down and fingers spread. "He's doing fine. The operation went well. We'll have to watch him carefully in the next twenty-four hours, to see if the bypasses take properly." Mrs. Stallo let out a soft "Ohhhhhh" and seemed to partially deflate; her face and shoulders sagged and for a second she became elderly. "Thank God. Can we see him?"

"Not now, but at about six tonight you may see him for a few minutes while he's in intensive care. Just so you know, he won't look good—he's been through a lot—and the visit has to be short. He probably won't be able to talk."

"Oh thank you, Dr. Streeka. Thank you so much."

"Not a problem," Dr. Streeka said, expressionless. He turned around and walked out.

"Congratulations on the good news," came a low voice from the back of the room. The woman with the square glasses was about to say something else when Dr. Almo entered, dressed the same as Dr. Streeka.

"Is anybody here from the Garzella family?"

"Yes, I'm his daughter," the woman said. She got up slowly and took a few tentative steps toward the doctor.

"We finished a few minutes ago. He's doing okay. The next twenty-four hours are critical."

"He got through it?"

"So far so good." His tone was as nonchalant as Streeka's. "It was a big operation, so he's not completely out of the woods yet. But so far, so good."

The woman blinked several times. Her eyes glistened. Dr. Almo left the room quickly, and for a few seconds there was silence.

"I guess we both made it," Mrs. Stallo said to the woman. "Or they made it. We, they—what's the difference, right?"

"Yes," the woman said, smiling through tears. "What's the difference."

VII.

There were two patients lying in the intensive care unit when Ralph and his mother were given the okay by the nurse to enter, at around 6:30 p.m.

The patient on the left looked about forty; under the thin white garment the outline of his compact, athletic figure could be seen, and he breathed evenly and peacefully, eyes closed.

Next to him, the body of Ralph's father, larger at every point than the other man and protruding at the middle. He was pale and sallow and wired up with IV tubes.

Ralph had expected to see this difficult sight, he had braced himself. But the one things he did not expect was how each breath of his father's would be so long and fitful. Each breath made his father's chest rise ominously and then, at the peak, the chest would shake hard before falling. The shaking sent tremors through his father's limbs, so that his father's arms seemed in danger of disengaging themselves from the IV tubes.

Oh Jesus, Ralph thought. Please don't die.

While Ralph stared, frozen, his mother approached the head of the bed. When his father opened his eyes, he was looking into hers. She put a light hand on his shoulder.

"You made it sweetie," she said. "You made it."

For a few seconds Ralph's father and mother looked at each other, motionless. Then his father blinked a few times and his eyes shifted to the foot of the bed, where Ralph had moved.

When their gazes met, Ralph searched his father's eyes for a few seconds. The look he found there seemed to him to be one of embarrassment, almost shame.

LOWELL JAEGER

WE'D PLANNED

to pull the blinds,
uncork champagne,
jitterbug naked
—your mother and I—
inside the empty nest.

You slammed the hatch
on your Subaru, its bursting load
of fantasies and mysteries boxed,
pillowcases stuffed
with plush bears.
Smiled, waved, honked,
and sped away. Our last,
at last
college bound.

We stood at the window
—your mother and I—
inhaling, exhaling.

She simmered a Mexican stew
later that afternoon, which
side-by-side across from your place
at the table, we sipped
with tender bewilderment,

spoon by spoon.

SOME THINGS PASS BY AND NEVER COME BACK

Late October afternoon, trees
flashing colors and leaves falling.
Need to slow your busy-ness, my sister says,
meaning one morning frames a glimpse
of yellows and reds . . . next glance,
nothing but branches gone bare.

We're sipping coffee, relaxing
on deck chairs, reminiscing.
She'd promised she'd fly out to visit
after Dad's funeral, and she's nothing
if not a woman of hard-won words.

I'm confused about Dad,
I say, meaning I can't find him in my memory,
can't picture him earlier than he faded
so quickly. Who was he before
he morphed into that stooped-over
miserable little stickman pushing a walker?

My sister frowns. *He had a good life,*
she says, meaning I wasn't around
to watch his decline. I was busy
elsewhere, and when I turned to look,
he'd already mostly passed.

We sit quiet. *It's beautiful,*
I say. *Yes,* she says, *beautiful.*
The leaves let go. They flutter downward.

Next one, next one, next.

WHO'S THAT?

She's posed like a tabloid starlet, one foot
lifted to the running board of a lustrous black Pontiac,
lips spiced with a flirty smile, an outlaw Bonnie
stepping toward the edge of infamy
as Clyde exits the bank in a firestorm
with sacks of cash, and the couple dash
into the deliciously dangerous and romantic yonder.

Instead, she marries our father, a soldier
home from combat, settles into what must have seemed
a monotonous routine—diaper bags, spit rags, heaps
of laundry, floors to sweep, never ending
cycles of meals to concoct and sinks full of pots and pans.

Who's that? my siblings and I ask, paging
through a moldering family album
of black and white scalloped edge
box camera snapshots.

She's just past teenage in the photo,
showing off for the lens. A puzzling contrast
to the woman we knew who stood back
and looked downcast when the flashbulb flashed.

MARY KAY RUMMEL

SON ET LUMIÉRE: CHARTRE

Walking the medieval city,
buildings crumbling and black,
rows of blowsy yellow roses, I feel
cracked old walls absorbing heat.

Outside the great Cathedral,
I lean back far enough to glimpse
workers scraping scaly soot
from stained glass.

Inside I study pantheons
of light and blue illusion
where the Madonna seems
to look on me with kindness.

In her window she floats in lapis lazuli
of a southern sky, while sunlight falls,
burning, like this moment, from inside out.

When my mother at eighty was dying
she asked me to be sure my father
didn't marry that woman from church
who wanted the money she'd let him save
instead of giving her the new kitchen
she longed for.

ADULT CHILDREN: Mary Kay Rummel

I'm sorry now that I laughed—knowing
it would never happen—my mother
fought against the hardest thing—
letting go, letting go
as the seas rose in her lungs.

Now I hold mother, father together
in my body and in my mind—a talisman.
Here, across a rising sea from home,
I feel closer to them. And to her.
Beside these walls I feel like a child
holding shards of history,
blessed by the sacred haloing of light
as it falls through the Madonna,
through her sea's twelfth century cobalt.

Tonight's offering, light and music
near the great Last Judgment doors.
Angel acrobats will fly across stone faces
of the saved and lost.

I'll wake in the morning,
cold, neck-sore, stiff-boned—
these things tell me the world is *here*
saying goodbye.

RETURNING

He sits beside me facing the sea,
young evangelist looking like a crow in his suit.
He follows me on the boardwalk,
I just want to tell you that god loves you.
What? Do I look so needy? Go away,
I want to say, but I once wanted to be holy.

Now my children follow
their own aureoles,
going where belief takes them.
They walked off the way fishermen
in the gospel stories turned,
leaving nets on the beach.

I am going, each announced.
I tried not giving advice.
I tried waking early to write.
Watching them grow I grew strong,
small and watchful as a lighthouse.
Their courage overcame my fear.

These days I'm letting the sea do my praying,
knowing it doesn't love me.
I love the sea in its thundering concentration,
not like the seal that slides in like oil,

but like grown children who
love a parent as separate
but still part of themselves,
the same way someone sent off
comes back to be with you,

the way last night's full moon,
leaping from mountains,
filled the Pacific with billions of stars.

MELODIE CORRIGALL

WINTER BIRDS

Maria studies her family clustered around the table, hopeful not of food but of deliverance. She is stretching her arthritic limbs towards a decision—albeit not in the direction her family anticipates—but the last few inches are excruciating and perhaps the goal is unobtainable.

A peacemaker and the core of a happy family all her life, Maria longs for a new role. But with so few years left, she wonders whether she should upset the apple cart. From her family's elated faces she realizes that inviting Mr. Walters was a mistake.

Resurrected by the arrival of the unexpected guest, the family celebrates the evening like comrades after uncertain battle—calling for drinks and remembering old songs. The guest, a usually grim farmer, savours the attention. He hasn't been treated so well since his wife's funeral two years earlier.

Anxious eyes monitor the old man closely for encouraging responses, flying gratefully to the weathered face like winter birds to scattered seeds.

Maria—mother, widow, homemaker, and this afternoon, hostess—refills empty glasses and carries in more food.

"You're a shrewd one, mother," her son teases, nodding towards their guest.

"The old coot could do with a home-cooked meal," Maria admits. And a little company she thinks.

She knows what it is to be stuck behind curtains in an empty house watching weekend visitors' cars drive by. And weekdays when even before lunch, her chores are complete. With only the motley cat to advise on the weather, she busies herself picking leaves off pampered plants and organizing meals in case one of her children visits.

"Sorry, Mom, Buddy has a baseball game."

"I have to bone up for a Monday meeting."

"Jenny's coming down with something."

"The car is acting up . . . the weather is bad . . . it's a long drive . . . sure you don't mind?"

Sunday is the worst. More from habit than conviction, she and her late husband attended church, weather permitting. Then rain or shine, after a midday meal, they hiked across the familiar terrain, commenting on the growth of the cedars, the height of the marsh grass, or the work to be done on the back pasture. "Like God on the seventh day," Paul would chuckle contentedly, snapping off a dead branch to clear the path.

Widowed three years, Maria misses the companionship—the shared ritual of instant coffee and toast before turning in for the night, the Sunday walks, and the mutual memories. She misses returning to a warm house after penning the chickens and finding her husband reading the paper. But she does not miss her role as chief cook and bottle washer.

Till her husband's death, Maria had never lived alone. Even when Paul was outside working, she was on call. Now her life is her own or almost. The children still have their say, of course. When she considered moving into town, her daughter protested.

"You'd hate to live anywhere but here, Mom."

But would she? She pictures a small apartment near the park and the shops. Maybe she'd learn to do something—to paint or speak Spanish. Her sister Bea had started university at sixty-three.

"Fine for Bea, she's different, Mom. You like looking after people, having your chickens."

Truth be known, she hated chickens: ugly, noisy ingrates that pecked at your hands. Paul had insisted they were worth the effort but as soon as she got the energy, she'd cheerfully initiate a beheading.

Watching Mr. Walters joke gruffly with the kids even with the false promise he brings, she is glad she invited him. He is no hero, always complaining about something and never lifting a hand to help. But since Peggy's death he is friendlier—needs must. They both have had to learn new dance steps.

Like her, he has been left to drift, all the routines disrupted, the familiar patterns destroyed. When a few weeks earlier at the local K-Mart, Maria noticed him forlornly staring at babies' wear, she had taken pity and helped him choose a gift for his grandchild.

The following week she had spotted him at the supermarket checkout counter: his clothes needing ironing, his jacket frayed. He was staring at the frozen meat pie in his basket, "I sure miss her pies," he sighed, prompting Maria's invitation to Thanksgiving dinner.

"The kids would love to see you," she lied. "We'll be having turkey and pie."

The old farmer squinted cautiously. "Sunday?" he muttered as if scanning a busy calendar. "Okay," he nodded indulgently, and then smiled, "I'd like that."

"Another helping, Mr. Walters?" Sharon encourages, tempting him with a generous slice of blueberry pie.

He declines. "Lord no, I've eaten more today than in a month."

The man nods appreciatively down the table at Maria who looks away, then comments pointedly, "I don't have much occasion for making pies these days."

Her children flinch.

"Do I hear wedding bells?" Betsy whispers to her sister.

"They're pie-eyed," Sharon giggles.

Later, when the house empties—"Don't forget to take some turkey." "Where is Arnold's hat?" "Are you coming up next weekend?" "Thanks for everything, mother"—Betsy and her mother cozy up on the sofa. Outside, the persistent snowflakes bury the footprints to the road.

"I always hate to see everyone leave," the older woman sighs. "I'm like a skeleton rattling around."

Betsy squeezes back her impatience and smiles. "You can change all that now, Mom."

"Move into town, you mean?"

"No, of course not, re-marry."

"Re-marry? Why?"

"You need someone to look after."

"I have the cats to look after."

"Be serious, Mom," the girl cautions. "You're not like me; you've always had someone to cook for, to care for. That's what you like."

"Maybe I don't."

The girl winces. "Don't what?"

"I cleaned and cooked for you kids and Dad but I don't want to do it for some stranger."

The girl gasps. They'd pinned their hopes on the old man. After all, her mother had invited him and he'd settled right in. Sharon would be furious. Even Bill wouldn't be able to hide his disappointment. The future they had talked of in which their mother settled down with a companion was fading like water colors in the rain.

"You like being a farmwife," the girl coaxes.

"Would you?"

The girl sighs. "Then you and Mr. Walters?"

"I'm better off alone."

"But is it fair?"

Turning from her daughter's crumbled face, Maria slowly rises, takes off her faded apron, folds it, and places it beside the others in the drawer. A certainty is growing inside her. Her heart pumps like a fledgling bird, timid but determined as it meets the cool air for the first time.

She glances out the window at the snow collecting on the bird feeder, and then stares through the lacy curtain of snowflakes at the ghostly silhouettes beyond. By morning the smaller birds will have to struggle to get seed. And when she moves into town, they'll have to fend for themselves.

ACKNOWLEDGMENTS

Carol Barrett's "Portrait" appeared previously in *The Switchgrass Review*.

Gayle Bell previously published "Homegoing" in *Mad Swirl* (2019) and "Down Home Blues" in *Blues and Jazz Mix* (Amazon, 2019).

Terri Berry's "On Guard" previously appeared in *Not What I Expected*, ed. Donna Currie Arias and Hildie S. Block (Paycock Press, 2007).

Melodie Corrigall"s "Winter Birds" was previously published in *Toasted Cheese Literary Journal* (2011).

Joan Dobbie's "My Mother IS Alive" first appeared in *Women's Struggles, Women's Visions*, ed. Cathryn Heisman (1992).

Joan Gerstein previously published "Dead Weight" in *Theories of Relativity* (Garden Oak Press, 2021).

Stephanie Hart's "Birthday Cake Dress" was first published in *Mirror Mirror: A Collection of Memories and Stories* (And Then Press, 2012).

Lisa Molina previously published "When We Held Hands" in *Ancient Paths Literary Magazine*.

Debbie Peters first published "Delinquent Account" in *The Writers' Cafe Magazine* (2019).

Sharon Lask Munson previously published "If By Chance" in *Poetica Magazine* and "Oh Mom" in *Manzanita Quarterly*.

M.K. Punky's "Precious Boy" was first published in *The Great Lakes Review*.

Mary Kay Rummel's "Returning" previously appeared in *What's Left Is the Singing* (Bright Hill Press, 2010).

Sherry Shahan's "Little House in the Red Woods" has also appeared in *Hippocampus Magazine* (2021).

Paul Sohar previously published "My Crutch" in *In Sun's Shadow*.

Gary Young's "My youngest son considers" originally appeared in *Chiron Review*.

Images by Heather Tosteson. Many thanks to the contributors, family, friends and passers-by who contributed images to art with no idea what was coming next. Particular thanks to Geanie Brown, Jan Callner, Alisa Childress, Melodie Corrigall, Sybil Gilmar, Janice Hume, Kerry Langan, Michele Markarian, Lisa Molina, Joanell Serra, Sherry Shahan, Paul Sohar, Penelope Starr, and the Brockett and Tosteson clans.

The Wising Up Writers Collective Editorial Group—Kerry Langan, Michele Markarian, William Cass and Murali Kamma—provided invaluable assistance in bringing this anthology to print. We could never do what we do without them.

CONTRIBUTORS

Patricia Barone's recent poetry book is *The Music of this Ruin* (Taj Mahal Press/Cyberwit). *Your Funny, Funny Face* and *The Scent of Water* are from Blue Light Press. *Handmade Paper* received an award from New Rivers Press. Short stories are in Wising Up Press, Peter Lang, and Plume/Penguin anthologies. She received a Loft-McKnight Award of Distinction and a Lake Superior Contemporary Writers Award.

Carol Barrett coordinates the Creative Writing Certificate Program at Union Institute & University. She has published two volumes of poetry (*Calling in the Bones* and *Drawing Lessons*) and a recent book of creative nonfiction (*Pansies*, a finalist for the Oregon Book Awards.) She is indebted to her family for inspiring many poems.

Gayle Bell's work has been featured in numerous anthologies. In 2018 she performed "Black Betty, That Thangs Gone Wild" with Cara Mia's "Storytellers, Building Communities." In 2013-2014 she was a co-docent for "My Immovable Truth—A Dallas Lineage." She facilitated her and other GLBTQY's oral history and performance, sponsored by Make Art With Purpose and displayed at the African American Museum in Dallas TX.

Terri Watrous Berry's work has appeared over the past thirty-five years in several anthologies, journals, magazines and newspapers, and has received recognition from The Hemingway Competition, The Des Plaines/Park Ridge NOW Feminist Writer's Contest, The Amelia Islander Literary Competition, The Tallahassee Writer's Association, Sky Blue Waters Poetry Competition, and The Poetry Society of Michigan, where she lives.

Mark Blickley is a proud member of the Dramatists Guild and PEN American Center. His videos, *Speaking in Bootongue*, and *Widow's Peek: The Kiss of Death*, represented the United States in the 2020 year-long international world tour of *Time Is Love: Universal Feelings: Myths & Conjunctions*, organized by esteemed African curator, Kisito Assangni. His latest book is *Dream Streams* (2019).

Paula Brown is a poet and a writer and a perennial student of the Writers Studio. Her work has been published in the *Tiny Seed Journal, Adirondack Review, North Dakota Quarterly, Whitefish Review,* and *South Dakota*

Magazine among others. She lives in Tucson, AZ with her husband and a pack of dachshunds.

Jan Callner has created over twenty musical plays for young audiences. Her award-winning, fully-recorded *The Frog Prince* and *The Magic Fish* are available through various venues. "Okay God" is an excerpt from her memoir. Jan is a professional soprano, actress, pianist, composer, playwright, and teacher. Her work has been published in *Writing in a Woman's Voice* and *Central Coast Journal*.

Alisa Childress writes creative nonfiction and personal essays. She has an MS in clinical psychology and now works as a case manager for persons with developmental disabilities. A proud nerd, multi-hobbyist and brand-new empty nester, she lives with husband and animal menagerie in Louisville, KY. Her work has appeared in the *Potato Soup Journal* and several Medium publications.

Beth Christensen is a mental health counselor in private practice in New Orleans. She has a few publications in professional journals and textbooks, both in counseling and in her previous profession of nursing. She has published short stories in *Thema* and her college literary magazine, *Calliope*, and has an upcoming story in *Avalon Literary Review*.

Lori Closter has written several published stories and five short educational films produced for National Geographic. Her unpublished works—a story collection, a YA novel, and the novel's accompanying screenplay—have been recognized in multiple contests and are wending their way toward the public eye. A lifelong Northeasterner with degrees from Cornell and Temple, she recently moved to North Carolina.

Melodie Corrigall is an eclectic Canadian writer whose stories have appeared in *The Whole Wide Word, Blank Spaces, Halfway Down the Stairs, Blue Lake Review, Corner Bar Magazine, Sybil, Bethlehem Writers Roundtable, Little Old Lady Comedy,* and *The Write Place at the Right Time*.

Alexis David is a poet and fiction writer who holds a BA from Hobart and William Smith Colleges, an MS from Canisius College and an MFA from New England College. She has published short stories, poems, reviews and nonfiction. She has a chapbook called *Animals I Have Loved* with Dancing Girl Press.

Sera David published a short story, "Unmasked," in the *Potato Soup Online Literary Journal* earlier this year.

Pamela Brothers Denyes is published in multiple Virginia writers' journals, *Shakespeare of Today, Wondrous World: Poems that Spark Magic, Vallum, Barstow and Grand V*, and several international collections by *The Poet Magazine*. Her poetry has won awards in several competitions. Retired now, Pamela is harvesting forty years of poetry, song-writing, journals and travelogues to create new works—and fun!

Joan Dobbie, MFA, co-hosts The River Road Reading Series in Eugene, OR, presently on Zoom. She has two full-length poetry books, *Woodstock Baby, A Novel in Poetry* (2013) and *The Language of Stone* (2019), several chapbooks, and many online, small press and anthology publications, including poems in Wising Up Press's *Love After 70* and *Surprised by Joy*.

Joan Gerstein has been penning poetry since elementary school. A retired educator and therapist, Joan taught creative writing to incarcerated veterans for five years, until the pandemic, and hopes to resume. Her poetry has appeared in over thirty anthologies, journals and online zines. Joan's first book of poetry, *Theories of Relativity*, was recently published by Garden Oak Press.

Laura Glaves, RN, BSN, BFA, is an award-winning photographer and graphite pencil artist. Her poetry has been published by *Open Door Poetry Magazine, Pure Slush Lifespan Series, The Fieldstone Review*, and *The Outrider Press 2021 Play Anthology*. Her nursing career spanned thirty years and eight specialties. She enjoys writing poetry about the human experience.

Madlynn Haber lives with her dog, Ozzie, in a cohousing community in Northampton, MA. She writes memoir, poetry, and essays. Her work appears in *Mothers Always Write, Mum Life Stories, Buddhist Poetry Review, Dissonance Magazine, K'in Literary Journal, Borrowed Solace, Ariel Chart International Literary Journal, Muddy River Poetry Review,* and other journals.

Janet Lunder Hanafin grew up on a South Dakota farm, transplanted herself to St. Paul, MN for college, and grew deep roots. Her writing has appeared in local and metro-wide publications including the *St. Paul Almanac*. She and her husband have two children and five grandchildren (all above average) and enjoy the companionship of two very fine cats.

ADULT CHILDREN: Contributors

Stephanie Hart is the author of the book *Mirror Mirror: A Collection of Memoirs and Stories* (And Then Press, 2012) as well as a young adult fiction novel. Her work has appeared in anthologies such as *Goodness* (Wising Up Press), and literary magazines, including *The Sun*, *Jewish Currents*, *And Then*, *Home Plant* News, and *ducts.org*.

Pamela Hartmann spent most of her adult life in big cities (Athens, Seoul, Los Angeles), teaching and writing textbooks. Now she lives in a small coastal California town, doing wildlife rehabilitation and writing fiction. More than a second act for her, it's an entirely new play. This is her fifth published fiction story.

Catherine Hayes is a recent graduate of Emmanuel College in Boston, MA where she obtained her degree in English Literature and Communication & Media studies, and minored in creative writing. She's currently attending Bridgewater State University for her English MA. Her favorite authors include Charlotte Bronte and Madeline Miller. This is her first publication.

Thea Heard is a fiction writer who cherishes their adult children, inner and outer, and also finds themself developing an irrepressible irreverence as they ages. Their motto is: *It could always be worse. Just imagine . . . and lighten up.*

Lowell Jaeger (Montana Poet Laureate 2017-2019) is founding editor of Many Voices Press, author of nine collections of poetry, Grolier Poetry Peace Prize winner, and recipient of fellowships from the National Endowment for the Arts and the Montana Arts Council. He was awarded the Montana Governor's Humanities Award for his work in promoting civil civic discourse.

Richard Leis has had his poetry published in *Impossible Archetype*, *The Laurel Review*, *Manzano Mountain Review*, and speculative poetry journals. He has been nominated for the Pushcart Prize and was a finalist in the Tucson Festival of Books Literary Awards in 2018 and 2021.

Kate Meyer-Currey moved to Devon, England in 1973. A varied career in frontline settings has fueled her interest in gritty urbanism, contrasted with a rural upbringing. Her first chapbook, *County Lines* (Dancing Girl Press), comes out this autumn. Her second, *Cuckoo's Nest* (Contraband Books), is due in February 2022.

Lisa Molina is a writer in Austin, TX. She has two chapbooks forthcoming in 2022, published by *Fahmidan Publishing & Co.* and *Sledgehammer Literary*

Journal. Her poetry can be found in print and digital journals such as *Beyond Words Magazine, Trouvaille Review, Neologism Poetry Journal, The Ekphrastic Review, Ancient Paths Literary Magazine,* and *The Orchards Poetry Journal*.

Sharon Lask Munson is a retired teacher, poet, old movie enthusiast, lover of road trips, and with many published poems, two chapbooks, and two full-length books of poetry. She says many things motivate her to write: a mood, a memory, the smell of cooking, burning leaves, a windy day, rain, fog, something observed or overheard—and of course, imagination. She lives and writes in Eugene, OR.

Jennifer Palmer is a 2016 graduate of Converse College in Spartanburg, SC. Her work has appeared in *Balloons Literary Journal, Writings to Stem Your Existential Dread, borrowed solace, Tales from the Cliff,* and *Dread Naught but Time*. She has also written the YA fantasy novel *Burst* under the pen name H. C. Daria.

Debbie Peters is an attorney by profession, living in New York City. "Delinquent Account" was inspired by and written in honor of the poet, Mary Oliver. Other work by Debbie has been published in *One Sentence Poems, DASH Literary Journal, Misfit Magazine, Pure Slush,* and *Embryo Concepts*. She dedicates all of her work to her beloved Gerson Lesser.

MK Punky is a frequent contributor to Wising Up Press anthologies and the author of thirteen books of poetry, fiction and nonfiction, most recently *The Unexpected Guest*, a memoir of befriending and housing a homeless neighbor. MK's *The Year of When*, a 365-poem cycle about 2020, is currently being produced as a multi-media art exhibition.

A.P. Quilt is a retired teacher. She holds a double master's degree in Education. Her work has been published internationally, and her first full collection of poetry was published this year.

Melanie Reitzel has published her poetry, fiction and CNF in such journals as *Poet Lore, North American Review, Tulane Review, Popshot Quarterly, ZYZZYVA, Fourteen Hills, Berkeley Poetry Review, 5x5, Barrier Islands Review, The Adirondack Review, The Prose-Poem Project, Naugatuck River Review, A River and Sound Review, Forward Movement,* and in various anthologies.

ARooney was an associate professor of writing in India at Jindal Global University. His fiction and poetry have been published all over the U.S. and internationally. His most recent novel, *The Autobiography of Francis N. Stein*, was published in 2019 by Madville Press. He is currently working on a novel about birdfeeders.

Mary Kay Rummel's ninth poetry book, *Nocturnes: Between Flesh and Stone*, has recently been published by Blue Light Press. Her first book, *This Body She's Entered*, won a Minnesota Voices Award from New Rivers Press. *The Lifeline Trembles* won the Blue Light Award. She is Poet Laureate emerita of Ventura County, CA and divides her time between Minneapolis and Ventura.

Judith Sanders' work appears in such journals as *Pleiades, Modern Language Studies, Chautauqua,* and *Calyx,* and on the websites *Vox Populi* and *Full Grown People.* Her poems won the Hart Crane and Wergle Flomp Humor prizes. She taught English at universities and independent schools, and in France on a Fulbright Fellowship. She lives with her family in Pittsburgh.

Deborah Schmedemann taught writing to law students for decades and now teaches English to new Americans. Her essays are in anthologies on such topics as the meaning of home, exploring nature, responding to change—and in Wising Up Press' *Surprised by Joy.* She lives in Minneapolis but often visits her two adult daughters and their families in the Chicago area.

Joanell Serra is a poet, playwright, novelist and essayist from Northern California, with work published in *Eclectica, Blue Lake Review, Black Fox Literary Magazine, Manifest-station, Poydras Review,* and elsewhere. Books include *The Vines We Planted* (Wido, 2018) and *(Her)oics Anthology*, a collection of women's essays about the pandemic (Regal House Publishing, 2021). Her work has won multiple writing contests.

Sherry Shahan's novel in free verse, *Purple Daze: A Far-Out Trip, 1965,* highlights a tumultuous year in history. Her personal essays have appeared in *Critical Read, F(r)iction, Hippocampus,* Oxford University Press, *Exposition Review, Confrontation* and elsewhere. She earned an MFA from Vermont College of Fine Arts and taught a creative writing course for UCLA Extension for ten years.

Laurence Snydal is a poet, musician and retired teacher. He has published more than a hundred poems in magazines such as *Caperock, Spillway, Columbia* and *Steam Ticket.* His work has also appeared in many anthologies including *Visiting Frost, The Poets Grimm* and *The Years Best Fantasy and*

Horror. Some of his poems have been performed in Baltimore and NYC. He lives in San Jose, CA, with his wife Susan.

Paul Sohar has been writing and publishing in every genre, including seventeen volumes of translations, and his own poetry: *Homing Poems* (Iniquity Press, 2006), The *Wayward Orchard* (Wordrunner Press Prize winner, 2011), and *In Sun's Shadow* (Ragged Sky Press, 2020). Awards: first prize in the 2012 Lincoln Poets Society contest, two nominations for Pushcart Prize. Magazines: *Agni, Gargoyle, Rattle, etc.*

Penelope Starr, founder of Odyssey Storytelling and author of *The Radical Act of Community Storytelling: Empowering Voices in Uncensored Events*, writes fiction, personal essays, and an occasional poem. A SoulCollage Facilitator, she offers workshops for writers and other creatives. Penelope lives in the foothills of the Tucson Mountains with her partner, Silvia.

Melvin Sterne has published two novels, *Zara* and *The Shoeshine Boy*, and two short stories collections, *The Number You Have Reached* and *Redemption*. He has published more than thirty stories, with work in *Quarterly Literary Review of Singapore, Best New Writing, Eclectica, Lalitamba, Soundings Review, StorySouth, Natural Bridge, Blue Mesa Review*, and *South Carolina Review*. He lives in Singapore.

Mark Tarallo is a Washington, D.C.-based writer and journalist. His poetry and fiction have appeared in *Abbey, Asphodel, Angelface, Beltway, Innisfree Poetry Journal, Manorborn, Red Mountain Review*, and the anthologies *District Lines, Insulatus, Connected, Surprised by Joy, Goodness*, and *Quintessence*. His book *Management and Leadership: Best Practice Essentials* (CRC Press) has just been published.

J. West has always told stories. It feels marvelous to finally publish one, especially in the company of so many fine poets and writers.

Nancy Wick worked as a writer/editor for many years at the University of Washington in Seattle. Now retired, she writes personal essays and other nonfiction and enjoys volunteering and being active in the beautiful Northwest. Her work has appeared in journals such as *Minerva Rising, Persimmon Tree, Summerset Review, The Broken Plate,* and *Longridge Review*, as well as several anthologies.

Chris Wood resides in Chattanooga, TN with her husband and several fur babies. She works as a lease maintenance manager for a real estate management company, and is a member of the Chattanooga Writers' Guild, where she currently serves as their treasurer. Her work has appeared in several journals and publications, including *Poetry Quarterly*, *Haiku Journal*, and *American Diversity Report*.

Gary Young is the author of several books of poetry, most recently, *That's What I Thought*, and *Precious Mirror*, translations from the Japanese. He has received several grants and awards, including the Shelley Memorial Award from the Poetry Society of America. He teaches creative writing and directs the Cowell Press at UC Santa Cruz.

EDITORS

HEATHER TOSTESON is the author of nine books of fiction, poetry and non-fiction, including most recently the poetry collection *Source Notes: Seventh Decade*. She has worked in health communications with a focus on communication across disciplines, racism, social trust, and how belief systems develop and change. She has an MFA (UNC-Greensboro) and PhD in English and Creative Writing (Ohio University).

CHARLES D. BROCKETT has a PhD from UNC-Chapel Hill and is a recipient of several Fulbright and National Endowment for the Humanities awards. A retired political science professor, he has written two well-received books on Central America and numerous social science journal articles and book chapters. With Heather Tosteson, he is co-founder of Universal Table and Wising Up Press and co-editor of the Wising Up Anthologies. They recently co-authored *Sharing the Burden of Repair: Reentry After Mass Incarceration*.

KERRY LANGAN is the author of three collections of short fiction, *Only Beautiful*, *Live Your Life*, and *My Name Is Your Name*. Her short stories have been published in dozens of literary magazines and anthologized often. Her non-fiction has appeared in *Working Mother* and *Shifting Balance Sheets: Women's Stories of Naturalized Citizenship and Cultural Attachment*. She is currently at work on her next collection of short stories. She resides with her family in Oberlin, Ohio.

MICHELE MARKARIAN is a short fiction writer and playwright. Her work has appeared in *Bridge Eight*, *Bright Flash Literary Review*, *The Furious Gazelle*, *Coffin Bell*, *Daily Science Fiction*, *The Journal of Microliterature*, *Moida Magazine*, and in five anthologies by Wising Up Press. A collection of her plays, *The Unborn Children of America and Other Family Procedures*, is available on Amazon.

Visit our website and learn about our other publications,
our readers guides, and calls for submissions.

www.universaltable.org
wisingup@universaltable.org

P.O. Box 2122
Decatur, GA 30031-2122

CPSIA information can be obtained
at www.ICGtesting.com
Printed in the USA
LVHW031619201121
703955LV00001B/54